THE ORIGINS OF POST-WAR GERMAN POLITICS

The conference convened at Potsdam to determine the political future of a defeated Germany charged the allies with the task of preparing 'for the eventual reconstruction of German political life on a democratic basis and for eventual peaceful cooperation in international life by Germany'. This book discusses how the allies worked towards these goals. It outlines how the deep ideological divisions within the allied forces ultimately resulted in the division of Germany and discusses how indigenous political movements were impeded by a deeply felt distrust of German nationalism in all organisations. Yet these considerations are always seen in the context of the massive logistical problems faced by the allies in restoring order to the chaos of war-ravaged Germany. Focusing on the central experiences of Hanover, the book illustrates how post-war German politics are the result of a coalescence of distinct and at times even contradictory ideologies and interests, emphasising how the German political scene can only be understood in terms of the mutual interaction of personalities, beliefs and economics and of indigenous and foreign influences.

Barbara Marshall is a Senior Lecturer in the Department of History, Philosophy and European Studies at the Polytechnic of North London.

The Origins
of Post~War
German Politics

Barbara Marshall

CROOM HELM
London • New York • Sydney

© 1988 Barbara Marshall
Croom Helm Ltd, Provident House, Burrell Row,
Beckenham, Kent, BR3 1AT

Croom Helm Australia, 44-50 Waterloo Road,
North Ryde, 2113, New South Wales

Published in the USA by
Croom Helm
in association with Methuen, Inc.
29 West 35th Street
New York, NY 10001

British Library Cataloguing in Publication Data

Marshall, Barbara
    The origins of post-war German politics.
    1. Germany (West) — Politics and
    government
    I. Title
    320.943   JN3971.A2
    ISBN 0-7099-4690-2

Library of Congress Cataloging-in-Publication Data

ISBN 0-7099-4690-2

MB

Printed and bound in Great Britain by Mackays of Chatham Ltd, Kent

CONTENTS

ABBREVIATIONS

ACC:	Allied Control Council
AsD:	Archiv der Sozialen Demokratie. Bonn-Bad Godesberg
CCG:	Control Commission for Germany
CCG (BE):	Control Commission for Germany. British Element
CCS:	Combined Chiefs of Staff
CDU:	Christlich-Demokratische Union
COGA:	Control Office for Germany and Austria
COSSAC:	Chief of Staff, Supreme Allied Commands
DGB Archiv:	Archiv des Deutschen Gewerkschaftsbundes. Düsseldorf
DP:	Displaced Person
FDP:	Freie Demokratische Partei
GU:	General Union ('Einheitsgewerkschaft')
HHN:	Hannoversche Neueste Nachrichten
HP:	Hannoversche Presse
IG Metall:	Industriegewerkschaft Metall (Metal Workers Union)
JCH:	Journal of Contemporary History
K Det.:	Military Government Detachment for an urban district
KPD:	Kommunistische Partei Deutschlands
MG/Mil.Gov.:	Military Government
NB:	Nachlass Bratke (Bratke Papers)
NHK:	Neuer Hannoverscher Kurier
NLP:	Niedersächsische Landespartei
L/R Det.:	Military Government Detachment for a region
OB:	Oberbürgermeister

OP:	Oberpresident
OV:	Ortsverein (Local Party Branch)
P/Det.:	Military Government Detachment for a province
PRO/FO:	Public Record Office, Foreign Office files
PRO/WO:	Public Record Office/War Office files
RC:	Reconstruction Committee
Rpr:	Regierungspresident
SAH:	Stadtarchiv (Town Archive) Hanover
SCAEF:	Supreme Commander Allied Expeditionary Force
SHAEF:	Supreme Headquarters Allied Expeditionary Force
S Det.:	Military Government Detachment for a town
SPD:	Sozialdemokratische Partei Deutschlands
STAH:	(Lower Saxonian) Staatsarchiv Hanover

PREFACE

The research for this book was carried out in Britain and during the course of a sabbatical year in 1980/81, in Germany. In Britain the files of the Foreign and War Office were most productive although those of the Control Commission were sadly disappointing as they contain mainly circulars and do not allow the kind of insight into the working of the Commission which could be expected. I was able to interview (Sir) Ashley Bramall (16.10.1984), formerly an Industrial Relations Officer with Military Government in Hanover and (Lord) Annan (25.4.1985) who, although not directly involved in local affairs, was nevertheless one of the few officers of Military Government with an overview of German political organisations, opinions and intentions.

In Germany I came up against the difficulties which most researchers into the immediate post-war period encounter: the scarcity of source material. The destruction and disruption at the end of the war, coupled with an acute paper shortage made the keeping of records a low priority. Nevertheless, for Hanover the situation was more favourable in that here, in the Town Archive, the papers of the former Oberbürgermeister Bratke are preserved, as well as those of a number of other officials and prominent citizens. In the Lower Saxonian State Archive the regional government files were most useful. In addition there were Schumacher's personal papers in the Archiv der Sozialen Demokratie in Bonn and those of the leading Hanoverian trade unionist, Albin Karl, in the Archiv des Deutschen Gewerkschaftsbundes in Düsseldorf.

Many other records remain however in private hands. Thus the papers of the SPD Ortsverein Hanover are held by the Politische Seminar of the university. Many Works Archives of the Hanover firms either refused access or keep their files closed. The former was the case of the firm Continental where I was unable to work; the latter that of the Sprengel sweets factory, the files of which are lodged with the State Archive. The Chamber of Industry and Commerce, Hanover, refused access to its files which 'are still in some disarray' (Letter to the author 12.1.1981). I was however able to use their printed material.

The availability of material naturally affected the emphases placed in this book. For instance I would have liked to include more on the economy and to have gone into greater detail over denazification. Files relating to denazification are closed to the public by a law passed in the Lower Saxonian Diet, 'Concerning the conclusion of Denazification in Lower Saxony' of 18.12.1951. There was also very little to base an analysis of 'bourgeois' politics on; official sources are virtually unobtainable. I was however able to interview Dr K Pentzlin, the former director of Bahlsen's biscuit factory and a leading figure in Hanover's pre- and post-war economy. Although of intrinsic interest and merit, and adding to the historian's general understanding of the period, this interview did not provide enough substantive information for a widening of the perspective of this book. Researching it has been an experience in itself. Many people were reluctant to talk about their experiences, and this applied to older Social Democrats almost as much as to 'bourgeois' personalities. The former by 1980/81 had come in for such massive criticism from younger 'left' historians for their failure to 'make a revolution' after 1945, that in many cases they were reluctant to allow me access. That this was possible was the result of the help of the director of the Stadtarchiv, Dr Mlynek. I was able to interview H Hasselbring, Schumacher's aid and secretary in the first post-war phase (4.3.1981) and A Holweg, Schumacher's successor as the chairman of the SPD Ortsverein Hanover after the latter had moved on beyond the local sphere in 1946 (11.5.1981).

The diffidence of old 'bourgeois' politicians is of a different nature and will only be overcome by time. Both kinds of people were almost equally defensive in their attitude, albeit for different reasons - in itself a telling comment on the role of the past in present day Germany.

I was also greatly helped by Dr Franz Hartmann who allowed me the use of extensive copies of material which he used for his PhD thesis and which he was able to obtain in those archives which were closed to me. Lastly, it was a practical matter which made my work much easier: the use of a room in a small archive nearer my temporary home in Bovenden outside Göttingen to which the files from Hanover could be sent. This was made possible by Professor M Last, now sadly dead.

I was able to spend the whole of the academic year 1980/81 in Germany, on sabbatical leave from the Polytechnic of North London and with the financial aid of a European Studies Research Fellowship of the Leverhulme Trust. My thanks must also go to my research assistant, Cathy Schling, for helping me with the documents, and to my husband John for wrestling with the manuscript in a foreigner's English. I am indebted to Gertrud Erbach for the prompt and efficient typing.

INTRODUCTION

With unconditional surrender in 1945 'Germany' ceased to exist as an independent agent in international affairs. In the absence of a central German government the victorious allies became responsible for all aspects of the running of their former enemy's country. On moving into Germany the allies' first consideration was therefore, besides their own security, the establishment of law and order, as well as the restoration of basic services. Decisions on the political future of Germany were postponed to the conference at Potsdam (17 July - 2 August 1945), although the Soviets created certain faits accomplis in their zone with the licensing of political parties and trade unions on 10 June. The western allies, on the other hand, adopted the so-called 'Policy of Postponement' which, on the assumption that possible decisions at Potsdam must not be pre-empted, banned all political organisations and trade unions and thus effectively blocked any spontaneous German political initiative at the end of the war. The Potsdam Conference revealed that there were fundamental differences among the allies, not least in the interpretation of terms such as 'democracy'. However, these were covered up for the time being. In order to prolong the illusion of allied harmony over Germany the clauses referring to Germany's political future in the final Protocol of the Potsdam Conference were kept deliberately vague. Thus one of the purposes of the occupation of Germany was

> iv. To prepare for the eventual reconstruction of German political life on a democratic basis and for eventual peaceful co-operation in international life by

Germany.

Democratisation was thus conceived as a longterm objective and for a German nation state. However, as the relations between the allies grew increasingly strained and their willingness to run Germany jointly weakened, the different zones took on separate identities, reflecting in their political, economic and administrative structures the traditions of their respective occupying powers. A study of the origins of West German politics will therefore have to start with an analysis of allied planning for Germany during the war and their policies in the immediate post-war period. It will then have to examine the organisation of the occupation and occupation policies. German politics initially had to develop within the constraints set by the allies, and only gradually gained more independence. But the limitations imposed by the occupation powers were not the only ones. The experience of National Socialism and of military defeat, the destruction of the country and the daily struggle with shortages of all kinds put an enormous strain on the population, leaving little surplus energy for political activity, particularly at a time when the allies seemed still in total control.

At the end of the war Germany had effectively disintegrated into a number of unconnected localities. The complete breakdown of the transport system and the absence of higher administrative echelons meant that each town or community had to fend for itself. This isolation was overcome only gradually. It made it much more difficult for the emerging political groups to build up organisations beyond the local level. Politics for the first two years after World War II was effectively local and regional politics. The origins of West German politics are therefore best studied in one of these localities, and Hanover, in the British Zone, has been chosen. The choice was made for a number of reasons: Hanover seems to represent the average German town and similar developments would have occured elsewhere at about the same time. But Hanover is also of special interest because it was the centre of important new initiatives in the immediate post-war period: a united general trade union organisation was set up and the SPD of the western zones was refounded there - by chance, because of the presence in the town of Kurt Schumacher, later the leader of the West German SPD. Hanover also had an energetic local politician, Oberbürgermeister Gustav Bratke who like his better known colleagues Max Brauer of Hamburg or Konrad Adenauer of Cologne came up against British and later German administrative controls.

As mentioned above, the allies introduced into their respective zones their own political, economic and social systems. The Soviets from the outset furthered the political left by forcing the newly licensed parties to co-operate in an anti-fascist bloc, by fulfilling long standing demands of the left such as the breaking up of large agrarian estates in the east and by launching first changes in the economy. The Americans in their zone initially carried out a vigorous denazification programme, using the elimination of Nazis from all aspects of German public life as a means to carry out a social revolution. But their basic principles remained those of an American style democracy. Far from considering capitalism a threat to democracy, they held the two compatible; indeed democracy seemed to work better in a capitalist system. This attitude from the outset precluded any profound political and economic changes in the American Zone in Germany.

The British were in a special position. A Labour Government was voted into office in July 1945 which had a clearly defined policy of moving Britain towards socialism. A socialist foreign policy might have been expected to export this socialism to the area which would seem to have been potentially the most receptive: the British Zone of Germany. Yet, as the later Federal Republic was to show, British policy in Germany seems to have had little lasting effect. Indeed, there is controversy among historians whether the British even attempted to introduce socialism into their zone or whether their attempt failed either due to their own lack of determination or resources or because the growing impact of the Americans mitigated against this policy. (1) Leading Labour politicians had of course been closely involved in the political decision-making process during World War II and the demands of Realpolitik at the end of the war proved greater than the ideological commitment to socialism in foreign affairs. Foreign Secretary Bevin continued the foreign policy of his predecessor Eden. We know that for Bevin events in Germany were dwarfed by Britain's other commitments. At best Germany's importance lay in being a pawn in great power relations. Thus Germany provided one means of prolonging war-time co-operation with the Soviet Union which the Foreign Office hoped would provide a way in which Britain could compensate for her weakness. Germany also brought about the lasting engagement of the United States in Europe unlike the latter's hasty withdrawal after World War I with its disastrous consequences. Joint control of Germany played a pivotal role in Britain's relations with France: the latter had to be humoured and its position strengthened in order to create a counterweight on the continent to the potential threat from Germany and later to the overwhelming power of the Soviet Union.

The present study aims to show the objectives of British occupation policy as they affected the local level. What were the priorities of the British in Germany? It examines the planning and the preparations for the occupation done by the military because it was the latter rather than the civilian planners who actually carried out the occupation and the running of the zone. The link between the machinery in Germany and the government departments in London is analysed. Only in close co-operation could a consistent policy have been produced and carried out. Attention is then focused on the daunting tasks facing the often tiny contingents of Military Government personnel at the local level as well as the overall working of the Military Government hierarchy.

There were three phases of the British occupation. The first, from the first move of the allies into Germany, lasted until spring 1946. Its first three months were characterised by the 'Policy of Postponement' which avoided fundamental political decisions but established British control over all aspects of German life. Co-operation between the western allies was still close; control over Germany was still carried out jointly under SHAEF. This was illustrated, as we have seen, by the ban on 2 June 1945 of all German organisations in the western zones which hit the nascent trade union movement and all German anti-fascist organisations particularly hard. The impact of these early measures on German politics will be examined closely. After the Potsdam Conference the British published a series of directives on the basis of which a Local Government Reform was carried out and trade unions and political parties eventually emerged. This was a slow and bureaucratic process, which meant that the organisations spend much of their energies on gaining recognition from the British, rather than concentrating on policies and issues. Moreover, by treating all parties in the same way, the Social Democrats whose organisation had survived almost intact, were affected most. Underlying the British approach was a specific concept of 'democracy' which needs to be scrutinised. The wider question is whether the British imposed a system which the Germans, left to their own resources, would have rejected. Was there a "verordnete Demokratie", an 'imposed democracy'? (2) The contradiction of introducing 'democracy' by dictatorial means was already seen by the British at the time. (3) The legal nature of the occupation has therefore been described as a 'constitutional dictatorship', i.e. a dictatorship designed to bring about constitutional rule. Phase II of the occupation began in the summer of 1946 when the role of Military Government was taken over by a civilian Control Commission and control over German activities began to loosen. Elections to local and regional representative bodies took place. The third phase came in January 1947 with Ordinance 57 which gave the Germans back the responsibility for running their own affairs. Also in January 1947 Bizonia, the joining of the American and the British Zones, came into operation. At the same time the British Element of the Control Commission was reduced in numbers from its staggering size of 26,000 staff in 1946. The London end of the occupation was reorganised with responsibility for Germany now clearly with the Foreign Office.

The focus of the present study shifts according to this background. The initial chapters are exclusively concerned with the British aspect; the central sections deal with the interaction of British and Germans. Once the organisational frame work was established the British ceased to play a prominent role and the focus of the study is therefore more on the German trade unions and parties for whom the presence of the British was a reminder of their own impotence although they no longer affected their affairs directly. In this last section it will be examined whether the allies 'prevented a new order' (4), whether the Germans themselves lacked the political will to push harder for it or whether, given more support by the SPD and the left CDU, the British themselves might have been more positive in their approach to political change in Germany. Special attention will be paid to the SPD who not only emerged as the strongest party in 1945 but who seemed the almost automatic political heir to National Socialism with which bourgeois capitalism had been too closely associated to be entirely untainted by it. Did the German Social Democrats and the trade unions (and the British Labour Party!) fail after 1945? Finally, what were the results of the occupation? To what extent did the British shape the origins of German politics after World War II, or were specific German traditions and conditions more important in influencing matters?

NOTES

1. W. Rudzio, "Die ausgebliebene Sozialisierung an Rhein und Ruhr, Zur Sozialisierungspolitik von Labour Regierung und SPD 1945-48, in: Archiv für Sozialgeschichte XVIII, 1978. See now also the contributions by H. Lademacher and R. Steininger in: J. Foschepoth/R. Steininger (eds), Britische Deutschland-und Besatzungspolitik 1945-49, 1985.

2. T. Pirker, Die Verordnete Demokratie, Grundlagen und Erscheinungen der Restauration, 1954.

3. R. Ebsworth, Restoring Democracy in Germany. The British Contribution, 1960.

4. E. Schmidt, Die Verhinderte Neuordnung, 1970.

Chapter One

BRITAIN AND THE OCCUPATION OF GERMANY

WAR-TIME PLANNING FOR GERMANY

It was only after Germany's eventual military defeat emerged as probable at the end of 1942 that the western allies gave serious thought to their contribution to it and to the treatment of Germany after defeat. Roosevelt and Churchill met at Casablanca in January 1943 after the successful completion of 'Torch' in North Africa and with the fall of Stalingrad imminent. They decided on an allied landing in the west of Europe and they committed themselves to fight on until Germany surrendered unconditionally.

They thus made military decisions but refused to get involved into more detailed plans for the future of a country 'which had not yet been defeated.' (Roosevelt) However, certain aspects of the actual situation which would exist at the end of the war in Europe were anticipated: Soviet troops would advance into the vacuum left by defeated Germany; the Soviet Union would become the most powerful nation on the continent. This raised the question of the nature of a future German state: should a German nation state survive and, if so, with what political and economic structure or should Germany be divided between the allies into zones of interests?

No concrete decisions on these matters were ever made. For one, the harmony between the western allies which was the foundation of their close military collaboration did not extend to political planning for the post-war world. The USA's involvement in Europe after the end of hostilities was uncertain. As late as at the Yalta

Conference in February 1945 Roosevelt indicated that US troops would be withdrawn from Europe within two years. Instead, the American leadership had grander visions of a new world order based on the creation of the United Nations, on the concept of 'open markets' and on the break-up of outdated colonial structures. Britain's priorities were quite different: the restoration of Britain's status as a world power (temporarily lost, it was thought, as a result of her military weakness towards the end of the war) depended on the revival of the Commonwealth and with it on preferential trade and market agreements. Above all, Britain was closer to Europe, if not part of it, and the political settlements there had more direct implications for her.

Postponement of decisions about the future of Germany was also due to the fact that as long as Germany was the enemy which had to be defeated co-operation between the allies was guaranteed. Much of British thinking about post-war Germany was based on the attempt to prolong this co-operation by involving all allies in the responsibility for Germany. This applied particularly to the Soviet Union which by sharing the running of Germany was to be made to behave rationally - like a western power. This fixation on Germany had serious consequences for the British: it excluded all constructive thought about the realities of power in Europe after the war, about the future of Europe and about Britain's possible role in it, because it was assumed that "a unified Europe would in fact be found to be a German Europe". (1)

Everything German however, was automatically rejected. This was only partly due to ignorance about the nature of National Socialism and the mechanics of a totalitarian society. Partly it was due to the understandable revulsion at crimes committed by the National Socialist regime. But the 'Vansittart' approach had far wider implications. There was often open contempt for the former elites of the Weimar Republic, not only among officials of the (more conservative) Foreign Office but in the Labour Party and the TUC: even German Social Democrats in exile in London were considered to be Germans first of all, and then weak and ineffective because they 'had let Hitler in'. (2) There was no 'better Germany' which allied planners could revive:

It was an illusion to imagine that there was a normal Germany to which one could revert. There had been no normal Germany for fifty years or more, except one governed by a centralised and militaristic machine. (3)

On the other hand, to create a new Germany by revolutionary means was equally unacceptable: any form of revolution by the Germans themselves would threaten the security and control of the British. Besides, the British had not fought National Socialism to see it replaced by an equally objectionable creed, communism.

There were thus few alternatives available for British war-time planners. Nevertheless, some plans for Germany had to be made. In view of the overall political uncertainty these were of a technocratic or military nature. Thus the European Advisory Committee (EAC) was set up in London after the Teheran conference. Of all the allies the British attached most importance to it: they alone were represented by a permanent high level Foreign Office figure whereas the Americans and Soviets sent their ambassadors to Britain. It was a British initiative which led to detailed proposals for an armistice with Germany, comprising no less than 70 articles. (4) The British also produced the plan for the division of Germany into zones of occupation. After months of painful negotiations throughout 1944 EAC accepted a British proposal to set up an interallied Control Commission for Germany (CCG) which was to be organised in parallel to the central German government with CCG Divisions corresponding to the Reich ministries which they were to control. The divisions were to be staffed by all three (later four) allies, the highest echelons being the Allied Control Council made up of the military commanders.

The whole CCG concept was flawed from the beginning. It was based on the existence of a central German government machinery, although the proclaimed western war aim of 'unconditional surrender' implied that such a machinery might no longer exist. This confusion resulted in major problems when it came to setting up the 'British Element' of CCG. The concept lacked general credibility and government departments such as the Treasury were reluctant to make scarce resources available for the venture. I. Kirkpatrick of the Foreign Office who was given overall responsibility for the recruitment of CCG personnel (in liaison with General Kirby from the War Office) complained of the Treasury's 'stone-walling tactics'. (5) Other ministries were reluctant to make specialist staff available. With the end of the war rapidly approaching, a

3

clear decision was vital for the efficient working of the system.

> I feel that the time has now come when on the return of our team from the Crimea we should make the effort through the S/S and the PM to get proper priority for this Commission. So far as I can gather the Crimean Conference decided to treat the problem of Germany as a matter of high priority but this does not appear to me to have filtered through to our government machine. The most important task of the CCG is surely the disarmament of Germany's war potential yet Luce of Labour does not allow volunteers to serve with CCG.

And with a note of desperation:

> In a word, the government must decide and decide quickly what importance is to be attached to the Commission. I am prepared to accept the ruling. But I do not think it fair to hold me responsible for the raising of this Commission on an adequate footing and at the same time to tell me that the Ministry of Labour will make it their business to obstruct the necessary recruitment. (6)

The Commission never received priority; service with it did not even obtain equality of conditions and status with the Home Civil Service which could have been the simplest way of transferring specialist staffs. Instead, the CCG planners began training their own staff at a number of centres in the UK which produced many but not enough competent men who would serve in Germany on one year contracts - the most the Treasury was willing to relinquish.

One of the reasons for the low esteem in which the CCG was held was that the defeat of Germany, its occupation and first measures of control were quite obviously the responsibility of the armed forces. It was here that most constructive planning took place, not only for the military campaigns but also for the situation in Germany in which allied troops would have to operate.

In preparation for the Normandy landings and the eventual occupation of Germany a new military formation, 21st Army Group, was set up in July 1943, followed by 1st Army Group in October. The inter-allied command structure was created with COSSAC (Chief of Staff, Supreme Allied

Commands) under CCS (Combined Chiefs of Staff) who were directly responsible to Roosevelt and Churchill. Besides the military operations the invading forces faced the problem of getting basic services in liberated countries going again and, for Germany, of building up a system of ongoing control. For this purpose both at the Pentagon and in the War Office a Civil Affairs department was created. In the British case the Civil Affairs Directorate under General Kirby was a new departure, for in the past, when they had occupied a country the British had seen no need for Civil Affairs using 'indirect rule' and left the natives to run their own affairs. There was also planning for Civil Affairs at COSSAC, and at 21st Army Group, the latter creating a special branch of the General Staff for Civil Affairs (G-5). In all there were thus four centres of planning for Europe and Germany.

When Germany's rapid military collapse became a possibility, later in 1943, these arrangements were changed again: more thought had to be given to what to do with Germany after her surrender. In December 1943 General Eisenhower became Supreme Commander Allied Expeditionary Force (SCAEF). In January 1944 COSSAC was turned into Supreme Headquarters Allied Expeditionary Force (SHAEF). In February 1944 G-5 of SHAEF was made responsible for the entire planning of Civil Affairs/Military Government for Western Europe and Germany. G-5 formed for Germany a 'German Country Unit' with the task of working out plans for a Military Government of Germany. But there were other centres working on such plans, such as the German Department at Shrivenham which consisted of 150 American and British officers. It published a 'Basic Handbook for Military Government of Germany' in June 1944 which approached the task in Germany with 'constructive pragmatism', demanding a fundamental reorganisation of German government structures and the elimination of the German war potential. Military Government should help to build up a German peace economy, and in the first instance overcome post-war difficulties.

Although these plans were conceived in a political vacuum in the absence of high level concrete decisions about the future of Germany they made clear that whereas 'Civil Affairs' were operating in friendly, liberated countries, Germany was to come under 'Military Government'. Thus the CCS Directive 551 of April 1944 ("Combined Chief Staff Directive for Military Government in Germany prior to Defeat or Surrender") determined:

> Military Government will be established and will extend over all parts of Germany ... progressively as the forces under your command capture German territory ... your rights in Germany prior to unconditional surrender or German defeat will be those of an occupying power. By virtue of your position you are clothed with supreme legislative, executive and judicial authority and power in areas occupied by forces under your command ... Military Government will be effected as a general principle through indirect rule ... The principal link for this indirect rule should be at the <u>Bezirk</u> (region) or <u>Kreis</u> (district) level; controls at higher levels will be inserted at your discretion. (7)

The difference of treatment reserved for the Germans was also expressed in the plans of G-5 of 21st AG for 'Operation Eclipse' (the occupation of Germany)

> The conduct of affairs vis-a-vis the civil population is totally different in liberated, friendly territories and in Germany. In the former we are dealing with our Allies and it is only the accident of war that brings us in their country ... In Germany on the other hand, it is the duty of the commanders to impose the will of the Supreme Commander upon the German people ... Germany will be made to realise that this time she has been well and truly beaten in the field by force of arms, and must now do as she is ordered. Military Government is the instrument, so far as the civil population is concerned, by which this will be conveyed and enforced. (8)

How exactly this was to be done remained vague. Thus the 'Political Guide' of the Directive stated

> The administration shall be firm. It will be at the same time just and humane with respect to the civil population so far as consistent with strict military requirements. You will strongly discourage fraternization between allied troops and German officials and population. It should be made clear to the local population that military occupation is intended. (9)

The "Handbook for Military Government in Germany" which SHAEF published in August 1944 was conceived in this spirit, so was the 'Germany Handbook' of October 1944 which was produced in Britain. The latter consisted of 38 directives, entitled "Germany and Austria in the post-surrender period: Policy Directives for Allied Commanders in Chief".

This phase of 'positive planning' for Germany was brought to a halt by the intervention of US Secretary of Finance, Morgenthau, who, claiming that allied planning had so far been 'too soft on the Germans' put forward his own plan to reduce Germany to an agrarian economy. Although this plan was only temporarily endorsed by Roosevelt and Churchill at Quebec (11. - 19.9.1944), it did result in the SHAEF Handbook being withdrawn. At the end of 1944 there were therefore no agreed interallied concrete plans for the treatment of Germany. CCS 551 technically remained in operation.

One lasting effect of Morgenthau's intervention was however the change made in the CCS's instructions to SHAEF concerning the German economy. Here stringent controls by the allies were introduced, and although controls did not accord with Britain's pragmatic approach to overall 'indirect rule' it is noteworthy that the British consented to these controls despite fears at SHAEF that these might lead to economic chaos and severely hamper Germany's economic recovery. (10) JCS 1067 which was issued in April 1945 for the treatment of Germany in the post-surrender period incorporated many of Morgenthau's ideas. It was religiously adhered to by the British whereas the Americans considered it unworkable and soon flouted it openly. In general however the British did not accept JCS 1067 but preferred their own 38 Directives as the basis for occupation policies.

As the end of the war approached there were thus two groups ready to move into Germany: the staff which had been recruited for the CCG and the Civil Affairs personnel of the army. Neither were adequately prepared for their task; both were desperately short of staff. Their functioning was impaired even further by the hostility between them because the Military Government establishment often poached CCG staff waiting in the UK for their time to go to Germany, and also because the civilians of the CCG were inferior in the eyes of the soldiers.

The difference on the British side (came) on account of

the simultaneous and somewhat independent planning by the Control Commission and by 21st Army Group. The latter was naturally solely responsible for organising Military Government in the areas won by it in the course of its advance, its personnel being drawn largely from those originally recruited and trained by the Civil Affairs Directorate of the War Office. Already before May 1945 officers of the Control Commission had been sent forward to work with Military Government officers under the Army, so as to pave the way for the essential transfer of duties. Meanwhile it was only natural for there to be at the beginning a tendency on the part of some officers in the field to dislike the advent of members of an outside organisation, the Control Commission, which was, moreover, to take over in due course the very functions the Army had organised from the start and had carried through with a great measure of success, in the face of appalling difficulties during the period of chaos following the German surrender. (11)

The occupation got off to a bad start.

THE LONDON END OF THE OCCUPATION

The Place of 'Germany' in Britain's post-war international obligations 1945-47

When military victory was finally achieved it became clear that the price Britain had had to pay for her involvement in World War II was horrendous: a quarter of her national wealth, or £7.300m. From the position of the world's most important creditor, she had declined to that of greatest debtor. High imports, notably of food and raw materials were not matched by an increase in exports which resulted already in 1945 in a balance of trade deficit of £654 million. (12)

Her economic and financial weakness was to affect fundamentally her foreign policy in general and that towards Germany in particular. Although Britain had de facto declined to the role of junior partner in the war-time alliance, it was assumed, as we have seen, that this was only a temporary setback which would be overcome in due course. Her world-wide obligations therefore remained the basis of the foreign policies of both Conservative and Labour governments. Economic weakness however forced on them a reassessment, and the subsequent withdrawal from untenable overseas positions such as India and Palestine.

In view of the massive problems which British policy makers faced it was not surprising that Germany initially was not a priority. Indeed, on assuming office Bevin established a list of the areas in which Britain would have to make important decisions. These were: (1) the Commonwealth and Empire, (2) the international economic system, (3) an international security system, in particular in order to control atomic weapons, (4) post-war settlements in the Mediterranean and Middle East, (5) peace settlements in Europe, and in particular what was to be done with Germany. (13) 'Germany' thus figured last on this shopping list of foreign policy priorities; this is also underlined by the fact that institutionally 'Germany' was treated as something of a sideshow, with much of the responsibility for Germany allocated to a minor Government department, 'COGA' (see below). There was also no overall plan, nor was a machinery for planning established - a hectic workload for the officials involved (14) resulted in a 'pragmatic' approach. This lack of clear foreign policy lines was frequently criticised in Britain, such as in the Commons debate of 22 October 1946, or in the censure by the Labour Party's Foreign Affairs Committee of November 1946. ("Keep Left"). In Germany where initially the British had won the admiration of the population this 'muddling through' was met with increasing consternation. (15)

If this pragmatic approach was due to British weakness at the end of the war which seemed to recommend flexibility and responsiveness to changing situations, there were nevertheless broad policy directions: British security had to be guaranteed, first against Germany and later against the Soviet Union. Moreover, in view of Britain's economic weakness these objectives must be achieved as cheaply as possible. This entailed a further policy aim: to involve as far as possible the United States in Europe who could take on some of the burden for not only the security in Europe against the Soviet Union (Greece, Turkey), but also the cost for the running of Germany. (Bizonia)

Both considerations, 'security' and 'costs', directly influenced British policy in Germany. In the initial post-war period with Germany as the perceived threat to British security, co-operation with the allies on the basis of German economic unity was pursued. Only a balanced economy in the whole of Germany would minimise British costs there. Where however British supplies such as food to Germany might become necessary the so-called 'first charge principle' should apply, i.e. these imports should be offset against German exports before the latter were taken into account for reparation payments. (16) At the Potsdam Conference Britain was therefore the most determined advocate of German economic unity.

However, allied co-operation did not function. No satisfactory joint import/export agreement was concluded, nor a fair distribution of German resources between the zones achieved. Britain did not succeed in obtaining allied agreement to the raising of the level of German industrial production. It became increasingly evident to Foreign Office officials that German economic unity was not only unrealistic but that the existing arrangement was working to the detriment particularly of the British and also of the Americans.

In the spring of 1946 the Foreign Office began to consider plans 'for the eventual division of Germany into two States' although at this stage the Cabinet was reluctant to change course and therefore maintained the British line that efforts should be made 'to keep the way clear for the re-establishment of more harmonious relations with the Soviet Union'. However, the economic argument soon prevailed. At the Paris Conference in July 1946 Bevin declared Britain's readiness for four power co-operation,

> but insofar as there is no reciprocity from any particular zone or agreement to carry out the whole of the Potsdam protocol my government will be compelled to organise the British Zone of occupation in Germany in such a manner that no further liability shall fall on the British taxpayer.

A direct response to this statement can be seen in the offer made by US Secretary of State Byrnes in September 1946 of fusion of the US zone with any other which was prepared to co-operate (17). In January 1947 the Anglo/American Bizonia emerged.

The short term economic benefits of this development were doubtful, although in the longterm it was hoped that a sharing of the economic burden in Germany was in prospect. There is evidence moreover that for the British this policy shift had also a political dimension: a divided Germany had the additional political advantage of keeping the Soviet Union out of the western part of Germany. Indeed, it has been suggested that by 1946 "political-strategic" motivations were ultimately more important in deciding the course of British policy than economic considerations. This might explain the determination with which the British, more than the Americans, blocked Soviet attempts to keep the question of Germany's economic unity, reparations etc. open. Already early on the British had chosen 'the clear option of a separate (German) state in the west.' (18) There is no doubt however, that for the economic recovery of the British Zone clear decisions were required and that the end of the by now fictitious allied co-operation was a necessary precondition.

In keeping Germany divided, if this was their intention, British policy makers were completely successful. They succeeded also in their second objective, to involve the United States permanently in Europe. The possibility of their withdrawal from Europe, leaving the Soviets in a position of overwhelming power was a continuing nightmare for British policy makers. A full American commitment to Europe was not made until May 1946 when the US gave the Soviet Union a guarantee to keep Germany demilitarised for 25 years. (19) If this signalled understanding for Soviet security needs it was nevertheless also the recognition that security based on four power control of Germany could no longer be taken for granted. Inter-allied co-operation over Germany was breaking down. Indeed, almost simultaneously came the American offer to join the American Zone in order to pool resources and to run this bigger unit more efficiently. For the British it meant that the Americans were now thinking along similar lines to themselves and although in economic terms, the newly created Bizonia only brought gradual benefits to them, it was a step in the right direction. Others followed such as the Trueman Doctrine and Marshall Aid in 1947. The 'German problem' was now seen as part of a Europe-wide issue. The limitation of these schemes to western Europe only reinforced a development which culminated in the division of Germany.

Growing US involvement in Germany also meant a lessening of British influence there. This was particularly relevant to the introduction of 'socialism' into the British Zone. The Labour government which had been voted into office in July 1945 with an explicitly 'socialist' programme raised the expectations of many, including the Germans in the British Zone of Germany, that a distinctly 'socialist' foreign policy might be pursued. But the involvement of both Attlee and Bevin as members of the war-time coalition in many foreign policy debates led to an approach to foreign policy which continued the line of the conservatives: a Labour government acted first and foremost in the national interest. On the other hand there was throughout Europe the expectation that at the end of such an upheaval as National Socialism and the war represented, a new social and economic order was only natural. This expectation was particularly strong in Germany were in some way the old capitalist order was made responsible for Hitler's rise to power. The British moreover were now in control of the largest industrial conglomerate in Europe and not only ideological, economic or political but also security considerations required a reorganisation of the Ruhr.

On the other hand it was precisely because of its enormous economic but also security importance of the Ruhr that the British were never entirely free in making policies of their own choosing there. The Potsdam conference had singled out the Ruhr as one of the areas in which not only dismantling and demilitarisation was to take place; it was from here that reparations should be taken. Moreover, German industrial production was severely restricted to prevent her from becoming a security risk again. As we have already seen it was the latter which caused the British to follow a more independent line in their Zone. Once they were in a position to look at the Ruhr in isolation the possible introduction of socialising measures was more seriously considered. By this stage the lack of more drastic measures had caused great frustration in Germany; with the Social Democrats threatening the withdrawal of all their officials from public office at all levels unless progress in the introduction of 'socialism' was made soon. This was no doubt one of the reasons for Bevin's announcement, in his speech to the Commons on 22 October 1946, that 'socialism' would be introduced in the Ruhr industries. It did not silence the criticism in his own party, as mentioned above. Whether Bevin's statement was simply a 'declaration of intent' (20) or expressed further reaching policy decisions (21), unilateral British action seemed again impossible. There was the difficult question of what 'socialism' in this connection actually meant. If nationalisation then there was no national government to take the industries over. Besides it would have strengthened this government to such an extent as to undermine the original intention of weakening the country. Furthermore, there was now no German nation state and the transfer of control of such vast enterprises to a provincial government, even of a large one such as that of North-Rhine - Westphalia was a dubious solution. Additional difficulties arose from the international investments in the Ruhr industries which would have to be compensated.

While therefore in theory there was a great deal of interest in the 'introduction of socialism' in Germany in practice the British did little. Socialism was too important to be imposed on the Germans, or 'to ram it down the Germans' throats'. (22) Ultimately the Germans themselves would have to make this decision. It was however not only a specific liberal notion of democracy which led the British to be cautious but also, as a result of their financial weakness, consideration for the views of the United States. They were not in favour of socialism, rejecting it for reasons of economic efficiency but also on ideological grounds: capitalism had in fact been beneficial for the growth of democracy in the States. Bevin's proposals for the introduction of 'public ownership' of at least the Ruhr coal mines was therefore doomed to failure. After four weeks of unsuccessful negotiations, on 10 September 1947, in a joint communique responsibility for coal production was handed back to the Germans. Two months later, in Law No 75 ownership was also returned to the Germans albeit under an Anglo/American control group. The only tangible success for Britain and the German Left was the introduction of 'Mitbestimmung' (Codetermination) for the workers in the coal industry. Later, socialism was stopped by the allies in other areas too. Thus, when regional the Germans themselves in Hesse (American Zone) and North-Rhine - Westphalia (British Zone) voted in favour of the inclusion of the nationalisation of basic industries in their constitutions these paragraphs could not be prevented by the allies but their operation was suspended to a future date.

This was the price the British paid for having to rely on American involvement in Europe as a result of their economic weakness. It is arguable whether it was a 'sell-out to the United States' or whether their own determination to introduce socialism in Germany was not as strong as it needed to be, particularly early on in the occupation. The Soviets provided an uncomfortable example of what could

13

have been done.

But the introduction of Socialism would have required an enormous amount of British energy and, probably, resources neither of which was available at the time. Germany was not the priority it needed to be. Indeed many indications point to the fact that the British very early on aimed at the establishment of some form of West German state which would have to sort out its own problems, such as the organisation of the economy or the tackling of the problem of denazification - another area where the western allies failed to introduce comprehensive and consistent policies.

These attitudes presented however a major problem for those British who were in Germany with the official task of carrying out often contradictory or vague policies. To some extent they were left to fend for themselves without much guidance from above.

The Control Office for Germany and Austria

It was however not only lack of commitment to the task in Germany which led to the subsequent confusion over responsibility for the occupation. There were also tensions among Foreign and War Office, for while both wished to be involved in policy making neither was keen on the heavy additional administrative burden which the involvement in Germany would inevitably entail. During the war, as we have seen, both War and Foreign Office had taken part in the planning process. However, already in 1943 it had been envisaged that the War Office would take control of the occupation during the initial, largely military phase. (23) On 1 June 1945 therefore the War Office took control of the British Element of the Control Commission in Germany. In order to co-ordinate the London end of occupation policies it had been envisaged by the war time planners that a small office would be set up. The formation of this Control Office for Germany and Austria (COGA) was however delayed by the change of government. It was only on 17 August that a small ministerial committee under Prime Minister Attlee decided that COGA should be independent from other government departments and come within the responsibility of the Duchy of Lancaster. The War Office was to take on 'responsibility in parliament' for it. On 22 October COGA came into existence; Chancellor at this time was John Hynd.

It was based in Norfolk House.

From the beginning there were serious problems inherent in COGA's construction. Firstly, its responsibilities were not clearly defined. COGA was only intended to be responsible for the administration of CCG and not for British policy towards Germany as such which remained the prerogative of the Foreign Office. The areas where COGA could become directly involved were therefore: to act as a general 'clearing house' between the London ministries and CCG, the recruitment of staff for CCG and for British occupation policies inside the British Zone.

Even within these more modest terms however, COGA functioned only with difficulties. The Duchy of Lancaster and the War Office had no seat in the cabinet. Neither Attlee nor Bevin did much to help COGA overcome this handicap by inviting Hynd to attend at least those sessions of the cabinet when 'Germany' was on the agenda.

> The Chancellor of the Duchy feels that he should be present at the Cabinet when German questions are discussed. He (feels) that the Control Office has been left in a somewhat inviduous position as a result of ... discussion(s) in which the facts were somewhat misrepresented. It is understood that it was proposed to invite the Chancellor to (the) meeting (but) that the Prime Minister thought it unnecessary. (24)

There is ample evidence that Bevin in particular did not wish to have the 'German' case put too strongly at a time when solutions of German questions were seen by him entirely in an international context. His dislike of Germans is also well documented. (25) This government attitude towards Germany also explains the fact that it refused repeatedly to give Hynd a base in Germany and thus create a special 'Minister for Germany', a demand which was frequently put forward by COGA itself and observers who recognised the weaknesses of British occupation policies. COGA therefore always played an ambiguous role of being seen to be responsible for Germany without being given the means to carry out this task.

Secondly, the institutional confusion resulted in COGA's frequent exclusion from the normal channels of communication. Despite the fact that COGA by March 1946 had grown into an organisation of over 3000, COGA civil servants and their opposite numbers in the CCG often did not know of each others' existence. CCG personnel were still corresponding more often with their respective ministries than with COGA. The latter did not even receive copies of the regular 'Activity Reports' which the different CCG branches were producing. Field Marshal Montgomery's divers' addresses 'to the German people' were not distributed to Norfolk House. All this seriously limited the amount of up-to-date information available to COGA, leading to rather crude jokes in parliament and the press about COGA as the 'hyndquarters' of the occupation. It also prevented COGA from making its views known in time to affect decisions taken in Germany on important matters such as the voting system to be introduced in the future West German state. (26) COGA's activities were also circumscribed by the lack of direct contact between it and the lower levels of Military Government. These were generally routed via headquarters in Berlin, leading to serious congestion there and further isolation of COGA. The latter was seen by CCG as simply a service department rather than a centre where political decisions were being made. Criticisms which CCG levelled at COGA referred therefore to matters such as the latter's inability to provide the right staff quickly rather than a lack in political guidance. The latter was expected to come from the Foreign Office and the cabinet but in the event this often did not materialise. Important decisions such as the length of the occupation (some members of CCG thought of 20 years) or to what degree the British Zone should be run directly or only indirectly by the British were never taken.

The personal qualities of Hynd may therefore not have played such a decisive role as has sometimes been suggested. (27) He had been a railway union official before the war and was the MP for Sheffield. Although he spoke good German he lacked experience of foreign affairs and in particular the kind of personality which might have given his office the weight with Bevin which it lacked formally. On the other hand, when Hynd was replaced by Pakenham (Lord Longford) in April 1947 the representation of German interests did not have more success with Bevin despite Lord Longford's more flamboyant style. Within the constraints of his office Hynd worked extremely hard, conducting Reisediplomatie, a ceaseless journeying between Britain and Germany although because of his rather reserved manner with only limited success. It was really only under Pakenham that British goodwill was brought home to the Germans on a wider scale.

A third problem for COGA was the inevitable overlap between its own terms of reference and the overall responsibility for Germany of the Foreign Office, as part of Britain's foreign affairs. As noted above the links between Military Government and Foreign Office were always closer than those with COGA. Although COGA prepared the government White Paper of May 1946 it required the approval of the Foreign Office. Policy papers concerning Germany such as Cabinet Paper 46 of 6 September 1946 which anticipated the devolution of power in the British Zone to the Germans were drafted by the Foreign Office without significant input from COGA. This reflected the decision which Attlee had taken already in August 1946

> that in regard to political German questions, the Chancellor of the Duchy should regard himself as being under the direction of the Secretary of State (for Foreign Affairs) and as virtually responsible to the FO. (28)

COGA was now recognised as what it had always been: an anomaly in the British government structure. It lingered on till April 1947 when, in the process of a general reshuffle it was taken over into the Foreign Office where it formed for a time an enlarged German Section which was gradually reduced in numbers over the next few years.

THE BRITISH MOVE TO GERMANY

The End of the War and the Establishment of Military Government in the Zone

In the spring of 1945 north-west Germany which was to become the British Zone was occupied, as planned, by 21st Army Group under Field Marshal Montgomery. This consisted of the first Canadian Army, the Second British Army and the 9th US Army. Whereas the Canadians and British moved north and north-east respectively (the British cutting off the Soviet advance into Denmark as well as the influx of German soldiers and civilians into Sleswig Holstein), the Americans moved into the centre of Germany until they linked up with Soviet troops on the river Elbe near Magdeburg, (see App. I: Map).

The advance of allied troops was swift. (29) 21st AG

consisted of 35 well equipped divisions against, on the German side, one parachute army with 10 divisions which had only 40 tanks operational. Between 23 March, the beginning of the crossing of the Rhine, and 3 May, when the German High command began negotiations for a partial surrender in Lüneburg the whole of North Germany came under allied control. On 4 May Montgomery and the German General Von Friedensburg signed the "Instrument of surrender of all German Forces in Holland, North West Germany, including all islands and Denmark". The Second World War in the region ended officially on 5 May at 8 a.m. Montgomery had refused to negotiate the surrender of troops fighting on the eastern front. The unconditional surrender of all German forces took place on 7 May at Eisenhower's headquarters in Rheims, and early on 9 May at the Soviet headquarters, Karlshorst in Berlin.

With the end of the war a reality, the British faced a number of tasks: (30) they had to disentangle from the conglomerate of fighting troops those military formations which were to stay in Germany to provide military back-up for Military Government; the headquarters of 21 Army Group had to become the headquarters of the British zone and all military units which were to remain in Germany had to be brought under its command; the areas of the British Zone which had been occupied by non-British troops had to be put under British control; the Military Government structure had to be built up at all levels. These four tasks were tackled simultaneously. When they were completed the mobile phase of the occupation had ended.

It had been planned that each former Prussian province should come under the control of one Army Corps and should be administered by one provincial "(P)" Military Government Detachment. This plan had to be modified when the creation of a French zone out of the British and American zones was accepted at the Yalta Conference. The southern part of the originally British Rhine province was allocated to the French and the northern half linked with Westphalia to form a new province, North-Rhine-Westphalia. However, the four provincial Military Governments were preserved, so that the British Zone had the following arrangement:

I Corps District

307/308 (P) Military Government Detachment: Province Westphalia, Land Lippe, Land

Schaumburg - Lippe

714 (P) Military Government Detachment:
Province North-Rhine

<u>VIII Corps District</u>

312 (P) Military Government Detachment:
Province Sleswig - Holstein, Hamburg

<u>XXX Corps District</u>

229 (P) Military Government Detachment:
Province Hanover, Land Brunswick, Land
Oldenburg

The provincial Military Government headquarters were situated in Münster, Düsseldorf, Kiel and Hanover whereas the Corps headquarters were at Iserlohn, Plön and Nienburg respectively. (31) Below the level of provincial (P) Military Government, detachments were in accordance with German administrative levels - the (L/R) Military Government Detachment (small 'Land' or Regierungsbezirk) and under them were the country or town district units: (L/K) or (S/K) Military Government Detachments (Land- or Stadt-Kreis). The British often just used the term 'K' Detachments to describe the lowest level of Military Government.

However this hierarchical system only emerged gradually for while it worked on the provincial and the next lower, the Regierungsbezirk, levels, the local Military Government units remained under the control of local military units. In one way this arrangement made sense as often local Military Government detachments were exceedingly small - not more than 5 or 6 men for a whole city in some cases - so that it was more important for them to co-operate with local troop commanders than with the remote (and due to lack of communications often unapproachable) higher Military Government echelon. But this was initially even the case with a local Military Government Detachment such as that in Hanover where the higher echelons were close at hand. Military Government Detachment 518 (S/K) remained under a variety of military units until its withdrawal at the end of May. Its Diaries illustrate well the way in which such detachments were set up, the enormous tasks they faced with their tiny numbers and the high turnover of their 'masters' whose help they

19

accepted gratefully: there were six changes between 10 April and 22 May.

In the long run such a system was no solution particularly as it cut off the higher levels of Military Government from Military Government on the ground. Thus the leader of the provincial Military Government in Hanover, Colonel Bruce complained:

> All (K) dets are placed under command of local formations. In some cases they were further allotted to regiments ... This system has, in my view, been extremely unfortunate as it has resulted in my being divorced from all detachments in this area which have been allotted to important towns. For four weeks I have had no control of the doings of the detachments in the towns of Hanover, Hildesheim and Brunswick while I never had any say in the affairs of Hamlin and Göttingen.
>
> Meantime an unknown and ever changing number of American Detachments and Military Government officers have been working at <u>Gemeinde</u> level. It has proved utterly impossible to keep trace of their movements, especially as they were operating under the command of various Divisions and even lower formations.
>
> The presence of this kaleidoscopic array of troops on the ground has rendered the reactivation of the civil administration at <u>Regierungsbezirk</u> and <u>Provinz</u> level extremely difficult. It does not help if a food official is sent out three times in a car to do a particular job and each time returns afoot despite the liberal plastering of his various vehicles with every conceivable kind of authority, both British and American. (32)

Eventually, on 27 May a division of labour between 21st AG and the provincial Military Government commander was drawn up on the basis of which the latter took on responsibility for most Military Government matters with a small liaison staff at Corps HQ. By the end of June the Military Government build-up was complete.

The CCG in Germany

With the official end of hostilities the British CCG

20

contingents began to arrive in Germany and initially congregated in the Hanover area. (33) It was decided to set up the commission's zonal headquarters in 5 small Westphalian towns rather than in one of the larger towns which were too devastated and in many cases still teeming with roaming DPs (34) and other disorderly elements.

Simultaneous with deployment in the zone an advance party went to Berlin to prepare the establishment of the four power Allied Control Council (ACC), and of the British Element (BE) of the higher CCG levels there. After the Soviets allowed the western powers access to Berlin on 1 July - the first session of the ACC took place on 30 July - four power control of Germany had begun.

For the British Element two tasks required attention: the transfer of control of Military Government to it and the transformation of the Military Government field organisations from military to civilian units. The latter was a gradual process, by adding civilian specialists or recruiting demobilised soldiers for a job which they had done previously as a soldier. The transfer of control took place on three levels: 21st Army Group became, as British Army of the Rhine, a purely military formation on 25 August 1945. It was divested of all Military Government functions. On 3 September the chief of Military Government affairs at 21st AG, General Templar, now became Deputy Chief of Staff (Execution) at the main headquarters of the BE, responsible to Montgomery as Chief of Staff (British Zone) and Montgomery in his other capacity, as British member in the Allied Control Council.

The second transfer took place in London when COGA was created to take over CCG business from the War Office and other Government departments. The third took longest and was the transformation of Corps Commanders who had also been Military Governors of 'their' areas, into civilians. Their Military Government functions were transferred to the provincial (P) Detachments. In April 1946 the corps commanders were replaced by civilian Regional Commissioners. (App 2. CCG (BE) in full deployment, September 46). However, for a long time the overall character of the British in Germany remained military, particularly as even civilian members wore uniform to give them status in the eyes of the Germans. It seems therefore that the whole 'civilianisation' concept was somewhat unnecessary, only adding confusion and layers of officials. From the beginning of its operation, already in the autumn of 1945 the CCG came in for criticism from the more able people who had gone to Germany with high hopes and who found themselves utterly frustrated because of the CCG's complicated structure, (its top heaviness leaving able people at lower levels without a job), and the incompetence of many senior officials. There were also complaints about pay and allowances and about the 'colonial spirit' which pervaded the CCG, when 'officers' refused to mix with the other 'ranks' socially - let alone with Germans.

The feelings were expressed in a private letter to General Robinson, Deputy Military Governor, at the beginning of 1946. The letter was later circulated in a shortened version in COGA, the FO and WO and led to considerable soul searching as to 'the need for examination of the organisation and principles of the German Commission'. In a memorandum produced for Sir A Street, top civil servant of COGA, by COGA's four heads of department, the lack of direction and leadership of British war time planning and post-war policies in Germany was revealed. According to the document, before the end of the war the commission had been directed to adopt the method of 'indirect control' in Germany. As things turned out at the end of the war the Commission '... had been compelled to embark on much more direct control ...'

> The question now (in March 1946) was whether there was not some reluctance to abandon direct control methods which were working satisfactorily and hesitation to risk failure and inefficiencies which might result from early handing over to the Germans.

But before the Commission could be restructured COGA felt that

> ... it did not appear that there was a sufficiently clear definition of the fundamental policy of HMG - for instance how long is occupation of Germany to be maintained, how much latitude can be expected in the development of the German economy and politics, how far can inefficiency of a new-founded German administration be tolerated ... (35)

The contradiction was clear: on the one hand the 26,000 staff of the CCG, costing £80 million in 1946, urgently required a drastic cut, on the other hand even that inflated personnel was insufficient to directly administer Germany. According to A. Bramall newly elected MP for Bexley and formerly Military Government officer in Hanover, there was among CCG members

> ... too much colonial spirit, and too much imbued too with the spirit that, because we have conquered the Germans, the individual German is a person to whom no attention need be given at all ... (36)

It remained to be seen how this mixture of lack of overall policy, a cumbersome occupation structure, over-staffed but lacking in expertise and often pervaded by a 'colonial spirit', would affect emerging German political life.

German Preparations for the End of the War and Allied Occupation

As the allied armies advanced further into Germany the vast majority of Germans believed that military defeat was inescapable, hoped that the end would come quickly and that the western allies would occupy most of their country. They were terrified of occupation by the Russians and although the different German attitudes towards the western allies and the Soviets owes something to Nazi propaganda which had depicted the Bolsheviks as 'Untermenschen', it was mainly the different standards of behaviour of the troops which impressed the German population: reasonably disciplined in the west but often not so in the east. There was one objective shared by most Germans: the will to survive and to procure food and shelter. Apart from this there was general war weariness and lethargy. (37) On a more practical level it is possible to single out a number of German preoccupations immediately before the arrival of the allies: (38) to hide food and valuables, to evacuate the majority of civilians from urban centres and often even from villages where fighting was expected; the Volkssturm (Hitler's last recruits, the old, infirm and young under the control of the NSDAP and SS) and, where still in existence, regular Wehrmacht units made preparations for a last ditch defence; the higher Nazi leadership fled or committed suicide; lower party ranks destroyed all incriminating evidence such as NSDAP files, badges, uniforms etc. Once occupation by the allies had taken place, after or without a last ditch battle, the civilian population returned full of curiosity about the allies and with a mixture of relief that it was all over and apprehension about what was in store for them.

The city of Hanover, on which this study will increasingly focus, illustrates the process. Here on 5 April NSDAP Gauleiter Lauterbacher published an appeal to the people of Lower Saxony "Rather dead than Slave" in which he called all to "fanatic endeavour: the enemy has passed through Hesse and Westfalia and stands with tank and infantry units on the borders of our Gau."

> Our homeland is in extreme danger ... We are willing and determined to use all means and possibilities without pity to protect our Lower Saxonian land, our women and our highest and most precious good, our children, from the reach of the Anglo-Americans and the jews, negroes, prison inmates and gangsters who will follow them.

In response to the popular belief that treatment might be more lenient in the west, Lauterbacher declared

> Mad is everyone who believes in the possibility of an honourable peace, and a difference between Anglo-Americans and Soviet hordes. We have already been deceived in 1918 ...
> After a German defeat there would be no Anglo-American West and Soviet East Europe. The dictator of the allies is Stalin. Europe and Germany will fall victim to inner Asian vultures and Dsingistans, and with that our homeland and we all will be obliterated ...

All preparations for a determined defence effort were going to be made; defeatism would incur the death penalty. "Germany lives in us and our Führer". (39)

Reality was different. Gauleiter Lauterbacher disappeared in the Harz mountains the next day. His crazy appeal, echoing Hitler's 'scorched earth' order of 19 March, was not heeded. On 9 April the Volkssturm was about to carry out instructions to blow up one of the sluices of the nearby canal which would have flooded vast areas and slowed down the approaching Americans. This was prevented by the Wehrmachtkommandant of Hanover city. The commanding district officer was then approached by the leading local government officials who appealed to him to surrender. This was agreed, but the civilians even at this stage felt they needed confirmation from 'higher authority' and contacted the area Wehrmacht command. If this was typical for German attitudes, so was the reaction of the High Command: refusal to talk to civilians but the threat of court martial for the local commander if Hanover surrendered without a fight. Hanover however did surrender unconditionally.

In the early hours of 10 April the first groups of soldiers of the 9th US Army entered the city, cautiously for their vision was restricted by fog. There were only few casualties although snipers continued to be active for a few more days. A sea of white flags greeted the occupiers; the population was subdued, but not hostile. Only those actively persecuted by the regime greeted the allies as 'liberators'. 100 heavy air raids between 10/11 February 1941 and 28 March 1945 had left the city centre so devastated that it was difficult to house the numerous allied personnel who now poured into the city. There was little water, less gas and no electricity, sewage and roads were blocked. Liberated prisoners of war, and freed political prisoners roamed the city in search of alcohol and revenge. This, without exception was the situation in all major German cities.

The British in Hanover

We have already noted that British Military Government personnel followed the fighting troops, indeed 518 S/K Detachment under Major Lamb (RA) established itself in the Town Hall on 11 April. On the same day 229 (P) Detachment, responsible for Hanover province took up its functions in the building of a Hanover firm which produced stationery, GEHA. They were joined on 12 April 1945 by the 'intermediate' layer of Military Government, 504 L/R (Regierungsbezirk) Military Government Detachment.

There was thus on the face of it an impressive array of British personnel in the city, yet Germans who lived through the period hardly remember them at all. (40) Apart from possible specifically German reasons (an attempt to blend out unpleasant memories), this illustrates the fact that the actual numbers involved were extremely small. Thus Major Lamb describes 518 S/K Military Government Detachment as consisting of eight men, including himself. These eight men were to control and restore basic services in a city of 216,000 inhabitants and over 50,000 DPs. This was only possible with the help of the fighting forces be they Americans, Canadians, British, Polish or Dutch. But even so the workload on these men was immense, as expressed in the shorthand of the War Diaries:

> 12 April ... Detachment very busy with British Ex PW 800 located in near vicinity of Hanover, the majority of whom had been prisoners nearly five years. Control of DPs commenced. Approx 60,000 in Hanover all nationalities, half being Russians and Poles ...

The same applied to 504 L/R and 229 (P) Detachments. The former, by the end of June 1945 was still without an Education Officer to oversee the reopening of the schools. (41) The latter by the end of April 1945 consisted of 58 officers and 71 men. On 8 September the total strength of the entire Military Government for 229 (P) Region was 1,212 officers and 1,637 other ranks, but in spite of these impressive figures Military Government was still short staffed in certain areas such as labour, finance and legal affairs. Moreover by September demobilisation was beginning to have its effect: the legal department was going to lose 11 British officers by the end of the month, and seven Canadians were to leave shortly. Worst of all, those men who were available were hindered in their work by an avalanche of paper.

> Schools are being reopened everywhere and the main function of every Education Officer at this time should be to inspect, advise and control. This he is completely unable to do for every day involves the reading of new instructions and the reproduction of them in a form suitable for action by non specialist officers and by GERMAN authorities. Real control of education can be exercised only in schools and unless the specialist officer can be relieved in his office this control cannot take place ... (42)

Complaints about the increase and growing complexity of the paperwork to be undertaken by the reduced numbers of Military Government officers was also voiced by 504 L/R Military Government Detachment

There is an enormous amount of paper work and shortage of staff is serious. The situation will be aggravated by demobilisations in the near future. This shortage is particularly marked at K Det level. The amount of detail and the technical complexity of the functional returns (statistical) now being called for necessitate a lot of work in conversion, first into simple ENGLISH and then translation into simple GERMAN. Unavoidably most of the information has to be obtained by the K Dets on the ground. The same applies to policy instructions now coming out which again require simplification before issue to the untrained GERMAN official on the ground who eventually has to implement these politics ... (43)

Colonel Bruce commented on this report:

I urge that constant effort be made to reduce correspondence and to keep within bounds the natural demands for precise information, the collection of which entails great labour without any corresponding degree of accuracy.

These complaints by Military Government officers on the ground are a good illustration of the way in which a vast but aimless bureaucratic machinery came into existence. It was only because of the devotion of the 'men on the ground' that impressive practical results were achieved. This was also the opinion of Sir W Strang the Political Advisor to Montgomery:

I have seldom met a body of men who are more obviously enjoying the work in which they are engaged, though they have to do it with inadequate staff, working long hours, and often in the absence of the requisite instructions. The skill, good humour and common sense with which they are guiding the local German administrations which are growing up under their care may derive from a traditional aptitude for government, but they also reflect credit upon those who planned and conducted the courses of instruction under which our military government officers were trained. (44)

However, even 'traditional aptitude for government' could

not disguise the fact that other than their own common sense, local Military Government Detachment commanders had little to turn to for guidance. Thus, in Hanover, Colonel Pownall who replaced Major Lamb at the beginning of June introduced an almost regal style into his public announcements: "I, Frank Hugh Swanwick POWNALL ("Military Cross" was crossed out) ... hereby order ..." (45)

It was not until after the Potsdam Conference that CCG (BE) produced the important 'Directive on Administrative, Local and Regional Government and the Public Services' which became the basis for local government reform and the eventual licensing of trade unions and political parties. But what local commanders needed most was some indication of how this Directive was to be interpreted. The average commanders even in January 1946 still

> ... (thirsted) for political guidance, but a chronic lack of experienced personnel has made it impossible to satisfy it. It has not hitherto been possible to maintain a special staff at Lubbecke to deal with problems arising from German political activity ... (46)

All that could be recommended from higher levels of the CCG to local officers was to be 'more liberal' in their interpretation of political ordinances (see below).

Military Government at the local level was most effective when dealing with immediate problems. We have already noted that the first problem facing the occupying forces was law and order, food and restoration of basic services. According to an eye-witness report this brought about a noticeable shift of attitude among allied personnel from an initial sympathy with DPs on the basis that 'the Germans are getting what they deserve' to the realisation that the threat to allied security did not come from the Germans as had been assumed but from thousands of undisciplined foreigners. (47)

> Very busy days ... for all his officers. Main activity to which everything else had to be subordinated has been dealing with DPs - French, Belgians, Dutch, Italians, Russians and Poles of whom there are many thousands in the area ... (48)

Likewise, the resumption of basic services produced

grudging allied admiration for German endeavour and expertise. Indeed, Colonel Pownall found German willingness to co-operate almost comical:

> During the period under review I have had the opportunity of contacting for the first time many individuals in the RB (Regierungsbezirk) administration. In all cases the eagerness to 'do the right thing' has been quite astonishing. The masochistic zest with which they accept defeat would be impossible in any other country. Where they fail, the reason can best be summed up by a recent classic mistranslation by a German MG interpreter: 'The ghost is willing but the meat is weak.' ... signed: Pownall (for Colonel Hume who is on leave.) (49)

The setting up of a German administration, the creation of a democratic police force, denazification and eventually the supervision of the emerging political groupings were to be the longterm tasks of Military Government, and are best seen in the German context.

NOTES

1. L. Kettenacker, Grossbritannien und die zukünftige Kontrolle Deutschlands, in J. Foschepoth/R. Steininger, op.cit.
2. A. Glees, Exile Politics During the Second World War, London 1982, p.131 passim.
3. Kettenacker, op.cit., p.37.
4. Kettenacker, op.cit., p.35.
5. FO 936/389 Chancellor - FO 19.9.1944.
6. FO 936/362 Kirkpatrick - Harvey 16.2.1945.
7. F.S.V. Donnison, Civil Affairs and Military Government North West Europe 1944-1946, London 1961, p.191/2. Pre-surrender Directive, issued by Combined Chiefs of Staff.
8. Donnison, op.cit., p.205.
9. Donnison, op.cit., p.197. This was one of the more shortsighted decisions of the Allies. Once in Germany after unconditional surrender the British discovered that non-fraternisation deprived them of an excellent opportunity of 're-educating' the at the time more receptive population as is expressed in a report from Hanover of August 1945.

I think, on the whole, that the majority of Germans welcome the opportunity of being able to talk to our men, and that they will be glad when they can ask them into their houses. As it is our object to educate the German people in our way of life, to make quite certain this time, that they are never under delusions as to who started this war in 1939, and to bring home to them the fact that they are responsible for all the bestialities of the Nazi regime, I feel that the sooner our men are allowed to enter German houses the better. The man who has been fighting is surely the one who is best fitted to mix with the Germans. If further relaxation of fraternisation is delayed too long, we shall find that most of the men who have borne the heat and burden of the day have been demobilised. The Germans will not pay the same attention to young soldiers out from England who have never fought. (WO 171/7879 HQ Military Government Hanover Region Fortnightly Report, 1-14 August, quoting a report from 722 (K) Detachment, Hanover City).

Already in July Detachment 504/720 (L/R) Military Government Detachment had reported that

The non-fraternisation order continues to amaze and bewilder the average German. Having been told by our propaganda ad nauseam that the majority of the German people were a prey to their unscrupulous leaders, the present argument that they were responsible for the same leaders strikes the normal German mind as a non-seqir (sic). Much more education in self-government is necessary before the German mind will accept the arguments of experienced democracy. (Wo 171/7990).

10. Donnison, op.cit. p.202.
11. FO 936/659 S/Gen/52/21 9.6.49. Brigadier van Cutsem, Genesis and Development of the Control Commission.
12. S. Pollard, The Development of the British Economy 1914-1967, London 1976, p.331/3.
13. A. Bullock, Ernest Bevin, Foreign Secretary, Oxford 1985, p.112.
14. Frank Roberts, 'Bevin and Eden: some personal impressions'. Conference on 'British Perceptions of Power in

Europe 1945-52: from Bevin to Eden.' Organised by the University Association for European Studies, King's College, London 27.9.1984. According to the speaker at no time had the FO staff worked harder.

15. B. Marshall, 'German Attitudes to British Military Government', in Journal of Contemporary History, vol. 50, 1980.

16. J. Foschepoth, Grossbritannien und die Deutschlandfrage auf den Aussenministerkonferenzen 1946/47, in, J. Foschepoth/R. Steininger (eds), op.cit., p.65 passim.

17. For the argument whether Byrnes' proposal can be seen as an 'offensive' US initiative in Germany or a 'defensive' response to the British threat of 'going it alone', see J. Foschepoth in op. cit. p.70 who follows the interpretation of J. Gimbel, "Byrnes und die Bizone-Eine amerikanische Entscheidung zur Teilung Deutschlands?, in W. Benz/H. Graml (eds), Aspekte deutscher Aussenpolitik, Stuttgart 1976, p.193-210.

18. Foschepoth, op.cit. p.84. The link between the 'economic' and the 'political' argument is also made by W. Strang, Montgomery's chief Political Advisor. In response to the Chancellor of Exchequer's remarks in the Mansion House speech of October 1946, that Britain was paying reparations to Germany rather than the other way round, he commented: "The cost of the British Zone should not, if I may say so with due deference, be regarded wholly as reparations to Germany ... We have to stay in Germany at least until the work of disarmament and demilitarisation is complete ... it would presumably not be practical politics to leave our soldiers and civilians in Germany among a starving population. We must therefore either pay to feed them or get out, and getting out now would mean letting the Russians in ..." (FO 371/55578/C 12660 Telegram to FO 20.10.1946).

19. Bullock, op. cit., p.269.

20. W. Rudzio, 'Die ausgebliebene Sozialisierung an Rhein und Ruhr. Zur Sozialisierungspolitik von Labour Regierung und SPD 1945-48'; in: Archiv für Sozialgeschichte XVIII, 1978, p.1.

21. W. Lademacher, Die Sozialisierungspolitik im Rhein-Ruhr Raum, in: Foschepoth/Steininger (eds), op. cit., pp.101-119.

22. FO 371/65444/C1537. Intelligence Report, November 1947.

23.   U. Reusch, 'Die Londoner Institutionen der britischen Deutschlandpolitik 1943-48. Eine behördengeschichtliche Untersuchung', in: Historisches Jahrbuch 100/1980, p.379.

24.   FO 941/4/CS 4/3. Extract of Cabinet Minutes 7.2.1947. At the time the timber supply in the British Zone was discussed.

25.   He could not forgive them for the war because he felt they had betrayed the efforts of British trade unionists after World War I to bring about relations of trust between British and German trade unionists.

26.   U. Reusch, op.cit., p.403.

27.   J. Thiess "What is going on in Germany? Britische Militärverwaltung in Deutschland 1945/46", in C. Scharf/H.J. Schröder (eds), Die Deutschlandpolitik Grossbritanniens und die britische Zone 1945-49, p.29. See also the contribution by W. Patterson and J. May in the same volume.

28.   Reusch, op.cit., p.401.

29.   U. Schneider, Britische Besatzungspolitik 1945. PhD Thesis, Hanover 1980, p.19 passim.

30.   Schneider, op.cit., p.26.

31.   Donnison, op.cit., p.226 with map.

32.   PRO WO 171/7955 War Diary 229 (P) Military Government Detachment May 1945 Appendix XIII.

33.   PRO 371/46697/C2637 Minute O'Neill 25.5.45.

34.   DP = Displaced Person. Foreign workers brought to Germany to work in factories there during the war and now liberated but homeless.

35.   FO 936/236. S/Gen/2/9 Memo COGA HoDs to Sir A Street, COGA, 16.3.46.

36.   HoC 29.7.46.

37.   M. Steinert, Hitler's War and the Germans, 1977, p.302.
It is interesting to note that apathy and despondency was greatest among the middle class whereas the working class simply carried on working even under awful conditions, their criticism reserved for the leading Nazis for not having excluded the 'lame' middle class from influence much earlier by a social revolution.

38.   Schneider, op.cit., p.23 passim.

39.   SAH, Poster Collection.

40.   Interviews, Projekt Arbeiterbewegung (PAH) der Universität Hannover.

41.   WO 171/7990 Monthly Report of Det 504/720 for

July 1945. App (N) Education 1 July.

42.   WO 171/7990 Appendix "F" to Fifth Fortnightly Report by Military Government Hanover Region, covering period 30.8.-13.9.1945 Education and Religious Affairs.

43.   Loc. cit. "Paper Work". Already in July the Hanover Education Officer had commented:

> The amount of paper seems to be steadily increasing and returns called for have at times credited SOs Education with a gift of prophecy. Assessments of what is likely to occur as a result of action that may be taken by higher authority are pure guesswork and not very informative for the recipients. (WO 171/7990 Monthly Report of Det. 504/720 for July 1945).

44.   FO 371/46933/C3858 Sir W. Strang - A. Eden 13.7.1945.

45.   SAH, Poster Collection.

On 28 August there was a changeover at the highest level of the provincial Military Government when Brigadier Lingham took over from Colonel Bruce. Although much more constructive in his attitude to the Germans, he was totally unprepared for his post in Germany. He had expected a posting in the Pacific. (WO 171/7879. War Diary of HQ Mil Gov Hanover Region, 1-31 August 1945).

46.   FO 371/55610/C 11763 Office of Pol. Adviser to C-in-C, Adv HQ Berlin - Rt Hon E. Bevin, FO 12.1.46.

A 'German Political Branch' was in fact set up at Zonal Headquarters but according to its head, Noel (now Lord) Annan it consisted of only three men. They were not only to maintain an overview over political developments in the Zone, but also to advise Military Government personnel and Germans alike. (Interview 25.4.1985).

47.   P. Moseley, Report from Germany, 1946, p.75.

48.   WO 171/7990 Military Government Detachment 504 L/R Diaries Entry 17.4.1945.

49.   Loc.cit. Monthly Report for September.

Chapter Two

LOCAL LIFE UNDER MILITARY GOVERNMENT DURING THE 'INTERREGNUM': APRIL - AUGUST 1945

The allies' shock at the extent of devastation suffered by the city of Hanover is born out both by the statistics, and by the Town Administration's own reports. The Allies had started bombing the town as early as 1 August 1940, with the first heavy raid on 10/11 February 1941. After their decision of January 1943 to carry out the 'Combined Bomber Offensive' the raids were stepped up with American target bombing during the day and British area bombing at night. In all the city was subjected to one hundred raids and over 800 air attack alarms with their profoundly upsetting effect on the population. About 5000 people were killed in these raids, and many more had fled into the surrounding countryside, reducing the number of Hanover's inhabitants from 472,000 in 1939 to 217,000 in 1945. The town centre was so completely destroyed that the German officials, when reviewing the damage, considered 'whether it would not be more sensible to rebuild the city somewhere else than to try and bring order into this chaos.' (1) (Appendix III: Statistics)

The reason why Hanover suffered so particularly from bombing by the allies was the fact that it was of prime strategic and industrial importance. Geographically, it was situated at the east-west/north-south intersections of the railways and motorways. It was also served by the east-west Mittellandkanal which provided cheap links with the industrial areas of the west of Germany. This favourable position had before the war brought steady economic growth and prosperity to the town. It had developed modern industrial plants and during the Second World War produced vital military equipment, mainly in its light metal industries: aircraft, tanks, and ammunition. It also had a large rubber plant, the Continental Works.

Now, at the end of the war, the number of businesses was drastically reduced from 19,048 in 1939 to 7,776 in 1945. Many would never recover, particularly the smaller ones and by 1950 the general trend was also noticeable in Hanover: the growth of the service industries at the expense of manufacturing industries with an accompanying change in the social structure, an increase of white collar as against blue collar workers. For the immediate post-war years, however, the remarkable feature was how quickly seemingly devastated industrial plants could take up production again. This is illustrated by numerous accounts of how plants were cleared up and restarted in the summer of 1945.

The first task of the allies as they entered the city was to find reliable Germans whom they could use to bring some order into the existing chaos. Immediately, on 10 April, when the Americans had established themselves in the Town Hall they were approached by three members of the Hanover 'underground', a loose network of people who had always opposed National Socialism and who had prepared themselves for precisely this event: the collapse of the Third Reich. On their recommendation the Americans made two key appointments: Gustav Bratke (2) as Oberbürgermeister who was to build up and head the German town administration, and Emil Barth (3) as chief of police whose help was indispensable to the allies in the troubled times that followed. According to the account of one of the three men from the underground the Americans instructed him to involve himself actively in a third area: to form an ad hoc Reconstruction Committee (RC) from among his political and trade union friends to assist both the allies and the German administration and the population in as many practical ways as possible. (4)

When the British took over from the Americans one day later, they endorsed the American decisions, albeit with some misgivings: Bratke, although obviously politically irreproachable and vastly experienced as an administrator was nevertheless a man of strong opinions which given his age, might spell trouble. Barth's appointment was made a temporary one, he was to be released as soon as a 'more experienced' police officer could be found. The fact that Barth had been Director of the Hanover police before 1933 did not, in the eyes of the British, constitute 'police experience' as he had been purely a civil servant and had not risen through the ranks.

With these Germans installed the main tasks could be tackled: law and order had to be restored, basic services repaired, the German administration built up and first denazification measures taken. All these took place simultaneously.

THE RESTORATION OF LAW AND ORDER

One reason why Hanover was not militarily defended was that behind the lines looting had already begun in some of the suburbs which the overstretched German authorities could no longer control. The allies themselves of course quickly discovered the dimensions of the problem of law and order. There were large numbers of DPs in the Hanover area and, to a lesser degree, in Hanover itself: 215,611 in the district and over 50,000 in Hanover city (45,786 in November 1945). (5) 167,294 were from the Soviet Union and Eastern Europe; they were reluctant to return home and were particularly incensed by the recent discovery that the SS, as late as 8 April 1945, had shot 200 Russians. (6) The statistics for the period show an alarming rise in the cases of violent crimes: between 10 April and the end of May DPs committed 34 accounted murders in Hanover alone. (App. III). One problem was that the DPs, as members of the victorious allied nations did not automatically recognise the authority of Military Government. Numerous posters in the town reminded the DPs - in Polish, English and German - that 'all persons except members of the Armed Forces are subject to Military Government Law.' (7)

In several meetings Major Lamb and OB Bratke discussed the situation. (8) A first measure was to give ceremonial burial to the 200 murdered Russians; known Nazis were made to dig the graves and the whole population was forced to take part. Although this was psychologically most important as an act of retribution and demonstrative punishment, it did little to bring the situation under control. This only happened after the DPs had been put into camps where they came under the authority of members of their own nationality, and where they enjoyed a comparatively high standard of living with double the food ration of the German population, which could be sold profitably on the quickly flourishing Black Market. In all 270 such camps were created.

One reason for the protracted difficulties made by the

DPs was the comparative weakness and lack of experience of the security forces. Public order after the end of hostilities fell to the domain of Public Safety Officers who were usually recruited from the police forces of their native countries. Thus one of the two British Public Safety Officers serving with 518 (K) Detachment under Major Lamb was Police Constable Wintherbotham from Cambridge who until the war had been responsible for traffic offences in Cambridge. This was hardly an adequate preparation for the tasks in Germany. Although supported by Dutch, Belgian and Scandinavians they were hopelessly outnumbered which made it imperative that a German police force should be built up. The Germans after all knew the geography and, in many cases, the physiognomy of crime and the criminals.

The job of building up a politically reliable and efficient police force was entrusted to E. Barth, as noted above. Special care was required as Nazi infiltration of the police had been particularly successful. It had become much more centralised and particularly during the war, strongly militarised. Initially therefore the men for the new service were handpicked and came under the close control of the Public Safety Officers for practical operations, and for administrative purposes under the German Oberbürger-meister. Their numbers initially were small. They were unarmed and recognisable by an armband in the case of new recruits; older men carried on wearing their green uniforms until the British insisted they were replaced by blue ones at the end of 1945. Very soon it became apparent that a small, unarmed force was ineffectual in the face of often armed trouble-makers. It was therefore all too easy, as more police were required either to take the place of allied personnel or simply to enlarge the force, for politically dubious elements to drift back into the service. But initially this did not affect the relationship between German police and British Public Safety officers where the common task of fighting crime soon created an atmosphere of camaraderie. Moreover, the German police became the indispenable executive organ of Military Government in such a variety of areas that the service developed into the 'girl Friday of the occupation', which in turn solicited the respect of Military Government officers.

However, the political background of the German policemen soon had no more significance. Faced with the choice between efficiency and political purity the British as well as Barth clearly plunged for the former. There was little doubt that the Hanover police was efficient but its political composition was so blatantly in conflict with openly professed allied policies of 'denazification' and 'democratisation' that there were endless attempts to get Barth to make changes. Thus Kurt Schumacher, the leader of the emerging Social Democratic Party approached Barth so as not to let slip a golden opportunity to eradicate undemocratic elements from the force; indeed Barth was betraying his party allegiance by his actions (see below). Eventually, through the services of Germans in exile in London, Schumacher had the matter raised in the House of Commons in May 1946.

As a result a special Denazification Panel for the Police was set up and a number of men were dismissed, but the initial damage could not be redressed.

THE RESTORATION OF BASIC SERVICES AND SUPPLIES

On 1 May 1945 only 11% of the area of Hanover city was supplied with water and 25% received electricity. By 1 June 55% and by 1 July 96% of all houses had water and electricity reconnected. (9) Military Government Engineering Service together with the German experts could show astounding progress in the reconstruction of the gas and sewage pipes, as well as the restoration of railways, roads, bridges, refuse collection and street cleaning. By 15 October, or just six months after the occupation of the city, a situation approaching normality had been created. While British reports mention this achievement with some pride, (10) those of German administrators written three years later do not refer to a British contribution at all. (11) With hindsight, the unsolved problems loomed larger: 6 million cubic feet of rubble still remained to be shifted, and while the main roads had been relatively quickly cleared, an acute housing shortage still existed; there were only inadequate supplies of building materials to carry out urgent repairs to damaged houses and there was even less labour. There were also from the beginning precariously low stocks of food and heating materials.

Compared to the figures of 1939 the number of flats available in Hanover in 1945 had decreased by 45% and that of rooms by 55%. The situation was made bearable only by the sharp drop in the population. However, as people drifted back and life resumed, the only available accommodation was in the suburbs and here overcrowding was considerable with two thirds of all households having to share a kitchen with three or more people. (12) This situation also explains the comparatively low number of refugees who stayed in Hanover; those in November 1945 only made up 1.5% of the population (as against 6.5% foreigners). Compared to the surrounding countryside the town's permanent intake of refugees was small.

Reconstruction of destroyed, and more urgently, the repair of damaged housing was therefore of paramount importance. The magnitude of this task and the problems involved are well expressed in a note from the Municipal Building Office. Shortages of building materials and labour were only part of the problem. There was also the lack of an overall building plan and the fact that any action by Germans had to take Military Government wishes into account. Under the circumstances it seemed almost futile for German officials to spend much time on working out detailed plans for reconstruction, but this was nevertheless necessary.

> Even if it seems that at this moment there is no possibility of carrying through such measures, an attempt to do this must still take place, since otherwise the town administration could be justifiably reproached for neglecting (its duties) ... (13)

By August 1945 Military Government had established a system of tight controls in the building sector; it simply stepped into the functions previously exercised by Reich authorities, such as the Reich Housing Commissioner and the Labour Front. On 13 August in a meeting between German and British officials the Germans were informed that

> Overall control of reconstruction was to take place through the Oberpresident throughout the whole province ... British Military Government is to supervise these matters ... and to co-ordinate all authorities involved in this programme ... the provincial office will be responsible for all matters previously dealt with by the Reich Housing Commissioner, the Gau Housing Commissioner and the German Labour Front ... New Housing Offices for province, districts and towns will be set up ...

No building work could be carried out without approval from the provincial level. But as approval would only be given provided the necessary building material was available the Germans were in almost a 'Catch 22' situation. Moreover, in their attempt to control the supply of these scant resources the British initiated a comprehensive stocktaking exercise which required the German authorities to provide detailed information often at short notice. Thus in August 1945 they had to supply answers to the following questions within three days:

1. How many workers and how much material is necessary to deal with the minor damages?
2. How much for moderately damaged houses?
3. How much for the schools, hospitals, churches, vital businesses etc?

In addition, a summary of the total requirements is to be given again.

This information had to be incorporated into an overall urban reconstruction plan. (14) This rather cumbersome British approach appeared to the Germans to impose an unnecessary bureaucratic burden on their already overstretched personnel while adding nothing towards solving the real problems of reconstruction. In their frustration, the Germans felt that the British stifled German local initiatives and had actually delayed the rebuilding process. (15)

Next to the shortage of building materials the major problem was the shortage of labour. There were a number of obvious reasons for this: the smaller number of men as a result of death or removal as prisoners of war; the fact that traditionally Hanover had recruited much of its labour force from an area south-east of the city (known as the "Eichsfeld") which was now cut off because it was in the Soviet Zone; the knowledge that there was a shortage of adequate accommodation kept many men in the countryside. The British had made repeated promises that prisoners of war would be released to ease the situation but these were never made available in the numbers promised and required. The situation actually got worse as time went on because in the early weeks after the end of the war many industrial plants had not started up production and their workers could be used for urgent public works. Moreover, it was heavy work for which neither additional food rations nor special clothing was available. Thus the head of the city's Engineering Department informed OB Bratke

The position at the moment is as follows:
At the moment there are no longer any extra rations for overtime working and extra rations for heavy work are only available twice a month, so that those doing heavy work have to go without for two weeks in the month.

In the case of foreign workers taking part in clearing-up work, the industrial inspection board does not recognise the heavy nature of the work. As a result these workers do not receive any extra rations. In my opinion this is not fair, since workers who are clearing up not only clear the blocked streets with shovels, but they also have to carry out much heavy manual work, which is very dusty and dangerous. In my opinion they should be treated in the same way as demolition workers.

The workers employed are expressing great displeasure over the attitude of the industrial inspection board. Naturally their productivity is suffering; it must also be taken into account that they are starved anyway and therefore are very weak. (16)

In addition to these problems work for Military Government had priority and firms requisitioned into providing labour for the British were no longer available to the German authorities. There were many cases of abuse with German workers officially requisitioned for a job that had been done in or required only half the time claimed. While these workers were not available to the town administration they could be busy for their own benefit. (17)

On the other hand the town administration persistently refused to conscript known Nazis into removing the rubble which indirectly they had been responsible for creating. That they should do so was a popular demand, particularly with anti-fascists, trade unions etc. That this was not done more widely is connected with the whole approach to the problem of National Socialism (see below).

As noted above, one of the reasons for the shortage of labour was the scarcity of extra food to compensate those employed on projects involving heavy labour for their loss of energy. Indeed, the food situation for the public in general was not good. In April 1945 the average consumer had to live on 1540 calories a day, when medical opinion held 2000 calories to be the absolute minimum required by an adult to continue a normal, active life. By the end of May there was a further decrease in rations to 1150 calories which reflected the effects of the looting of food reserves and the almost complete breakdown of communications between Hanover and its food suppliers in the surrounding countryside, in particular in the Soviet Zone which had become inaccessible. A long report on the general supply situation in the city written in April 1947, (18) gratefully recalls the British contribution to getting looting under control and helping with transport to make food from outside the city available. But much of this precious food had to be diverted to feed DPs first, and what was worse in German eyes, the British were duped by the DPs excessive food demands; the latter simply diverted their supplies onto a Black Market where Germans had to buy back food which should have been rightfully theirs in the first place. Again, the Germans complained of exaggerated bureaucratisation of the system when the British insisted on introducing newly designed ration cards based on calories which were unknown in Germany, at a time when, in the eyes of the Germans, there were more important things to worry about, such as the actual delivery of food.

In many ways the town administration continued its work of the war years. Just as it had had to accommodate and refurbish those who had been bombed out, they now collected - on a wider scale - clothing, furniture and other goods. But the situation was not helped by further demands, this time by the British to equip their accommodation, which they had requisitioned from the Germans. Indeed, requisitioning was very unpopular in the bombed out city and led, a year later, to protest demonstrations and petitions. Time and again it was German ingenuity in by-passing official channels which eased the supply situation, and overall the system of controls did not work satisfactorily from the British point of view. This applied both to inter-provincial trade which the British had banned and also to the working of their own systems of forms, claims and finance (see below). As late as November 1945 there was much confusion: 'The ... commander is calling a conference of all procurement officers in S/K and L/K Hanover to clarify the situation ...' (19)

THE BEGINNING OF THE GERMAN ADMINISTRATION

The practical problems outlined in the previous sections had to be tackled by Military Government officers who had only a rudimentary knowledge of local conditions, and by Germans who were demoralised and, before the official end of the war, often reluctant to come forward to co-operate with the 'enemy'. In Hanover, Bratke from the moment of his appointment plunged into tireless activity and it was to some extent due to his determination that other German experts came forward so quickly. (20)

Already during the war the British had given some thought to the kind of administrators they wished to appoint and had collected information from Germans in exile in the UK for this purpose. Thus a former Assistant Secretary in the Prussian Ministry of Finance had a list of 83 names of 'possible candidates for posts in local administration.' (22) This information was supplemented in November 45 by a further list of 'senior administrative officials in Germany (British Zone)'. (23) Once in Germany, the British did in fact appoint men from the war-time list although many, such as Bratke, had not figured, their names being added later. It was clear that whilst the British thought in terms of a purge of personnel they did not at this stage plan the change in the administrative structure which was proposed later and, in the form of Local Government Reform, put into practice (see below, Chapter 4).

The old Prussian administrative structure was simply revived. This had consisted of a clear channel of command from the Prussian Minister of Interior to the Oberpresident (OP) of a province to the Regierungspresident (RPr) of a district comprising several small towns or rural districts. The RPr held a watching brief over the local administrators in his district.

At the lowest level was the Oberbürgermeister (OB) of a town, and the elected local town councils enjoyed a measure of autonomy although their minutes and many of their decisions had to be submitted to the RPr.

Once they had moved into Germany and with OB Bratke installed, the British next appointed a RPr (H Kopf) on 5 May to co-ordinate the district business, and this was followed on 11 May by the recruitment of an OP for the province of Hanover (E. Hagemann). (24) As Prussia no longer existed, the British assumed the position of the former Prussian Minister of Interior: this became particularly important in financial matters. On the face of it 'normal' administration could thus begin. But there were a number of problems to be overcome: as all three layers of administration were actually located in Hanover accommodation proved difficult to find, and working conditions particularly in the winter were terrible. Also, by making these appointments the British pre-empted alternative administrative arrangements. Many Germans at the time believed that the historically evolved Prussian structure was no longer right in the post-war situation. Lastly, conflict also arose between the men appointed: although Bratke and Kopf were members of the SPD, Bratke was a staunch advocate of local autonomy and had campaigned during much of the Weimar Republic for more independence for the cities from the watchdog, the RPr. Moreover, OP Hagemann stood politically on the right as a member of the former Guelph Party.

Once the appointments were made the German administration in the British Zone started up precisely where it had left off under Hitler. Even the Gemeindeordnung (Local Government Statutes) of 1936 were left in force, except for obviously Nazi provisions. OB Bratke, like his predecessors, carried out instructions from above ('Auftragsverwaltung').

If there was thus initially no break in the running of local government the population also had more immediate evidence that little had changed. Local officials were as rude as ever, or even more so, given the much more difficult circumstances in which they had to operate. British observers were stunned and reminded by this behaviour 'of the worst excesses of the Third Reich.'

> Whenever one observes ordinary Germans ... the first thing that strikes one is their complete disregard for one another their ruthlessness, and above all their complete and utter absence of any consideration for their neighbours ... I had occasion to see German officials at work ... Their contempt, rudeness and lack of interest that were encountered, defy description. (25)

One British Control Commission official reported that as to the ordinary German there seemed to be little difference between the rule of the Nazis and that of Military Government, jokes began to circulate.

> Gott gib' uns ein fünftes Reich
> Das Vierte ist dem Dritten gleich. (26)

For the next nine months Bratke wielded considerable power in Hanover. He provided the link between the British and the German population. (27) He controlled the administration and the police and was responsible for supplies to the population and the denazification of all sections of society. Every communication between Germans and British passed through him and needed his endorsement. His workload was accordingly immense: the files are bulging with requests and pleas for help. In addition to this workload there were daily meetings with the local Military Government commander to discuss a wide variety of issues; it was only in September that the meetings were scaled down to one a week.

One of the main problems turned out to be finance. With the Reich and Prussian Governments gone, it fell upon the cities to take over their financial obligations. Thus, Hanover now had to pay for what previously had been provided by central funds such as war pensions and the police, in addition to the costs emerging from the special circumstances of military defeat and occupation. One of the greatest burdens was the supply and support not only of the population of Hanover but also of DPs. The DP camps alone cost the city RM 2 million a month - an intolerable burden. Already at the end of April Major Lamb conceded that eventually these costs would have to be born by the Reichskasse or failing that by some other central fund. (28) There were also a great number of homeless people and refugees who, although just passing through the city required vast expenditure. Indeed in 1945 this was the largest single item in the city's budget.

On the other hand the city's revenues were much smaller than before and during the war. The British, on arrival in Hanover, had blocked all reserves; taxes were not being collected because of the general destruction. Soon the city had run up an enormous deficit, rising to 25.5 million RM by March 1946. One of the first measures of Military Government was therefore to order Tax Offices to start operating even though most of their buildings were destroyed and with them all financial and legal records. The German officials very much resented the manner in which they were told to work and, in particular, the detailed instructions they received. This comes out clearly in the account written in 1950 by an official of one of the tax offices:

> On the day on which Allied occupation troops marched
> into Hanover the three largest municipal tax offices ...
> were completely destroyed by enemy action ...
> everything that was necessary for productive work, ...
> was destroyed ... In order to comply with Military
> Government instructions, the department had to begin
> work again ... in spite of outrages by the mob in the
> streets, left-wing elements and foreigners and in spite
> of the difficulties imposed by the occupying power ... In
> the winter 1945/46 the ... officials worked in
> completely inadequate and unheated rooms ... with an
> abundance of extra work due to complicated allied
> legislation ... 40% of the employees suffered first and
> second degree frost bites in their hands and feet ... (29)

The tax which was eventually assessed and collected
with such difficulty turned out to be as expected much
lower than in previous years, as the level of taxation had
been fixed in 1943 and the number of people and businesses
able to pay tax had now been severely reduced. For the
immediate needs it was important to preserve the banking
system as such by avoiding a complete drain of bank
reserves. As early as April 1945, before the end of the war,
this problem was tackled, with a joint appeal by all Hanover
banks to settle much of the salaries and wages due 'in kind',
with the banks' decision to block all withdrawals from saving
accounts and not to pay out more than one third of civil
servants' salaries.

> From the statements of the banks it was apparent that
> there was not enough cash available to satisfy the
> expected demand for payment if more or less normal
> cash movements were allowed and that the Reichsbank
> (in Hanover) did not have sufficient cash, since its
> supply was falling ... (it) was laid down that for the
> time being no payment from savings accounts should be
> made. This decision has been welcomed by the savings
> bank, since even the paying out of small sums would
> doubtless have closed it down within a few days. It was
> also established that the existing supply of cash would
> not meet even the present limited wage needs and that
> a quick recovery of the sums given out was not to be
> expected. It was therefore decided, and left to the

banks and credit institutions, only to allow firms one third of their current wages or salaries bill in cash and otherwise to leave it to the individual firms how they wanted to distribute this third to the individuals entitled to it. Even the municipal savings bank thought that this recommendation would allow it to satisfy the demands of its customers for wage payments - the largest of these being the town administration itself.' (30)

Three weeks later the British had established control of the financial system and were giving detailed instructions about payments to prison inmates, the raising of loans by the city, and the appointment of responsible finance officials after denazification. An important provision was that 'the payment of family allowance is to cease.' Where necessary, the local Welfare Office had to intervene. (31)

It was very much in the spirit of normal administrative procedures that the Germans, in May, raised the question of compensation for those house and flat owners in whose property members of Military Government were billeted. (32) Far from treating this as preposterous on the part of a just defeated enemy the British accepted it and developed an intricate system of claims and forms with the help of which the occupation was put on a proper legal, accountable basis. (33) The form (21st AG 80 G) on which claims were to be made came in triplicate, in three different colours for the different channels the form had to go through. It has reached justified fame as embodiment of much of British occupation policy in Germany. It was so complicated that as late as October the Germans still needed additional explanations of how to work it. (34)

DENAZIFICATION

Besides the provision for daily needs and the organisational reconstruction, the allies had declared that denazification was one of their principal objectives in Germany. In the early phase of the occupation the treatment of Nazis was relatively simple. Based on the Anglo-American SHAEF Law No 5 which was backdated to 18.9.1944, the day on which the occupation of the west of Germany began, the NSDAP, its organisations and para-military groups were banned. One NS organisation to survive intact was the National Socialist welfare organisation, the NSV (<u>Nationalsozialistiche</u> <u>Volkswohlfahrt</u>) the vast financial commitments of which were reluctantly taken over by the local administrations. Another, the Reich Food Estate, continued to operate almost without interruption. Leading National Socialists however either fled, committed suicide or were arrested by allied troops immediately.

What was far more difficult to handle for the Allies was a denazification programme which went beyond the first wave of security measures. Denazification was another area in which the lack of overall political guidelines made itself felt: not much thought had been given to how National Socialism was to be eradicated from the mass of the German people. Basically, this required a political approach, a systematic replacement of Nazis or all those who had sympathised with them by known anti or non-fascists. We have already noted that this approach was not taken in the first weeks of the occupation by the British in Germany when a pragmatic 'muddling through' was the general method. But to apply a denazification programme based on political criteria was not acceptable to the western allies later either, mainly because they distrusted German anti-fascists (after all, they were still Germans who were kept at arm's length with the non-fraternisation rule) and also because they feared that a general shift to the left might open the door to civil unrest and advance communism.

The general political approach was not adopted, and instead membership of the NSDAP became the yardstick by which implication with the regime was measured. This personalised, 'legal' approach from the beginning had obvious flaws: it was going to be bureaucratic and slow which was psychologically wrong when the general public (Nazis included) had prepared themselves for a 'big bang' of drastic actions during which the members of the Third Reich were going to be dealt with. The 'legal' approach also did not take account of all those who were known to have benefited from the regime without being officially party members, whereas thousands of innocuous party members would be penalized.

The Germans, more than the allies initially, were aware of the complexity of the problem. It was for this reason that the leading member of Hanover's underground groups (on whose recommendation Bratke and Barth had been appointed) submitted to the British a memorandum in which a definition of Nazis, supporters (although non-members), beneficiaries etc. was attempted. It showed that membership in itself was not a useful concept as in many cases this had been the precondition for keeping or obtaining a job. By its very nature it was a lengthy and complicated document, and the British refused to act on it. (35)

Having removed well-known Nazis, Military Government for Hanover district could report the following by mid-July:

> The remains of the Nazi party and its sympathisers seems to fall at present into five main categories:
> (a) The 'big shots' almost all of whom are accounted for by mandatory arrests.
> (b) The young male rank and file who are so hard boiled as to be incapable of accepting any alternative.
> (c) The 'bread and butter' Nazis who, for personal reasons only subscribed to the faith and are equally willing to turn their coats to show a pro-British lining.
> (d) The disillusioned, in whose minds events immediately preceding the collapse have found room to stimulate the reasoning faculty and who sincerely admit that they were wrong from the beginning.
> (e) The women.
> Of these (a) can be ignored in a general survey, (c) are only likely to be a danger if conditions were allowed to deteriorate where rebellion might succeed and (d) a small but growing minority are a positive asset. (b) generally passive and time seems to be the only possible cure for them. (e) are the major problem. Mothers and potential mothers of young children are almost all ex-members of the BDM. Their hysterical worship of Hitler allows no room for the working of logic. Time alone will show whether fraternisation will act as a corrective to their present hostility ...

One major problem was the 'cleansing' of the German administration at all levels. The British charged the Germans themselves to carry this out. All those who had been members of the NSDAP and its organisations on or after 1 April 1933 were to be dismissed. For Hanover city this task fell on the <u>Oberbürgermeister</u>, Bratke. He was responsible for denazification not only in his immediate area, the city administration, but also for that of the medical service, the police and, even more unwieldy, that of the economy. From the beginning, Bratke protested sharply that a strict application of allied instructions 'would paralyse the town administration', and with this the British town commander concurred. It was this lack of political priorities which was resented by the Americans. On 3 May 1945 General Eisenhower sent another reminder from SHAEF that denazification was to be carried out rigorously, even where this meant administrative inconvenience. The British responded rather reluctantly. As Major Lamb put it, 'if it becomes apparent later on that the town administration needs more employees, then one can fall back on individuals who are not too badly compromised'. (36) Colonel Hume of 504 L/R Detachment confirmed: it was not the intention of the British 'to cause a holocaust of dismissals.' (37) For the time being the matter had to be played by ear. Particularly as except for the general SHAEF directive no further instructions had been issued.

On 19 June 1945 the Oberpresident sent out a circular to leading officials in the province requesting them to carry out the purge in their organisations. But progress seems to have been slow for on 23 July a reminder was necessary. (38) The basis for this purge was to be the innocuous British Military Government directive on how to treat 'Financial Institutions, public or private, Government Agencies, and the Officials and Employees thereof.' (39) According to this each employee had to fill in a questionnaire, and detailed instructions on how to do this properly were circulated ('All questions ... must be answered, that is every single one. It is not enough to put dashes ...' (40). This was then passed on by the superior with his comments ('according to the records of the institutions and their knowledge of the person concerned') to the appropriate Military Government Detachment. Predictably enough an avalanche of paper was produced, which slowed the process down considerably.

> Denazification is not everywhere proceeding as fast as seems desirable owing to the complete inability of Field Security to deal with Fragebogen (Questionnaires) in the numbers which are now being submitted to them. (41)

By August Military Government in Hanover could report that denazification was now being pursued vigorously and in spite of some loss of efficiency a number of intermediate civil servants were being dismissed who had in any case only been retained on a temporary basis until their successors were trained. (42) On the other hand, if denazification had really been thorough, there would have been chaos, for example in the teaching profession. Military Government felt that to carry out denazification on such a scale would prove counterproductive.

> The recent order ... that no member of the NSDAP may be employed as a teacher is considered to have catastrophic implications, and representations have been made to HQ 30 Corps District on the subject. In country districts between 80% and 90% of all teachers will have to go, in towns between 60% and 80% ...
> The German reaction to this method of dismissing teachers is certain to be unfavourable, NOT less on the anti-Nazi than on the Nazi side. (43)

The problem which denazification presented in Hanover's Town Administration is illustrated by Bratke's report to the (P) Military Government Commander in July 1945, that 'the city employed 12,000 civil servants, white and blue collar workers. Many had been employed for political reasons only, but it was difficult to get rid of the Nazis.' (44)

By November 1945 Bratke reported that 256 higher civil servants, 440 white and 165 blue collar workers had been removed from the Town Administration. The figures do not indicate the kind of posts these men had occupied. An analysis of the administration's telephone directories for 1943, 1945, 1946 and 1949 shows, however, who remained: the experts. Most of the Heads of Departments of 1943 had disappeared in 1945; of the 20 in post then only 2 survived. (The administration restarted with only 10 departments.) At the next lower level, Head of Division, far less change occurred with 25% of them actually remaining in post and 71% promoted to that rank from within the organisation. Only 4% were new recruits. Again, in the city's hospitals the leading doctors were replaced by junior men and 3 out of the five civil servants administering the Health Office (Gesundheitsamt) in 1943 carried on after 1945. Lower down the ranks there was almost no change: statisticians, building inspectors etc. remained. No 'holocaust of dismissals' had thus taken place.

The overall impression in the eyes of the general public that denazification had not been thorough enough, was therefore correct. This feeling was particularly strong in the working class and on the left generally, but Military Government was aware that the disillusionment over this aspect of their policy was widespread.

> A major problem is raised by the retention in relatively prominent positions both at RB and Province level of officials acceptable to us <u>and</u> previously employed in the same or a similar post under the NAZIS. The bulk of public opinion in this RB is in favour of a clean sweep and, ignoring administrative expediency, is perplexed at our retention of such borderline cases. The only real solution is their removal with the minimum disturbance to the workings of the machine and in this RB this is being done as far as administrative considerations will allow. (45)

Denazification in the eyes of many Germans was not only not thorough enough, there were indications that both German and British authorities combined to prevent it from becoming 'political'. This was the reason why British and Germans agreed on not employing known Nazis to clear the rubble in the street: they might be seen as martyrs and could become the focal point of possible opposition. A mild form of civil war might break out among the Germans, or an undesirable exodus of known Nazis to other areas with its unsettling consequences. (46) Everything had to be done 'properly', thus when anti-fascists tried to turn Nazis out of flats and allotments which the Nazis had taken from them in the first place, this was not allowed by the British, and Bratke concurred. (47)

This general attitude is also well illustrated by the experience of the Committee of Ex-Concentration Camp inmates (CECCI). This committee had been set up by the Americans - so its members claimed - to supervise the release from the camps and aid the reintegration into society of those unfortunate men and women who had borne the brunt of National Socialist persecution. In Hanover its members were leading representatives of the former SPD, KPD, the pro-republican <u>Reichsbanner</u> as well as of the Jewish community. The committee, from its creation had done an important job efficiently but on 2 June 1945 it was banned, together with all other committees (see below). Its application for re-founding perhaps under another name was rejected. The local Military Government commander suggested that its work be carried out by the town's welfare services. Eventually, CECCI's assurances 'that (it) pursues no political aims whatsoever and carries out no political propaganda of any kind' were successful, in that it was given permission to carry on operating as before while MG was waiting for 'guidelines'. (48) On 28 June it submitted to Military Government an impressive list of activities. But MG had already decided to hand this problem back to the Germans, this time to the provincial administration, as 'the activities of the CECCI went beyond the confines of Hanover city.' (49) The OP as a political conservative in turn used MG's general ban of committees to stop any further work by the CECCI. To make an exception would create 'a precedent'. Besides, released concentration camp inmates could always get help from official sources or even consult a lawyer. (50) This callous reply, together with the fear that the city might have to take on another set of obligations spurred the departments involved to emphatic declarations about the work of CECCI. The Food office expressed the desirability of 'one welfare centre'. (51) The Health Department praised the way in which CECCI attached photographs to ex-prisoners' records cards thus removing the possibility of duplicating benefits. (52) The police stated, rather ambiguously, 'that a <u>German</u> service would not be able to act with the same success in this area of security work'. (53) While the organisation was reluctantly allowed to continue its activities, Military Government's suspicions of it persisted. This emerges from the treatment given to the CECCI's application to commemorate all victims of National Socialism in the form of a solemn burial on 9 November 1945. The British refused permission for this ceremony as 'the object of this procession would seem to be to stage an Anti-Nazi demonstration rather than to give solemn burial to the victims of the Nazi regime ...' (54)

Given these British attitudes towards anti-fascists denazification of the economy would prove an even greater problem than the purge of the civil service. The priority here was for British and German authorities alike to maintain orderly industrial production and in particular, to prevent that workers should use denazification for political ends, i.e. to try and change the structure of the economy. This was of course precisely what the committed anti-fascists advocated, claiming that it had been the capitalist economy and the weakness of the working class in it which had brought National Socialism to power.

53

Denazification of the economy, if carried out at all, therefore had to be strictly controlled. In keeping with this approach, an anti-fascist list of National Socialist 'Musterbetriebe' (factories which the Nazis had honoured by this term for special services rendered to the regime) was not acted on by the British. (The only firm on the list which was dismantled later was affected because it had been involved in the production of war materials). (55) On the other hand the British instructed Bratke to oversee the process of denazification of the economy. On 4 June 1945 Bratke made first concrete proposals of how this could be carried out. In the absence of more precise legal guidelines from the allies, Bratke suggested that the problem should be approached pragmatically. A commission of three impartial men was to be set up, one of which must be a peer from within the industry to be investigated. This commission could examine the questionnaires filled in by owners, managers and employees and make recommendations to British Military Government. This approach of peer review and of 'keeping it all in the family' was supported by the industrialists and also recommended by the Chamber of Industry and Commerce. On the basis of the questionnaires owners, managers and employees were put into one of three categories by the British: M = mandatory removals; D = discretional; N = no objections. The few results which are known show the limited effect of the denazification of the economy: Sprengel (chocolates and sweets): 8 N; Günther Wagner/Pelikan (writing utensils): 1 M, 7 N: Hanomag (machinery): 1 M, 21 N: Clothing Industry (wholesale): 1 M, 20 N; Transport: 15 M, 6 D, 299 N. According to recommendations made by the Crafts Department of the Chamber of Industry and Commerce in October 1945 only 38 master craftsmen should be prevented from working (out of several thousands in the city!) because of their too close association with the previous regime. (56)

Until the end of 1945 each occupation power followed its own approach to denazification. It was only on 12 January 1946 that CCG published its Directive No 24 which laid down guidelines for denazification for all zones. This was followed on 17 January by the British Political Zone Directive No 3 defining the application of Law 24 in the British Zone. From now on all Germans between 18 and 65 were subject to denazification, and the Germans themselves were to play a significant part in the process. German Denazification Panels were to be set up which were to sift through questionnaires filled in by all Germans and make recommendations to the allies. Depending on the degree of involvement with National Socialism the individual was to be put in one of five categories ranging from 'guilty' to 'implicated' to 'less implicated' to 'followers' and 'innocent'.

In Hanover one Main Denazification Panel and a large number of Subcommittees (at one point over 50!) were set up. The latter were formed either according to urban districts or to vet specific organisations (such as the police). Their composition was to reflect society at large but from the beginning this was difficult to achieve mainly because of the reluctance in the public to get involved in a procedure which was held generally in low esteem. It was considered too bureaucratic, it came too late and was too open to abuse to generate much enthusiasm. It was therefore perhaps inevitable that in the end only committed anti-fascists provided the core of the Denazification Panels whereas 'bourgeois' members worked hard to avoid involvement. Every session of Hanover Town Council between March 1946 and the autumn of 1947 was preoccupied with approving a new composition of various Denazification Panels.

The procedure was ponderous and inefficient. Many cases which had already been heard the previous year were opened up again, and there were incidents of corruption on the basis of which the desired Clearance Certificate was obtained. The Germans called this the 'Persilschein': the term derived from the well known washing powder which, according to advertising of the time, washed 'whiter than white'. There were also cases in which individual well connected Germans successfully appealed to higher Military Government authority such as happened in the case of a well known hospital consultant. (57) The managing director of the Bahlsen biscuit factory, Pentzlin, who spoke excellent English having spent some time in the United States as a young man remained unmolested in his post. According to the communist newspaper he had been

> ... the right hand man of the war criminal Sauckel. (He) held seven important economic posts during the Third Reich. He was the prototype of the non-political expert. (58)

After the war Pentzlin again filled a crucial position in Hanover's economic life. The managing director of the rubber company Continantal, Konnecke, a member of the SS and the NS Gau Economic Council was only temporarily removed from his post after prolonged workers protests. He returned in 1946.

On the other hand there is evidence that those who co-operated in the procedure suffered social ostracism and political disadvantage. There was the case of Willi Schoreit who as a lifelong socialist had fought actively against Hitler. He had considerable administrative experience and seemed the obvious candidate for the post of Head of Administration and Personnel at Hanover's Labour Exchange, a post which had become vacant after the previous holder had been killed in an air raid. As the head of the overall Labour Exchange, a Nazi, was not removed, an intolerable situation arose ending with Schoreit's dismissal on 26 June 1945. According to the Labour Exchange's own report

> (Military Government officer) Major Mathers stated without giving a reason that he was not satisfied with (Schoreit) and that he (Schoreit) was dismissed with immediate effect. (59)

There is also the example of Dr T Nagel, another active anti-fascist who was subjected to repeated smear campaigns in the press; these culminated in the summer of 1947 in insinuations that the fact that he had been able to build a small house and possessed soap were indications of his immoral dealings. He had to mount a public investigation to prove his innocence. (60)

There were adverse political consequences from having served enthusiastically on Denazification Panels even for members of the SPD. This is illustrated by the career of Willi Wendt who was a prominent representative of the party's left wing. In 1948 he had to face a party court for having 'co-operated with communists over denazification' in 1947. Although exonerated he remained on the fringe of the party. Another prominent member, H. Hasselbring, (initially Schumacher's right hand man) was not re-elected to the SPD's executive committee in 1948. His positive stand on denazification was undoubtedly a contributory factor.

Lack of more detailed sources prevent a precise analysis of the impact of denazification in Hanover. But even a cursory glance reveals that it was ill conceived and carried out inefficiently. Well known Nazi activists were seen to be left unscathed whereas convinced non-Nazis seemed to suffer for their commitment. Denazification too often simply deteriorated into a process where denunciations were made to obtain personal advantages. In thus turning even members of individual families against each other for the basest of motives denazification was worlds away from the 'cleansing' of the German people which had been anticipated at the end of the war. It generated enormous bitterness and encouraged the 'ohne-mich' (without me) stance, the opting out of politics altogether of a large section of the German public for years to come.

NOTES

1. H. Plath, H. Mundhenke, E. Brix, Heimatchronik der Hauptstadt Hannover, Cologne 1956, p.308.
2. Gustav Bratke (1878-1949) a life long member of the SPD had been Bürgermeister of one of Hanover's larger suburbs, Miesburg, throughout the Weimar Republic until sacked by the Nazis in 1933. He had gained a reputation as an efficient administrator and as being particularly progressive in the area of Council Housing.
3. E Barth, Police President of Hanover during the Weimar Republic until dismissed by the Nazis. His reputation, of being tough on the far left, notably communists, made his appointment controversial from the beginning.
4. Nachlass Nagel. Wiederaufbauausschuss. A. Karl, Von der Untergrundbewegung.
5. Schneider, op.cit., p.153.
6. U Schröder, 'Der Ausschuss für Wiederaufbau und die antifaschistische Bewegung in Hannover', in: L. Niethammer, U. Borsdorf, P. Brandt (eds), Arbeiterinitiative 1945, p.472.
7. SAH, Poster Collection.
8. SAH II L 40 Unterakte a (1) Discussions between Major Lamb and myself.
9. Städtisches Presse- und Kulturamt Hannover (ed), "Anpacken und Vollenden", Hanover 1949, p.69.
10. N.H.K. 20.7.1945 "Der britische Bulldozer beseitigt Gefahren in deutschen Städten".
11. "Drei Schwere Jahre". Ein Bericht der Bauverwaltung der Hauptstadt Hannover für die Zeit vom Beginn der Besetzung (April 1945) bis zur Währungsreform

(Juni 1949), p.32.

12.   The report from Military Government for August 1945 states 'The overcrowding of the population remains a serious problem. In the city of Hanover, weatherproof accommodation, incl. houses still in need of slight repair, is 39% of prewar while the population is 59% (and) is increasing daily. Of the accommodation much is taken up by troops and DPs.' (WO 171/7879 War Diary of HQ Mil Gov Hanover Region, 1-31 August).

13.   SAH 20 Municipal Building Office - Town Councillor Muller 4.6.1945.

14.   SAH, NB 20. The problem of reconstruction was systematically tackled only after 1949 with the setting up of Reconstruction Society ('Aufbaugemeinschaft') in which all sections of the city's inhabitants were represented. Its work became exemplary. See: J. Diefendorf, "Organisationsfragen beim Wiederaufbau deutscher Städte nach 1945", in "Die Verwaltung", 18/4, 1985.

15.   Drei schwere Jahre, p.17 and p.21 for the following.

16.   SAH, NB 20 Hanover City Civil Engineering Dept - OB Bratke 27.6.45.

17.   SAH, NB 20 OB - Military Government Detachment 722 14.1.46.

18.   SAH, NB 10 Städtisches Wirtschafts- und Ernährungsamt, Tätigkeits- und Erfahrungsbericht. Hannover, im April 1947.

19.   WO 171/7990 Appendix J Military Government Hanover Region, November 1945.

20.   L. Moseley, op.cit., p.76.

22.   FO 371/46974/C 8336/4831 PID using 'reliable refugees in Great Britain'.

23.   An introductory note explains the origin of the information: "Note: The phrases 'it is reported' or 'according to reports', 'reliable sources' etc. should be taken to mean that the information derives from reliable refugees in Great Britain. Where such phrases do not occur, the information comes from Corps (BAOR) Summaries and other British or Allied Intelligence Reports." Of 79 names listed for 30 Corps District 23 were definitely known to the British before the end of the war but 28 appointed during the "Interregnum" were not. More revealing, by November 1945 there were 12 German officials in post in the zone whose identity was still not known in London.

See also Schneider, op.cit., p.42 passim.

24. In subsequent months it transpired that as a member of the NLP Hagemann stood politically too far on the right to be acceptable to Military Government. He was rather unceremoniously sacked. 'Commander had routine conference with the <u>Oberpresident</u> and informed him that, owing to his age and the pressing commitments of his work during the coming winter he would have to be relieved of his appointment as soon as a relief could be found. (WO 171/7879. War Diary of HQ Mil Gov Hanover Region, 15.8.1945).

25. BBC Written Archives, F.M. Blumenfield, Report of a Tour of the British Zone 30.12.1946.

26. R. Ebsworth, Restoring Democracy in Germany. The British Contribution, 1960, p.21 'Lord give us a fifth <u>Reich</u>, the fourth is too much like the Third.'

27. The way in which he used his position is illustrated by his comments on an application to the British for a manufacturing license by the 'Cement Producer Group North-West' of 4 June 1945. Bratke: 'I am not able to endorse this application (made by a strongly Nazi conglomerate)' SAH, NB 16.

28. SAH 11 L 40 <u>Unterakte</u> a(1). Discussions between Major Lamb and myself, 26.4.1945.

29. STAH ZGS 1/4 Finance Inspector Schroeder, 'Recollections of the Collapse of National Socialism in Lower Saxony in 1945', Hanover 1.10.1950.

30. SAH IIL40 g Town Treasurer Weber - OB Bratke 25.4.45.

31. STAH NdS 120 Acc 58/65 No 11 Record of the discussion in the building of the chief Finance President with Major Brown of Military Government 18.5.45.

32. Loc. cit. Memo random Town Treasurer Weber 30.5.45.

33. See also STAH NdS 120 Acc 67/67 No. 4 <u>Oberpresident</u> of Hanover Province - <u>Regierungspresident</u> Hanover 25.7.45 Re: 'Costs occasioned by Occupation Powers Requirements'.

34. SAH IIL40 g Minutes of meetings held in Room 134 on 19.10.1945. Subject: Form 80 G procedure.

35. SAH <u>Nachlass</u> Nagel. <u>Wiederaufbauausschuss</u>. A. Karl, <u>Parteizugehörigkeit zur NSDAP</u>, undated.

This was done very much in the spirit of Bevin, who when provided with German information on the situation in the Soviet Zone, refused to even look at it. 'It is early days yet to start dealing with Germans.' FO 371/46861/C 6451

Correspondence Bevin - Eden 20./26.10.1945.
36.   SAH IIL40 op.cit., 3.5.1945.
37.   SAH Niederschriften über Besprechungen mit den Dezernenten und dem Stadtbeirat. Speech to the district's administrative heads, 16.7.1945.
38.   STAH, NdS 120 Acc 58/65 No. 319.
39.   STAH, NdS 50 Acc 32/63 No 14, Schneider p.125.
40.   STAH, NdS 120 Acc 58/65 No 319 Regierungspresident Circular 29.5.45 'The Filling in of Questionnaires'.
41.   WO 171/7990 504/720 L/R Military Government Detachment Weekly Report for week ending 8 July 1945.
42.   WO 171/7879 HQ Military Government Hanover Reg. August 1945 contd. Fortnightly Report 1-14 August 1945.
43.   As (6, p.45) Appendix 'F' Education and Religious Affairs.
44.   STAH, NdS 120 Acc 32/63 No 90a I. Bruce - Bratke 16.7.45.
45.   WO 171/7990 504/720 L/R Military Government Detachment Weekly Report for week ending 8 July 1945.
46.   FO 1010/27. Report 504 Military Government Detachment. 31.1.1946.
47.   SAH IIL40b. Conversations ... 7.5.1945.
48.   SAH Conversations ... 11.6.45.
49.   Loc. cit. 13.6.45.
50.   STAH NdS 120 Acc 58/65 No 14 Oberpräsident - OB Hanover 11.7.45.
51.   SAH NB 9 Municipal Economic and Food Office - OB Bratke 19.7.45.
52.   SAH NB 9 Head of Health Department - OB Bratke 19.7.45.
53.   SAH NB 9 Criminal Administration - OB Hanover 20.7.45.
54.   SAH N B 22.
55.   SAH N B 4 Chamber of Economics - OB Hanover 13.8.1945.
56.   T. Grabe, R. Hollmann, K. Mlynek, Wege aus dem Chaos. Hannover 1945-49, Hanover 1985, p.54 passim.
57.   SAH N B 4 Report Dr. T. Nagel to OB Bratke 30.5.1945.
58.   VST 18.10.1946. These communist allegations were however never substantiated. Pentzlin was cleared by a Denazification Panel in September 1946 although persistent allegations such as the ones made led to further

investigations by Special Branch (FO 1010/27 Appendix 'A'
to 229/MG/13030/1/S/Gov 11.3.1947).
    59.   SAH NB 4 Labour Exchange - OB Bratke 5.7.1945.
    60.   STAH VVP 5/162.

Chapter Three

FIRST POLITICAL DEVELOPMENTS DURING THE 'INTERREGNUM'

THE LOCAL POLITICAL BACKGROUND

Although to contemporaries the collapse of the German nation state and the occupation by the allied forces signalled the complete break with the past in the area of politics, there was in fact considerable continuity: the activists of the pre-1933 period who had survived the dictatorship re-emerged. Political developments in Hanover's past would therefore have some influence on the emerging organisational structures and policies after 1945.

The point of reference is of course the Weimar Republic but the analysis of the town's political development during this period shows that although it was the only example of a democratic system available to the majority of the citizens it was itself not unproblematical and not necessarily the example which should be followed after the war.

In 1919 the revolution in the city had quickly been superceded by the establishment in the office of Oberbürgermeister of the leading Social Democrat, R. Leinert. Law and order had been restored. (1) The Local Constitution was amended (in the whole of Prussia) by the removal of the three class franchise and the property qualification; this made every inhabitant of the city a 'Bürger' with the right to vote in local elections. In the first of these in 1919 the Social Democrats obtained 35 out of 84 seats which gave them, as in the Reich, a majority in coalition with the left liberal DDP (8 seats). Together they carried out a programme of modest social progress, notably in the area of housing, but none of their actions were particularly controversial, their basic objective being the running of local affairs with as much consensus as possible. Although this was based on the assumption that much in local affairs required common sense irrespective of the party political background of the participants, it also meant that the first generation of post-revolution officials did not use the powers which the constitution gave them to their full extent. The constitution was only superficially adopted to the new democratic order by removing the restrictions of the franchise. As far as all other clauses were concerned the 'Revidierte Städteordnung' of 1858 remained in force. In practice this meant that the now democratically elected Council could still not remove the highest official, the Oberbürgermeister. Although the Council elected him he was appointed by the state authorities for 12 years and could not be voted out of office before the end of his term of duty. This situation was to be exploited in the later part of the Weimar Republic when a non socialist became Oberbürgermeister.

In many ways the local developments in Hanover mirrored those in the Reich as a whole. As on the national level the local Social Democrats avoided any display of 'ideological' radicalism but from this course they reaped little reward. In the local elections of 1924 their share of the vote dropped to 22 (DDP-3) out of 74 seats, as against 22 of a centre-right 'Ordnungsblock' which could mobilise additional support from a number of councillors representing small interest groups. In view of this situation OB Leinert resigned. In the election of his successor the SPD did not put up a candidate of its own preferring instead to support a centre-left government specialist from outside Hanover. As in the simultaneous presidential elections in the Reich the communists put up their own candidate who, without a hope of getting elected himself, succeeded in splitting the working class vote, thus guaranteeing victory for the bourgeois candidate. Although the latter, Arthur Menge, a member of the Guelph Party, in two ballots failed to get the necessary absolute majority, the majority of bourgeois town councillors simply declared his election valid - against the votes of the SPD. Menge was duly installed and conducted the city's affairs quite efficiently - so much that the Nazis did not remove him from office. The additional reason for this was that politically he was close to the NSDAP although not a member of the party. Before the Nazi ascent to power he followed a rigid course of 'balancing the books', ie of cutting 'unnecessary' expenses mainly on projects which would have benefitted the working class. The Great Depression therefore hit Hanover with unmitigated harshness and brought the NSDAP electoral success - as in the Reich on the whole. As Menge's expertise in local affairs and his authoritarian personality had already introduced the 'Führerprinzip' the transition to the abolition of the trappings of democracy in 1933 was made with ease. Menge remained in office until 1937 when the period for which he was elected came to an end. He was not sacked in 1933 but he was also not kept on longer, as he had always refused to join the NSDAP.

The remarkable aspect of local political developments in Hanover was the performance of the SPD who not only failed to exploit their strong position after the World War I, but also meekly surrendered the office of OB in 1924. Worse still, despite winning the absolute majority in the local elections in 1929 (51%) they were unable to remove Menge or make their weight felt in other ways. In part of course their hands were tied by the provisions of the local constitution but it seems that it was also due to the character of the party in Hanover. In its majority it belonged to the party's reformist wing. (When the USPD split in 1922 all its members joined the KPD rather than the SPD). There was a wide gap between the grassroot working class membership, with 18,328 or 4.1% of the population one of the largest in the country, and the leadership who were exclusively intellectuals or lower middle class. There was an air of respectability and even snobbism among them with a party run motorcycle club - an unusual feature for a working class party in the Weimar Republic - and this made it even less prepared to take dramatic and controversial action.

A party with this general outlook was ill suited to take on a radical political opponent such as the NSDAP. The more the latter grew, the stronger the demands were in the SPD, notably by younger party members to find more flexible strategies of fighting Fascism. One result was the formation of the Sozialistische Arbeiterpartei (SAP) under a young activist Otto Brenner (2) in 1931. He drew on the support of other republican organisations such as the Reichsbanner, a republican ex-servicemen's league, workers' sports organisations and the police formations ('Schufos'). The purpose of this co-operation was an active anti-fascist policy, if need be by taking on the Nazis in the streets, quite apart from providing protection for republican politicians and meetings. 'Everybody has to learn to shoot' was also the motto of another left group, the Internationale Sozialistische Kampfbund (ISK) which had a flourishing branch in Hanover.

The potentially most important ally of all of these groups and of the SPD in the fight against National Socialism was of course the KPD which had 9000 members and a vote of 13% in 1932. But in Hanover they pursued the same policies as elsewhere, attacking the SPD as 'social fascists' even after both their organisations had been destroyed by the Nazis. When they did offer to form a 'united front' on 23/24 February 1933 this was received with suspicion by the SPD's leadership, particularly as these local overtures were accompanied by attacks on the national level. The KPD's call for massive political strikes at the beginning of April found no support.

If there was thus no concerted effort to stop the rise of National Socialism it was almost impossible to oppose it once it was in control of the media and the repressive apparatus of the state. As all non-National Socialist organisations were banned or forced to dissolve themselves, the only form of opposition was that of clandestine underground activities, to at least circulate information and to keep in touch. Thus the ISK published the Reinhartbriefe and in small groups of four or five intensified its work in the local factories.

The most important opposition group was the Socialist Front. It had over 1000 members and was run in 12 districts which corresponded to those of the SPD. Its members came mainly from the former SPD and the socialist free trade union movement. The leader was W. Blumenberg, formerly the editor of the SPD local paper. From 1934 the Front was able to publish its own paper ('Sozialistische Blätter') which grew to a circulation of 500. It also ran a scheme of financial assistance for the families of the victims of Fascism.

Despite much ingenuity at disguising their organisations and activities, by 1937 the Gestapo had succeeded in penetrating all the groups. All leaders were either arrested or fled abroad. The former were given savage sentences and in several cases paid with their lives. It was the end of any kind of organised opposition to National Socialism in Hanover.

The only hope remained that somehow the regime would

disappear and that in preparation for that day, the non-fascists must remain in touch and begin to plan for a future Germany. Such a network of contacts did in fact come about. The most important link between different groups and personalities was provided by a trade unionist, Albin Karl, who under the guise of his new job as a salesman had inconspicuous access to a wide variety of people. (3) The network of contacts also included members of the middle class: bourgeois politicians, academics, churchleaders etc.

Although not very effective in terms of opposition to National Socialism the experiences during the Third Reich determined the political outlook of the participants in the post-war period. Thus, the most important lesson learned by the activists of the left was that their disunity had weakened them so decisively that they had been unable to stop the rise of Hitler. The desire for working class unity was therefore very strong and found expression for example in the so-called Buchenwald Manifesto of April 1945 which was issued jointly by communists and social democrats. There was also the aim of creating one unified trade union movement, not only overcoming political and religious divisions but also those between blue and white collar workers. Trade union leaders such as Hans Böckler in the west were so impressed by the one large National Socialist Labour Front that they envisaged its continuation after the war, albeit under a different political leadership. In Hanover Albin Karl became the main protagonist of the concept, and after April 1945, of the realisation of one General Union. When it transpired that in the political field the old divisions would re-emerge, many of the more energetic men such as Otto Brenner, while still working in the SPD as the only viable party of the left, put their main effort into the creation and operation of the General Union. (4)

The bourgeois politicians went through a similar experience, and it was this which made the overcoming of religious divisions possible in the form of the only new political party to emerge, the Christlich-Demokratische Union (CDU).

BRITISH ATTITUDES

As early as 9 November 1944 a SHAEF Directive promised the Germans that, once the evil of National Socialism was eradicated, a democratic trade union movement would be set up. On this basis German activists from March 1945 attempted to refound their organisations as soon as the advancing allied troops put them in the position to do so. In Hanover, Albin Karl, encouraged by individual Military Government officers sent out a circular in May to the unionists in the surrounding area,

> The question of organisation has become acute now that after the occupation by the allies, the German Labour Front has been dissolved and after the often repeated promise by allied Military Government that trade unions will be allowed and that their formation will be supported by them. (5)

A first meeting was held on 24 May in the presence of Military Government officers who were described as 'competent in union matters.' (6) However, the Germans soon discovered a significant divide between general high level SHAEF pronouncements and what was accepted by the allies in practice. Thus SHAEF itself declared, still in mid-May 1945, and after Germany's unconditional surrender, 'that the time was premature for the establishment of labour unions in Germany ... current SHAEF policy confine(s) such unions to those concerned principally with local issues.' (7) The ban of 2 June of all organised German activities put a stop to this first wave of union formation.

There seem to be a number of reasons for this obviously contradictory allied approach of first promising the establishment of unions and then not liking the German initiatives. In the first instance there was the attitude of Field Marshal Montgomery the British Military Governor, who was not in favour of the early establishment of German trade unions. 'The Russians supported trade unions. I decided not to do this.' (8)

There was also the general suspicion of Germans and this extended to German trade unionsts.

> Can it be that there are amongst German trade union leaders today those who see in a unified trade union movement a potential political weapon of enormous strength? (9)

Trade unions might be the guise in which German power would reassert itself and endanger British security. Moreover, the German proposals to overcome the past

67

political and religious divisions in the trade union movement by creating one General Union (GU) were derided by the British

> as typical of the Germans' lack of realism. The Germans seemed unaware of the enormous difficulties ... The magnitude of the task does in fact lend an air of unreality to trade union affairs ...

There was also little enthusiasm among allied personnel in Germany for simply reviving the old pre-1933 trade unions, albeit under a different overall structure. After all, they had lacked the moral fibre to stand up to National Socialism - a fact which the Germans appeared to be all too keen to forget. This sentiment was also shared by British trade unionists. Thus Sir F. Legett, Chairman of the TUC, commented on his recent visit to the British Zone

> ... in Britain, and he thought that he could express the view also on behalf of the TUC, there was considerable disappointment that the trade union movement in Germany had not made any response to earlier pleas made to them from 1931 to 1933 to resist Hitler and subsequently to prevent the German nation from going to war ... (10)

German attempts to explain the unions' problems under the totalitarian regime of National Socialism were brushed aside as 'a good deal of complacency (in) the attitude of the (German) Trade Union Movement ...'. What was worse, in the eyes of British observers now, after the war the Germans seemed to lack the proper degree of contrition.

> ... no doubt that the old Trade Union leaders wanted the outside world to look at the war period as a matter of past history and to shake hands and be friends as if nothing had happened ...

These compromised trade union leaders were now emerging again and seemed to be getting control of the new union structure. This was not what the British had in mind.

> In the Hanover area where a highly organised and upper hierarchy exists, the general impression is that these pre-1933 Trade Unionists are not what is wanted ... (11)

It was more difficult for the British to determine what they did want. The British certainly disliked this early German self assertion and saw the initial period of the occupation as one of soulsearching, thought and preparation for a future trade union organisation (and political parties). This was the advice given by Hanover's local Military Government commander at the time of the union ban. The unionists ought to welcome a 'period of reflection and preparation for the time when the unions could be built up on truly democratic principles.'

This was one of the key ideas which the British also applied to the development of the political parties: democracy somehow had to grow spontaneously, from the bottom upwards. While waiting for the impetus from below, no decisions on structures of organisation must be taken. But the only result seems to have been to frustrate experienced German unionists, while new forces were not forthcoming. (12) In fact, even within their own terms of reference the British approach was counterproductive, for far from discouraging old trade unionists the ban actually suited them, in that it strengthened their hold over the organisation. Clandestine operations were only possible within the surviving old structures.

> Throughout the zone the limitations placed on trade union organisers have been cheerfully accepted. This is particularly noticeable in respect of the political ban but it should be remarked that for the moment a political truce suits the book of trade union organisers interested in a unified trade union movement. (13)

It was clear that sooner or later the British would have to make changes. There was the German resentment at their forced inactivity as a result of the, to them, unjustified British distrust. There was also the example of the Soviet Zone where unions and parties were allowed to function. Moreover, this was the first time in German history since the 19th century that no working class organisation existed officially. On the other hand a host of welfare schemes depended on them.

> Owing to the absence of workers' organisations it has not been possible so far to carry into effect the main point of British policy, namely the reconstitution of the Social Insurance Funds on the lines of the pre-Nazi

system, under which the funds were autonomous and their administration (was) carried out by representatives of employers and workpeople, but a start has been made in this direction, in the case of the <u>Ruhr-Knappschaft</u> (the Ruhr miners' sickness and pensions scheme) and the experience gathered here may be such as to justify the hope that it will soon be possible to set machinery in motion for the re-establishment of democratic administration ... (14)

On 5 July a Directive for the 'Policy for the Formation of Trade Unions in the British Zone' was promulgated which allowed German workers to hold meetings to discuss the formation of trade unions. Inside factories they could elect spokesmen who however were not allowed to discuss wages or hours of work. For the time being the factory based Works Councils were to be considered as temporary unions 'until such time as properly constituted unions can undertake the work of organising the representation of works people in matters concerning their employment.' (15)

But before such councils were allowed to operate they had to be elected democratically, using British style democratic elections, complete with 'presiding officers', 'scrutineers' and 'constituencies' - all notions which were quite new to the German workers and which caused bewilderment among them. The British also stipulated that candidates for office had to have worked in the plant for one year and all those voting for six months. As this would debar all serving soldiers or refugees it seemed that the British intended to base their system on older workers and those who for one reason or other had been able to avoid service at the front.

Two aspects emerge: unions as conceived above remained quite meaningless because they were deprived of their most basic functions. It also becomes clear that the British were either unaware of the specifically German organisations of 'Works Councils' (representing the whole workforce in a particular factory, white collar workers included) or they remembered the more political role which these had played after World War I. In any case, as late as 1947 the head of the Manpower Division, R. Luce, appealed to German trade unionists to work towards a situation where labour relations could be managed exclusively by employers and trade unions. Works Councils should consist of trade unions at factory level. (16) It was therefore not surprising that Works Councils were not given the kind of influence in the running of their plant which they demanded (see below), and that when their status was eventually determined in Control Council Law No 22 of 10 April 1946, it fell far short of the rights and powers they had wielded under the Factory Council Law of 1920 (which in its day had come as a disappointment to the activists).

There is thus considerable evidence of a lack of understanding and sympathy for working class organisations among Military Government officers. According to one observer, this hostility was particularly widespread among the leading echelons of the Manpower Division who took their cue from the Head of Division, Luce. (17) But according to a report of a junior man in the Labour Division of P Detachment in Hanover this applied generally to the senior ranks. (18)

> It is only fair to state that these suspicions and complications are not due to the people who run the Industrial Relations section of the Control Commission. They are drawn from the conciliation staff of the Ministry of Labour and naturally have both knowledge of and sympathy with the Trade Union movement. Their hands are, however, tied by the higher direction which rests mainly in the hands of the regular military element who regard trade unions as a sinister force ...
>
> We spend most of our legislation to set at rest the fears of those whose ignorance in Trade Unionism matches their prejudice against it. There are in Military Government only a handful of officers who know anything of what trade unions mean or stand for ...

The General Union structure was, as we have seen, the result of the experience by German unionists of defeat and destruction under National Socialism which they believed would not happen again once a unified union structure existed. At the same time some union leaders, such as Hans Böckler in the Rhineland, had even wished to continue the Labour Front. This much more centralised structure of the Front had however been abandoned in favour of the GU, although even against this there was some German opposition, notably from the more powerful Metalworkers' Union in the west and north of Germany. On the other hand there was little doubt among observers that the GU was the structure which most German workers wanted at the time.

> Whether such a wider organisation is wise from the point of view of Trade Unionists is one question, but there can be no doubt that it is what the workers want. Any other form of organisation would be an artificial creation by the British authorities. (19)

However, it was not only the local British authorities who frustrated the German unionists. The rejection of the GU was also endorsed by the TUC. In fact it was the TUC which led the campaign to persuade German colleagues of the erroneousness of their ways. On 23 November 1945 a TUC delegation went to Düsseldorf to meet German union representatives. The TUC members welcomed the German proposals for overcoming religious and political divisions as this corresponded closely to what was being practiced in the UK. On the other hand they rejected the notion of a GU. This was after all not done in the UK. While conceding that there were perhaps too many unions in the UK, British unionists would nevertheless 'strenuously resist any attempt to create one Trade Union from the organisations affiliated to Congress ...' Even if this GU was what German workers wanted they did so for misguided reasons, out of the traditional German 'tendency ... to blindly obey instructions from Headquarters'. (20)

> We therefore, as the representatives of a great trade union movement which sincerely desires to see real democracy in Germany, ask you to modify your plan so that a small number of unions shall have complete autonomy over the industrial affairs of their members ...

As a result of such combined pressure the German union leaders in the Rhineland gave up the concept of the GU by the end of 1945. The rest of the British Zone followed only at the second zone-wide trade union meeting at Bielefeld, in August 1946 although the actual transition from one General Union to several industry based unions went on into 1947 notably in Lower Saxony. Albin Karl in Hanover took part vigorously in the controversy with Military Government. Their correspondence shows how little impact arguments put by Germans generally had (even when the matter discussed was denazification on which British and Germans should have been closest).

There was a great deal of dissatisfaction among

German trade unionists with the way the British were trying to teach them 'democracy' by forcing them to build their organisation from the bottom up. 'Nothing has been achieved by preaching to us that we have to start from below ...' (21)

They made it quite clear that in abandoning the GU they were giving in to British pressure. Thus Hans Böckler declared in his speech on 7 December that Military Government had forced him and his colleagues to accept autonomous industrial unions. How widely German unionists blamed the British for the confusion in the German organisation was expressed vividly at the second zonal conference in Bielefeld. (22)

Walter Freitag, leader of the zone-wide Metalworkers Union stated, 'that we shared the views of our friends in Hanover, but had to form autonomous industrial unions because Military Government wished it ...' The representative from Sleswig-Holstein reported that there the situation was still unclear:

... We still have the GU in some areas, but even there we are in transition to autonomous industrial unions. It is questionable whether this is right. On the whole we wanted the GU and we still have problems with Military Government ... The English demand financial autonomy for individual unions ...

A representative of Hamburg's Factory Workers' Association made it clear that '... Our difficulties were not created by ourselves but by the occupation authorities ...'

The argument surrounding the form of the German Trade Union organisation was only one aspect of the wider question of the role which the unions should play in the economy as a whole. This was another instance in which the division of opinion in Military Government itself became evident. It emerged in connection with the question of Trade Union representation in the Chambers for Industry and Commerce. The employers wished to treat the Chambers as their own pressure groups whereas the unions saw in them potential decision making bodies in economic matters in which they, the unions, ought to be represented. A paper drawn up in October 1946 by a Government Sub-Commission showed the Economic Sub-Commission of the Zonal Executive Office and the Political Division of CCG (BE) in favour of union participation, but the Commerce Branch of the Trade and Industry Division and the Manpower Division opposed to it. The latter had the support of the Americans who in their zone were opposed to trade union power sharing. This view prevailed. (23)

As far as the German political parties were concerned similar British attitudes as those towards trade unions emerge. The British did not have a high opinion of them because they had surrendered ignominiously to National Socialism. The treatment received by German political emigrés during the war reveals the measure of contempt even towards those Germans who were after all either opponents or victims of the odious regime. This extended equally to German Social Democrats and was shared by members of the Labour Party and the Trade Union Movement. Once the war was over, the British had no precise views as to Germany's political future and would have liked to postpone the emergence of political parties in their zone to a later date. But, as we have seen, they involved Germans in the running of their own affairs locally from the first days of the occupation, which of course meant giving them responsibility on the basis of some sort of trust. It was no accident that the men selected for these posts were more often than not Social Democrats, simply because they were untainted by National Socialism and therefore available. To deprive these men of political power was a political decision by the British. However, this is not how they tended to see it at the time. As we have seen, there was a very small number of men responsible in the CCG for supervising and advising both the CCG and the Germans alike on political developments and they consisted mainly of 'young idealists'. They were committed to the idea of starting democracy 'from the bottom up'. The Germans should take over responsibility without however involving themselves in politics.

> There was at this time a strong feeling among the western allies that we must somehow enable the Germans to take over political responsibility without permitting them to form political parties ... (24)

In the German context however this 'non-political' approach was eminently political: 'To be non-political meant either that one had been a Nazi or that one did not have the moral courage to show one's colours and was therefore a potential Nazi.' (25)

At the time however, British Military Government

officers felt that to allow early political parties would favour the SPD, whose organisation had survived in better shape than that of its bourgeois counterparts who had been far more disrupted by National Socialism. To allow the SPD to exploit this advantage would be tantamount to 'dictating' to the rest of the German people. This, it was felt, was incompatible with Britain's mission of teaching the Germans 'democracy'. (26) This approach seemed to have been vindicated by later election results which gave the CDU a slight majority; but it is a fact that the lack of encouragement given to the SPD must also have had longterm political effects. That 'no decision' had also short term political consequences was according to British observers also seen by Kurt Schumacher, the SPD leader in Hanover :

> ... the longer we (the British) refuse the Germans the right of political activity the greater the danger will be of Nazis and rabid nationalists covering their tracks and taking refuge in other groups, notably the Welfen, and of the politically uneducated Germans becoming even more misguided ... (27)

THE COMMITTEE FOR RECONSTRUCTION (RC)

The Committee for Reconstruction was perhaps the most important new organisation which emerged spontaneously at the end of the war; it was potentially very powerful in that at a time when all other organisational structures had collapsed, it provided a rallying point for the 'new Germans'. Although from the beginning its proclaimed aims were to give practical help to the allies, to the emerging German administration and to the population at large, it was nevertheless seen as a threat, firstly by the German administration because it had taken over some of its responsibilities, but also by the allies for it was an independent German organisation with its potential as a security risk. Given that the RC deprived itself of reaching further political goals by limiting itself to practical work, its existence, sandwiched as it was between the German administration which was growing in strength daily and a Military Government which grew more nervous about the RC's activities in some of the suburbs, was precarious and only temporary.

Its organisational structure already revealed that here was not a secret German power centre in the making: there was a central committee (CC or <u>Hauptausschuss</u>) of initially about 20 members and district committees in the different urban districts. There was however no strictly hierarchical structure with orders from the centre carried out at the lower level. Rather the CC assumed a co-ordinating role. It was moreover soon bypassed by an even smaller committee of 5, consisting of Karl, Bratke, Barth and two other members of the underground movement. Bratke and Barth thus played a double role as part of the traditional administrative structure and as members of the wider body. At times it looked as though there would develop a 'dual power' structure. (28)

That this did not happen and that the RC remained in its role of auxiliary was largely due to its party composition in which those who were disinclined to venture into new approaches predominated. Of the 20 members in the original RC about 2/3 were members of the SPD, 3 KPD, 2 DDP, 2 Centre Party and 2 ISK. It was indicative that only the communists saw the RC as a political body, enquiring on arrival in the Town Hall where their party's room was to be ('<u>Fraktionszimmer</u>'). (29) The RC's self imposed limitations as well as the generally fluctuating situation also explains the high turnover in the RC's personnel. With other organisations such as trade unions, political parties, and the Chamber of Commerce regrouping, the bourgeois members in particular drifted away. The RC, moreover, steadily lost its importance as Military Government and the German administration increasingly established a grip on the situation.

The development of the RC took a different course in the urban districts. Initially the leaders of 6 out of the 22 districts had been Social Democrats; indeed in some cases they had been identical with the SPD leaders in the area before 1933. In three districts the Social Democrats worked together with Communists. In another three however the Communists set up a rival and far more political anti-fascist committee. As Hanover had always been an SPD stronghold the militantly anti-fascist elements remained weak, although where they had the power such as in Housing Associations and in some factories they did take action in evicting Nazis from flats or allotments. These 'transgressions' were subsequently taken as the pretext by Military Government for the ban on 2 June of the RC as a whole. (As the ban was promulgated by the highest level, i.e. SHAEF for all western zones, local incidents were almost irrelevant).

Two factors emerge: the limited extent to which Social Democrats and Communists co-operated even at this early stage, and the way in which the RC's CC diverged increasingly from its area branches. As far as the relation between the two working class parties was concerned their growing antagonism seems to have developed at the grass roots inspite of the emotionally conceived need for unity. This in turn seems to have affected the leadership involved in the RC which when the RC had first been set up was described as 'not at all radical'. (29) Grass root opposition to unity by Communists is also hinted at by Schumacher in his first important speech to SPD functionaries on 6 May. (30) This preceded the discouragement of unification tendencies in the KPD Zentrale in Berlin.

If the RC considered its main objectives to lie in practical work its achievements must be measured by this yardstick. In a 12 point Action Programme these were expressed as follows: to secure food supplies (Pt 1), to provide the population with gainful employment (Pts 2 & 3), to restore communications (Pts 6 & 7), to reopen schools to remove the youngsters from the streets (Pt 10), and to secure housing and particularly important in a time of food shortages, the control of the allotments (Pt 11). Within this new order the position of the workers had to be safeguarded: Pt 4 therefore stipulated workers' representation in businesses and Pt 5 the setting up of trade unions. The only political objectives were expressed in Pts 8 & 9 with the demands for the cleansing of all administrative bodies and of trade and industry. But the RC never aimed at control over these organisations, being content with placing non-Nazis in influential positions. In this it was relatively successful. As we have seen, Bratke and Barth controlled the city's administration and police; an RC member was in an influential position in the Labour Exchange; the city's housing department was led by an RC member and the inspector for the reopening Primary Schools was appointed on the RC's recommendation. However, these first appointments were not always effective in the long run as is illustrated by the summary dismissal of the RC man Schoreit from the Labour Exchange (see above) and the gradual infiltration of the police by former Nazis which made repeated purges necessary in as late as 1946/7.

The RC adopted a similar approach to various commercial organisations, the building co-operatives and the Allotment Association. By the middle of May it had put RC members in charge of the political purge of the city's hotels and restaurants and of the butchers' trade, made proposals for new executive and managing committees for the coal trade and for the Chamber of Solicitors as well as for the Economic Chamber, as noted above. The latter in particular revealed the RC's limitations.

It was not successful in the modest attempt by Henkel to carry out a denazification procedure of the most incriminated Hanover factories. Already in April the Economic Chamber began to compete with the RC when it came to the issuing of licenses and permits. Individuals who had something to fear from an investigation by the RC found help in the Chamber. From mid-May the RC conceded defeat and handed the business of issuing licenses back to the Chamber (see below for the ease with which the Chamber was able to continue its operations at a time when all other organisations were banned). In the relationship between the RC and the Chamber one of the fundamental issues of post-war Germany was first touched upon. The RC, and even its most moderate members were basically committed to 'natural justice', i.e. wherever possible, the wrong done by the Nazis should be put right without much ado. Thus property, allotments etc. which the Nazis had taken over should be restored to their rightful owners. Members of the Chamber, the town's administration and the British on the other hand saw in this procedure a first step in the direction of a revolution because men were taking the law into their own hands, away from where it ought to be: with the courts. It was the thin edge of the wedge of 'socialism' and must be fought at all costs. Most members of the RC itself of course did not want an uncontrolled 'reckoning with the Nazis'. To this end they devised formal 'Principles for the enforced removal from accommodation, industrial plant and allotments of party members and others' (31) on the basis of which no action could be taken without the approval of the Central Committee. These principles were drawn up in response to more radical activities by some of the RC district organisations, but despite its moderation the RC was simply abolished. It is true that in some ways it had become an anachronism with the emergence of normal city government. But with it went also the most spontaneous response to the post-war situation, the attempt to deal with the consequences of National Socialism in a humane and fair way. Instead, as we have noted, the victims of fascism often had a rough deal. It is of course also true that the RC to bureaucrats in the German and British administrations represented an irregular element, no matter how useful it had been in the first weeks. This is illustrated well by the relief with which Bratke informed the RC of its ban. One sentence was enough to thank them for the services rendered. (32) Members of the RC were naturally shocked and bitter about the treatment they had received. It seemed undeserved.

> We, in the Main Committee for Reconstruction have from the beginning of our activity up to the dissolution of the Main Committee, its sub-committee and delegations, which took place today, on 2.6.1945 on the order of Military Government, made a serious effort to help in the reconstruction of the town of Hanover and also of Germany.
> We knew that our action has been a major contribution towards the creation of favourable conditions for this reconstruction and that the incidents which attracted the censure of Military Government and which are given as the reasons for the dissolution can be considered as unimportant compared to the positive and acknowledged achievements of the Committee and its organs, particularly in view of the enormously important economic and political events. (33)

WORKS COUNCILS AND TRADE UNIONS

In his account 'From the Underground Movement' Albin Karl claims that the Americans had asked him to build up the workers' organisations in the economy. The RC certainly tackled the problem very early on; it formed two subcommittees which were composed of experienced pre-1933 trade unionists for this task. The first sent representatives into the local factories to mobilise support for trade unions; the other worked out proposals for their future constitution. At the same time in the factories some form of 'Works Committees' emerged spontaneously, particularly in those plants where the politically compromised owners or managers had fled and where therefore the workforce itself took over the restarting of work, be it in the form of the first clearing up measures or the beginnings of a modest amount of production. The RC representatives usually endorsed the membership of these Works Committees and tried to co-ordinate between committees in different plants. In plants where no Works Committees had come into existence spontaneously, the RC men had the important and often difficult task of cajoling workers into becoming members of organisations which for them, faced with daily struggles with practical problems, were often not a priority.

All members of Works Committees in this early stage had been active in the Works Councils before 1933; as we shall see even after they were confirmed in the elections held on the insistence of Military Government, the continuity of personnel is astounding. There was also a close link between Works Council and Trade Union members; in many cases the experienced men from the factory floor were instrumental in building up the unions and were simultaneously union functionaries. Often they called the first union meetings. (34)

Besides the reconstruction of their organisations the workers' first demands were concerned with the reckoning with leading Nazis and, despite their official non-existence, with employers over redundancies and conditions of work in the inflationary post-war situation. With regard to their political demands the lack of action by the British remained a grave disappointment.

As far as the representation of workers' interests within the factories was concerned the situation presented, in the words of a British observer, another example of

> ... (the difference) between theory and practice ... (of the occupation) ... With the occupation in April Works Councils were elected everywhere in, as far as can be ascertained, a perfectly regular manner. In early June, however, these were all suspended until someone could decide whether they could exist and what they could be called as - it was stated - the term 'Betriebsrat' (Works Council) had an 'unpleasant connotation in some quarters' ... It was not, apparently, realised that employers were as dependent as workers on the existence of some form of contact organisation and therefore, the suspended councils merely elected one or two spokesmen who performed their functions and

> reported back by personal contact rather than by
> formal meeting ... (35)

The same discrepancy existed over the trade unions. A first
meeting of union officials took place on 3 May; we have
already referred to the principles on which it was hoped one
General Union would emerge. Preparations for it progressed
so rapidly that on 24 May a meeting of 200 'trade union shop
stewards' took place which was also attended by the Labour
officers of Military Government, OB Bratke, the Chief of
Police, Barth and other leading Social Democrats.

The latters' goodwill towards the British was expressed
when Bratke opened the meeting and thanked Military
Government for the liberation of the country. This was more
than paying lipservice to their new masters: Albin Karl saw
it as an 'honour' to be able to help in the reconstruction, not
only of Germany: a 'new German' needed to be created. The
emotional atmosphere was unmistakeable, the task ahead
immense.

The RC's subcommittee's proposals for the GU were
endorsed by the meeting. They found the support not only of
the social democratic unionists, but also and emphatically of
the representative of the christian trade unions. (36) The
immediate tasks of the GU were: (a) the reconstruction of
the economy with special reference to the social and
economic interests of union members (b) the maintenance of
existing wage and salary conditions by tariff agreements and
their adjustment to changing circumstances (c) the purge of
factories and offices of Nazi elements by Works Councils or
trustees of the unions (d) the entry of union members into
existing or future institutions of the state, local
government, industry, agriculture, commerce and the free
professions. The sub-committee had already prepared
application forms for membership so that recruitment could
begin immediately. (37)

The work done by the sub-committee was endorsed by
the meeting and a provisional executive committee of three
was elected without opposition (although there were three
abstentions): the committee was Albin Karl, Louis Böcker
(who had chaired the sub-committee) and H. Beermann. A
wider council of 11 was also voted into existence; each
member responsible for a branch of the economy. All of
them later played an important role in either the trade
union movement, the Bonn government or locally, e.g. as
town clerk. Politically only two belonged to the CDU, 1 to

the KPD, the remaining 8 were Social Democrats.

But, as we already noted this promising start was interrupted by the ban of 2 June. While the build-up of the organisation was delayed the unions nevertheless continued to operate where they were most needed, in negotiating for their members.

> ... while the Trade Unions have been theoretically non-existent they have in fact been carrying on, through the temporary Committee, their normal functions and have, in fact, saved a lot of trouble to Military Government by negotiating with a similar 'non-existent employers' organisation' on such difficult questions as the purging of Nazis from the factories and the heavy redundancy of office and supervisory staffs in factories which were carrying on during the war with inflated labour force of foreign workers. (38)

The need for working class organisations was clear even to Military Government officers. It remained to be seen whether the enforced 'period of reflection' would produce politically more acceptable structures.

THE POLITICAL PARTIES

Of all the manifestations of emerging political activity the political parties seemed the most irrelevant to the mass of the Germans and as noted above were treated by the British with even greater suspicion. The parties in the early post-war phase were seen to be irrelevant not only because of their own performance in the past but also because there seemed no way in which they could justify their existence by exercising power: the allies were in total control, and there was general uncertainty as to the very future of the country.

The RC's aim to help rebuild political parties was therefore of less immediate concern than its more practical measures but not, of course, to the political activists. As we have seen they had maintained close contact throughout the Nazi period; these contacts extended to closer links between them than had existed in the Weimar period. The emerging political parties would start from the shared experience of the Third Reich and have certain basic values in common on which they wished the new Germany to be built. These must be: a commitment to peace and international co-operation externally and to the creation of a fairer and socially more just society internally in which the suffering of those who had lost homes, limbs or lives must be alleviated by contributions from those who survived in more fortunate circumstances.

Beyond this common bond a fundamental difference was soon to emerge: This was the divide between those who wished to return to a basically capitalist economy with its emphasis on property, individual freedom and responsibility and those who advocated greater state or societal control over property for a fairer distribution of wealth and a safeguarding of democracy which - so it was argued - had been undermined by the connivance of big capital with Hitler. Within these two camps were a number of divisions and how these were overcome was to prove crucial for the future political development.

The divisions in the bourgeois camp centred mainly on the role which Christian values were to play, with the followers of the former liberal parties firmly committed to keep religion out of political life but a far larger, new grouping turning to Christianity as the only basis for the German people to go forward. The most significant development was that the call for unity, which had determined much of trade union thinking, was successful in this area with a joint protestant - catholic party emerging in the form of the CDU. In many areas there were, moreover, regional groupings which in a period where no central authority existed to act as a common bond, were bound to achieve at least temporary prominence.

In the 'working class' camp the first crucial question was whether the two main parties of the Weimar Republic, the SPD and KPD could now co-operate. The example provided locally in the RC Hanover boded ill for the future but it remained to be seen whether developments at higher level were to bring about improvements. The second was whether unlike after World War I, the left would achieve lasting power and introduce its desired changes into German society. Success would depend to some extent on the attitude of British Military Government to the German left, but perhaps more on whether the parties could generate sufficient appeal to the German electorate in future elections which alone could produce the democratic base of their power.

There was no general pattern according to which the

parties emerged. Every town had its own experiences. (39) Indeed, the end of the war came at different times and in different circumstances in different places. The developments in Hanover are nevertheless typical in several respects although, as in many similar German towns, there is not much source material available to trace the process in detail - a reflection of the chaotic circumstances at the close of hostilities and of the quickly growing paper shortage. As in most cities, political activities were started by men who had been active in this field before 1933. Leading figures, such as Dr Pfad (later CDU) or Franz Henkel (later FDP) had temporarily co-operated with the RC and were politically active in other ways, such as in the movement to create a 'Free Hanover'. Their respective parties however emerged only later after overcoming the often diverse objectives of their potential supporters such as, in the case of the CDU conservative protestant landowners in Sleswig-Holstein or catholic workers in the Rhineland; or, in the FDP, that division which in the Weimar Republic had manifested itself in two liberal parties, the DDP and DVP.

In the early summer of 1945, three political parties were operating as such: the SPD, the KPD and the Guelph Party. It was perhaps inevitable that the 'bourgeois' party which emerged earliest on the scene was the Hanoverian Guelph Party whose members had few qualms about their attitude to National Socialism. They sympathised with many of the Nazi ideas and continued to do so after the war, but they were able to dissociate themselves from the Third Reich by an easy expedient: National Socialism had grown up on Prussian soil and was thus thoroughly un-German (only non-Prussia qualified as 'Germany'). Now that Prussia was defeated, Hanover was free to pursue its own path from which it had been thwarted by Prussian tyranny. In a first appeal of May 1945 the pre-1933 local leader of the Hanoverian Party expressed these views. The creation of the administrative unit 'Hanover Region' by Military Government in June 1945 was particularly welcome as a first step towards the Guelph's long term aim of an independent 'Lower Saxony'. To achieve this 'support for the measures of the occupation powers' was the duty of every party member, not only out of gratitude because they had liberated Hanover from the 'weed' of un-German National Socialism but also because there had existed special links between Hanover and Britain since the early 19th century (sic!). This idea was expressed in a lengthy undated obtuse document written by a retired Professor Ludewig. Its language and the terms 'lower Germany' ("<u>Niederdeutschland</u>") as a 'symbolic England' are as flowery as they were irrelevant to the real situation in the country. Subsequently the Hanover leadership was relegated to second place in the party as a whole, and another branch built up in the northern small town of Stade, where F Hellwege determined the party's policies.

In Hanover however Ludewig played an important part in getting the party off the ground; it now called itself '<u>Niedersächsische Landespartei</u>' (NLP) to indicate its wider aspirations and was officially founded on 20.6.1945 during a meeting in Ludewig's house. An application for a license was made to the British on 23 June. It was of course turned down but the NLP had re-established itself with a wide network of contacts ranging from local landowners, to the former <u>Oberbürgermeister</u> Menge and the aristocracy. This was remarkable particularly because of the Party's ambiguous attitude to National Socialism which created some difficulties in the party's later dealings with Military Government.

There is unfortunately no source material relating to the KPD during this period. There is more information available on the foundation and organisation of the Hanover SPD because much of the party structure and many of its functionaries survived the war. The analysis of the party in Hanover goes beyond mere 'local' history because of the presence in the town of the future West German leader, Kurt Schumacher. (41) Not only is some of the information concerning the party contained in his papers, his relationship with local party officials sheds valuable light on the problems facing the SPD in the post-war period.

As noted above the links between former trade unionists and Social Democrats were particularly close. It was only to be expected that these members of the underground would wish to reinstate the SPD as an official party. It had after all been the only party to stand up to Hitler's bullying tactics over the Enabling Act and many of its functionaries had suffered for their continued opposition. The SPD of all parties therefore was felt to have the moral right to re-emerge as soon as it was possible. Already on 19 April a first meeting of party functionaries took place, arranged with the help of the RC and notably A. Karl, and under the watchful but not unsympathetic eye of Military

Government. (42) At this meeting Schumacher emerged as the leading personality although not a Hanoverian by origin.

The meeting on 19 April decided to 'tackle the rebuilding of our party organisation immediately' and already on 29 April a meeting of 80 functionaries took place in the working class suburb of Linden. (43) Schumacher addressed them on 'The Origins of 12 years of Nazi Dictatorship and the most urgent problems of party work'. This was the first of many speeches exhorting the German nation to recognise the causes which had brought about Nazi barbarism, destruction and immense suffering on Germans and the rest of Europe alike. Now was the time to bring about a new socialist Germany which would make a repetition of past errors impossible.

A meeting with 130 members on 6 May confirmed an executive committee with Schumacher in the chair, who again gave the main address. It was the most comprehensive analysis yet of the social, economic and political developments in Germany which had culminated in National Socialist barbarism. Now, the destruction of the country was total and the German people faced a standard of living 'the primitivity of which cannot yet be imagined.' Schumacher's approach to the German situation was one of utter realism; the allies had defeated Hitler without help from the Germans. The latter had no right to make demands ('demands can only be made by those who have contributed themselves. Revolutionary demands without revolution are empty phrases'); the allies had determined 'democracy' to be the firm frame within which German reconstruction was to take place. 'We are obliged to absolute honesty in filling this frame'. Social Democrats needed no lessons in democracy but it was the bourgeoisie which had to learn to think differently. For this reason he particularly rejected the notion of collective guilt which prevailed notably amongst many abroad. But while demanding recognition for the political stance taken by German anti-fascists, Social Democrats should have no illusions as to the reasons why they were now chosen to help with the reconstruction of the country. This did not signify 'a particular ... political preference' (on the part of the allies). On the contrary, it would be far more natural for the allies to use bourgeois circles as they shared common social origins and aspirations. 'But in Germany there are not enough bourgeois forces which are untainted by National Socialism'. On the other hand Social Democrats should not allow the bourgeoisie to avoid its responsibilities again as after World War I. 'It would be an unsurpassable stupidity to claim a monopoly to powerlessness'. Both power and weakness must be shared.

Three elements in the speech were to have lasting effect: the criticism of Military Government for pushing political parties 'from the clear atmosphere of party democracy into the darkness of conspiracy' set the tone for the SPD's relationship with the allies.

The second was Schumacher's view that at this stage in its development, political activity was necessarily limited to local government and administration. Without any practical possibility of putting 'democratic socialism' into practice, in preparation for it Social Democrats should gain an overriding influence at all levels of administration. In this the party had a measure of success at the local level with men such as Bratke and Barth, and eventually six out of ten departments of the town's administration were occupied by party members. Also, the offices of <u>Oberpresident</u> and of <u>Regierungspresident</u> were in the hands of experienced party members. At the lower level far fewer changes occurred either because the incumbents' expertise was needed or because the SPD lacked members with sufficient qualifications.

On the other hand, having a party member in post was no guarantee of adequate policies, as the example of Police President Barth demonstrated (see above II, 2a). Another case is that of Inspector of Schools, F. Deike. An old and experienced Social Democrat, Schumacher had used all his influence to get him appointed. However, he proved unsatisfactory. 'While loyal, conscientious and hard working (he) was not quite up to tackling the particularly difficult problems arising in the city'. (44) 'Personal politics' on its own could not and was not intended by Schumacher to replace political power. It was not possible for the SPD to dislodge great numbers of civil servants. It had neither the political control nor sufficient replacements to do so.

The third element in Schumacher's speech with lasting consequences was his belief that 'democracy' was irreconcilable with co-operation with the communists. Against all the professed desires for 'unity' the latter had established themselves as an independent party everywhere, including Hanover, and were tied to one of the occupying powers and were as undemocratic in their objectives as ever.

With Schumacher's increasing authority fully committed

against a link with the KPD the way was open for his own version of working class unity: the SPD should act as a 'magnet', attracting all smaller left groups into its fold and thus creating one large party. This was in fact what happened in the subsequent months but there is evidence that the process did not pass without some bitterness. Otto Brenner recalls:

> The remaining illegal small groups which were essentially SAP friends, Socialist Front and ISK had offered their active practical co-operation as soon as the Americans occupied the town. Political discussions about longterm objectives were pushed into the background. Realpolitik was the word. This found its manifestation in the so-called Reconstruction Committees. None talked about the so-called 'historical' parties. None believed they would reappear in their full 'glory'. The concept of the workers' movement was the unity of the working class as the lesson of the past. A new socialist movement ought to have been the consequence. That it came differently, we owe to the restoration efforts of the allies who knew no other aim but the reformation of the state of pre-1933. The Russians ... led the way. While we were still arguing about what kind of political movement could emerge from the committees, they created faits accomplis in their zone ... The question was which political party we should join ... We started from the precondition as to which party could provide the basis of a truly socialist party and a home for all socialists. We believe that the SPD is this party ... but we are fundamentally of the opinion that we take a long term view ... (45)

Attempts at creating a third workers' party were doomed and did not progress beyond first contacts, such as those between the SAP and KPD. (46) The ideal of working class unity was preserved in the concept of the one and united General Union, and it was to its creation that many activists turned while remaining often disgruntled members of the SPD. (47)

All those who had sought new, more radical responses to the disaster of National Socialism such as Blumenberg or Wendt, who had been most active in the Sozialistische Front, came to political grief. Blumenberg was prevented from returning to Hanover from exile ostensibly because no job could be found for him in the city - the precondition for a permit to enter it. (48) Wendt, although active in the local SPD always remained an outsider, as the difficulties he faced over his active involvement in the denazification system illustrated.

The period of 'semi-legality' between April and August 1945 was for the SPD, as for the other parties, a period of reconstructing their organisation. Thus the organisational structure, basing party membership on urban districts, (Wohnbezirke) was revived. The only change was forced on the party by circumstances rather than design: as the population had left the destroyed city centre in favour of the suburbs new district organisations had to be created, and old ones erased. One of the younger functionaries, Hermann Hasselbring, was busy collecting signatures in the (vain) hope that massive popular support would speed up the licensing process. (49) But when the SPD eventually obtained its licence the preparations made gave the party a good start over its competitors.

NOTES

1. Hannover im 20. Jahrhundert. Aspekte der neueren Stadtgeschichte. Beiträge zur Ausstellung aus Anlass des 75 jährigen Bestehens des historischen Museums am Hohen Ufer, Hanover 1978, p.118 passim.

2. Otto Brenner, born 1907 in Hanover. Son of a mechanic, was an unskilled labourer. 1921 member of SAJ (Socialist Youth organisation), 1926 SPD, from 1926 member of Metal Workers' Union, 1931 co-founder of SAP and its leader in district Hanover. 1933 reorganisation of SAP for illegality. Arrested end August 1933. 1935 convicted to 2 years prison for preparation of high treason. 1945 working party of SAP and ISK, unsuccessful attempt to form united party of SPD and KPD. Member of the Reconstruction Committee. End of 1945 leader of the Economic Group 'Metal' in the General Union in Hanover; in 1946 in Lower Saxony. From the beginning in opposition to union leadership. From 1952 leader of the Metal Workers' Union in the Federal Republic, initially together with Brümmer, from 1956 on his own. Died 15.4.1972. (F. Hartmann, Entstehung und Entwicklung der Gewerkschaftsbewegung in Niedersachsen, PhD Thesis, Göttingen 1977, p.521).

3.   A. Karl, Von der Untergrundbewegung. It has not been the intention to give a comprehensive description of all forms of opposition here. This would have to take other aspects, such as e.g. the Churches into account. In our context only those facets have been highlighted which seem relevant to political development in Hanover after 1945.

4.   Otto Brenner - Joseph Lang, New York 15.8.1947. In: H. Grebing/B. Klemm (eds), Lehrstücke in Solidarität. Briefe und Biographien deutscher Sozialisten 1945-1949, Stuttgart 1983.

5.   DGB Archiv Düsseldorf. Material 'Allgemeine Gewerkschaft Niedersachsen'. "Richtlinien der Allgemeinen Gewerkschaft", May 1945, p.2.

6.   Hartmann, op.cit. p.96.
Within the Control Commission the formation of the German unions was the responsibility of the Manpower Division and within it of the Industrial Relations branch. It employed 'Industrial Relations Officers' such as those who attended the meeting in Hanover on 24 May 1945.

7.   H. Pietsch, Militärregierung, Bürokratie und Sozialisierung. Zur Entwicklung des politischen Systems in den Städten des Ruhrgebiets 1945-48, 1978, p.80.

8.   Field Marshal B. Montgomery, Memoirs, 1958, p.364.

9.   FO 371/46829/C 8256/CCG (BE) Intelligence Bulletin No. 3, 20.9.1945 for the following.

10.   TUC London 943/200. Minutes of a conversation between H.V. Tewson and Sir F. Legett, 8.10.1945.

11.   FO 371/46933/C4198 Weekly Political Intelligence Summary No. 2, 14.7.1945.

12.   SAH N.B. 22 Mil. Gov. 722 (K) Detachment - An den Oberbürgermeister ... 27.6.1945.

13.   FO 371/46899/C 6710. 'German Morale and Attitude to Control.' Appendix 'L' to CCG (BE) Progress Report for August 1945. Manpower Division, Industrial Relations.

14.   FO 371/46899/C 6183. CCG Progress Report for July 1945, Appendix L, Manpower Division.

15.   SAH NB 22 Mil. Gov. 722 (K) Detachment - An den Oberbürgermeister ... 1.7.1945. LAB 13/165 Industrial Relations Directive No 1.

16.   DGB Archive. Correspondence DGB/BZ - Manpower Division. Manuscript of speech by Luce to German Trade Union leaders, 13.11.1947.

17.   M. Balfour, op.cit., p.364.

18.   TUC 943/911 Major E.A. Bramall - H. Tracey 15.9.1945.
19.   See also the CCG (BE) Intelligence Report No. 4, 20.2.1946: 'The British method has been made to prevail ... the main structure is to be on British lines ... In general ... German trade unionists are still wedded to the Einheitsgewerkschaft, and argue furiously against the rival system favoured by us.' (FO 371/55610/C 1332).
20.   TUC Annual Congress 1946. Report of TUC Delegation to Europe. Visit to Germany. Letter TUC Delegation - Hans Böckler, 27.11.1945.
21.   Protokoll der ersten Gewerkschaftskonferenz der Britischen Zone, 12 - 14.3.1946 in Hanover-Linden, p.9/10.
22.   Protokoll der zweiten Gewerkschaftskonferenz der Britischen Zone, 21-23.8.1946 in Bielefeld, p.20. The conference nevertheless voted with 267:78 votes in favour of autonomous industrial unions.
23.   FO 371/55620/C 12203. Appendix 'A' to GOVSC/P (46)71. 10.10.1946.
24.   Ebsworth, op.cit., p.22/23.
25.   Ebsworth, op.cit., p.23.
26.   Interview with Noel (now: Lord) Annan, 25.4.1985. Lord Annan was a member of the CCG Political Division.
27.   FO 371/46934/C 4772 21st Army Group, Political Intelligence Summary No. 6, for period ending 17.8.1945.
28.   A. Karl, op.cit. p.2.
29.   Schröder, op.cit. p.465.
30.   Schröder, op.cit. p.498.
31.   "Wir verzweifeln nicht".
32.   SAH, Nachlass Nagel.
33.   SAH N.B.6. The Oberbürgermeister - Herr A. Karl, 2.6.1945 'I thank you for the work you have done for the good of the town of Hanover and ask you to express these thanks to your colleagues on the main committee.'
34.   SAH, Nachlass Nagel. Minutes of the final meeting of the Committee for reconstruction, 2.6.1945.
35.   Hartmann, op.cit. p.107. The debate among historians whether Works Councils and/or trade unions sprang up spontaneously or were revived by a few experienced officials cannot be settled definitely. The evidence in Hanover suggests a mixture of the two. See S. Mielke, Der Wiederaufbau der Gewerkschaften: Legenden und Wirklichkeit, in: H.A. Winkler (ed), Politische Weichenstellungen im Nachkriegsdeutschland 1945-1953, Göttingen, 1979.

35.   TUC 943/911 Bramall, op.cit.

36.   Anton Storch, later to become Minister of Labour in Adenauer's cabinet.

37.   Hartmann, op.cit. p.88.

38.   TUC 943/911 Bramall, op.cit.

39.   A. Kaden, Einheit oder Freiheit. Die Wiedergründung der SPD 1945/46, (2) 1980, p.13.

41.   Schumacher happened to be in Hanover at the end of the war, having been released in 1944 from Neuengamme concentration camp on condition that he took up a clerical post with a Hanover firm and did not reveal his identity. He had been one of the most promising younger members of the SPD in Württemberg before 1933. He was a member of the Reichstag from 1930 onwards and in 1932 had risen to become a member of the parliamentary party leadership. He was arrested on 6 July 1933 and spent the next eleven years in concentration camps and prisons.

42.   Interview H. Hasselbring. Hasselbring became Schumacher's right hand man, who rendered invaluable practical services. According to Hasselbring he organised meetings with local functionaries to make Schumacher known, because 'he was not a Hanoverian'. Schumacher's personality was so impressive, his determination and clarity of view such that he emerged as local leader almost 'naturally'. The precise process by which Schumacher established himself remains however obscure. See G. Plum in: Westdeutschlands Weg zur Bundesrepublik, 1976, p.97.

43.   F. Hartmann, Geschichte der Gewerkschaftsbewegung in Niedersachsen, 1972, p.37.

44.   WO 171/7990 504 Detachment R/B. Monthly Report for October, 31.10.1945, Appendix E.

45.   Otto Brenner, Hanover - Joseph Lang, New York 12.2.1947, in: Grebing/Klemm, op.cit., p.145-149.

46.   Hartmann, op.cit., p.31.

47.   Hartmann, op.cit., p.28.

48.   AsD, Nachlass Schumacher J. 10. Correspondence Blumenberg - Schumacher, August 1945. Apart from political controversy, this episode also reflects the fact that in many instances party posts were handed out in the first weeks after the starting up of political activities, leaving anyone not at the right place at the right time outside (see Kaden, op.cit., p.22, Footnote 19).

49.   Interview Hasselbring.

Chapter Four

THE DEMOCRATISATION OF LOCAL GOVERNMENT

BRITISH ATTITUDES

During the first months of the occupation the British used German administrative experts to carry out their orders and help restore basic services and law and order. The legal basis for this system remained the National Socialist Gemeindeordnung with the most objectionable clauses declared invalid. It was clear however that this was a temporary mode of operation only, pending the fundamental decisions about the future of Germany to be made at the interallied conference in Potsdam. In this conference it was agreed that

> The administration of Germany should be directed towards the decentralisation of the political structure and the development of local responsibility. To this end:
>
> (i)   local self government shall be restored throughout Germany on democratic principles and in particular through elective councils as rapidly as is consistent with military security and the purposes of military occupation;

Points (ii) to (iv) referred to political parties which would be encouraged to adopt the principle of democratic elections on which regional and local assemblies should be based.

The Potsdam Agreement thus referred specifically to the 'restoration' of German local government and this was the basis on which the Americans and French proceeded in their zones. The British, however, in the meantime had adopted a fundamentally different view from the other allies on the nature of German local government prior to 1933. Whereas the use of the term 'restoration' implied that there had been local democracy which had been subverted by the Nazis, the British rejected this and claimed that local government in Germany had never been democratic and that this lack of basic democratic experience at the local level was responsible for the ease with which the Nazis had been able not only to take over local government but at the national level as well. What was needed in Germany was a lesson in basic democracy as practiced in Britain.

The political developments in Hanover during the Weimar Republic had shown that the British interpretation was not without foundation in Prussia, but these British views surfaced rather suddenly after the end of the war and were put forward by W.A. Robson, a Professor of Public Administration at the LSE and a close colleague of Attlee in the past. (1)

Robson was able to approach the Administration and Local Government Section of the British Element of CCG at the time of the German surrender when they were waiting in London for their departure to Germany. He spoke at as many meetings as possible and his views made an obvious impact. (2)

Robson reviewed the various systems according to which German local government was run (Magistratsverfassung, Bürgermeisterverfassung, Stadtratsverfassung) and concluded correctly as the example of Hanover demonstrated that each of them had a central weakness: they functioned efficiently but were basically undemocratic because the officials, and notably the Bürgermeister, were civil servants appointed for long periods if not for life and unremovable whatever decisions the elected councils might make. The Nazis had gained complete control of local government by ensuring that the officials were loyal to them.

> ... Any mayor or chief officer who did not profess or display the most complete loyalty and adherence to the Nazi regime could not have survived in his official capacity ... (3)

Indeed, according to Robson, the established bureaucracy was one of the four main pillars on which the Nazi regime was based, the other three being the Party, the Army and the industrialists. German local government had always been highly authoritarian in outlook. What was needed was a fundamental reorientation of the awareness of the German people on four points:

1. that bureaucracy, however efficient, was no substitute for self government;
2. that 'local self government' does not, as many learned German apologists have claimed, mean administration by local officials but involves effective control by popularly elected representatives;
3. that pre-Nazi government was not democratic;
4. that the expert and the professional administrator should be only the adviser and the instrument of executive action, and not the maker of administrative policy.

This was a major, long term objective. The men involved in carrying these proposals out compared it to the changes which Napoleon had brought about in Germany.

The ideas were incorporated in Military Government Directive on Administration, Local and Regional Government and the Public Services of 8 September 1945. The Directive envisaged the introduction into local government of the British 'dual system' with its elected Council and the Mayor as representative head elected by it, as well as the creation of the office of full-time, permanent Town Clerk which was hitherto unknown in Germany. Fundamental changes were also planned for the German civil service which was to be made more accountable and, on the British model, transformed into true 'servants' of the public. A further area of reform was to be the decentralisation of the overall administrative system with more power going to the elected councils away from the state authorities which had been particularly powerful in a large state like Prussia.

By 1947 the British approach had only been partially successful. It had worked where German resistance was weakest, namely in the institutional changes. Thus the functions of the former German Bürgermeister were now split between the new style mayor as elected head of the Council and that of the Oberstadtdirektor. The (to the British) dangerous Führerprinzip in local affairs had been avoided. As planned democratically elected Local Councils were playing their pivotal role in the new local government structure.

British policies were not successful where they met with more determined German opposition, such as that voiced against the proposed changes in the civil service, or where administrative convenience immediately after the war created certain faits accomplis which proved impossible to remove. Thus the Prussian hierarchical structure of Regierungspresidents (RPr) (responsible for several urban and rural districts) and of Oberpresidents (OP) (responsible for a whole province) was revived in May 1945 for reasons of temporary efficiency and then developed its own momentum which neither British local government specialists nor German local politicians were able to shift.

Three areas need more detailed investigation: (1) the change of the local constitution and the attempt to reform the civil service. (2) The problem of the decentralisation of the political and administrative system at large without which local self determination would remain truncated and (3) the issues of local politics will have to be examined to establish whether the system worked more democratically and, more importantly, benefited the local people.

POLICIES IMPLEMENTED

Changes in the Local Constitution and the Civil Service

German reactions to the announced proposals for change ranged from bewilderment to outright rejection. To clear up some of the confusion the British sent out further details in October 1945.

> The following instructions are sent to supplement the Directive of Military Government on Administration ... (of September) ...
> (a) The Bürgermeister in office will become chairman of the (Nominated) Council (NRC) provided that he agrees to give up his appointment as an official and to give up his entitlement to a salary or other financial reward. He will receive an honorarium.
> (b) If the Bürgermeister ... decides to become an official ... he can be appointed as a paid executive of the NRC. He is NOT a member of the Council ...
> (c) ... He will be nominated by Military Government. (4)

in view of German confusion - one immediate problem was the question of payment for the elected head - the British decided to proceed slowly. (5) One task which was however tackled speedily was the change in the status of the existing executive heads. Up to November, OB Bratke wielded considerable power in Hanover, as we have seen. However, although efficient he nevertheless seemed to display to the British everything that was wrong with German officials: he was authoritarian and accountable to no-one - the British included as they were unable to keep track of the minutiae of local affairs. Not without relish did they therefore inform Bratke that by the following day he had to hand over to them some of his duties such as all political correspondence, in order to alleviate the by now intolerably 'heavy burden of work'. (6) No thanks for the services he had rendered were expressed.

German officials continued to be unenthusiastic about the changes which were being imposed. Their reservations centred around two arguments which they put to the British up and down the Zone. Firstly, that the British directive imposed a foreign system without regard to the good democratic traditions which had existed in the communal self administration of Germany before the Nazis came to power. Secondly, that the British were wasting their energies on comparatively unimportant matters at a time when the 'Battle of Winter' was being waged in which fundamental German needs had to be met.

Although the second argument particularly expressed the justified impatience of harrassed officials who had to cope with the daily struggle for the most elementary needs of the population, British priorities were clearly fixed on the longterm aims of the occupation, the political re-education of the German people.

What ever democratic traditions you may have had in Germany it was not strong enough to withstand the attacks of Nazism, and it is therefore necessary to amend it ... We regard (the changes) as the cornerstone of our scheme for the political re-education of Germany, pending the introduction of the elective system ... (7)

On the other hand, support for the changes were also not forthcoming from those Germans who might have had a vested interest in the increased powers of elected councils:

the politicians. Thus Kurt Schumacher for example thought the proposals were disastrous ('verhängnisvoll'). (8)

As early as July 1945 Bratke had proposed the setting up of a small Advisory Council and through August the composition of this Council was busily debated, with the communists worried that they might not obtain any seat, as they had been excluded from all offices in the town administration. In September the British began to implement their reform programme by choosing the members of a larger but equally advisory Council. The Germans again seemed slow and unable to grasp the finer points of what the British intended.

> ... The organisation and selection of councillors for Gemeinde and Kreis Councils are now in full swing throughout the RB ... The German mind, never a highly flexible mechanism, is very slow to grasp the principles involved. This means additional explanation and supervision by Military Government (on) whose job in this respect would be much simpler if a press campaign could be started to initiate a still bemused public in the mysteries involved in governing themselves ... (9)

The selection of suitable candidates was made by the British on the basis of representation of all sections of German society but the German political parties - as yet officially non-existent - through Bratke tried to influence this process. The lack of publicity meant that no independent candidates came forward which from the beginning defeated the British objective of starting a new democratic system in Germany with men (and women) not contaminated by the experiences of Weimar.

Eventually an Advisory Council of 12 members met for the first time on 16 October. The Germans scrutinised the party political composition carefully. There were 5 SPD, 3 CDU, 2 KPD, 1 FDP and 1 NLP. The communists, predictably protested that they deserved more seats on the basis of their pre-1933 election results. But when the Council met for the second time on 6 November it transpired that far from listening to the KPD the Council had been widened by taking in representatives from two further interest groups. The entirely formal approach to German politics comes out well in the discussion between the Town Commander and OB Bratke:

In the discussion of the new Advisory Council the Colonel was of the opinion that it might be advisable under the circumstances to include women in the Council. We then agreed to take in 2 women and 1 representative of the refugees to increase the number of Council members from 12 to 15. (10)

The task of this first Council was naturally limited: to provide a link between town administration and the population. But even this was made more difficult by the adversities of the time. When the Council met for the first time to receive and discuss a report by the OB this could not be done because owing to the paper shortage it had not been possible to distribute it to all Council members beforehand. Instead they had to listen to a verbal report which was so gloomy that it left little for the councillors to do. According to Bratke in the last months 'the entire social fabric of our city has collapsed and has been plunged into deepest confusion.' (11)

It was a depressing review of shortages of all kinds notably in housing with 5000 weekly new arrivals putting an intolerable burden on already overstretched resources. The situation in food and consumer goods was bad because they were outside the city's control. The city's social services were unable to cope with the ever increasing number of cases seeking support. (12)

The small Advisory Council was only considered to be a 'practice ground' on which the Germans could learn the rudiments of local democracy before they progressed to a larger council with more extensive powers. With a slight delay - caused by the sudden death of the local Military Government commander in a traffic accident - the new body came into existence on 29 January 1946. Its elected leader was the industrialist Henkel, an acceptable choice for all concerned although not a member of the strongest party, the SPD. It was for this reason that the British especially approved of him. When on the other hand it was discovered that he was the leader of a political party he was almost sacked - such was the commitment to the 'non-political approach in German politics.

It has come to my notice that the new OB is the representative of a political party. He is the representative of the smallest group, the CDU (sic!). I was not consulted when he was appointed, but now that

99

he has been installed I think it better to preserve the status quo until after the elections. (13)

Bratke had chosen to stay on as <u>Oberstadtdirektor</u> (Town Clerk) as was to be expected.

After the ceremonial opening of the new session by a high ranking Military Government officer, Henkel replied on behalf of the Council. His address, delivered in awkward English, revealed again the limitations of German policies at the time: gratitude to the British and transferring loyalty to them was the only mode of operation. In reply the Military Government representative thanked Bratke for his work in the past and appealed to Council members not to be guided by party political considerations but to act as links with the population. This was extremely important, 'we are in the middle of the battle of winter'. Within these limitations they were the city Government. (14)

There were initially 48 NRC members and although they were again to represent occupations their political orientation was once more carefully scrutinised. The SPD had 16, the CDU 12, the KPD 6, the FDP 9, the NLP 1, and 4 did not belong to any party. Again protests were lodged against this composition, again mainly from the KPD:

> The vast administrative tasks can be fulfilled only by the antifascist, democratic parties ... In these circumstances it would have been better to make up the Council of representatives of recognised political parties. A schematic transfer of democratic experiences from one country to another by-passes the requirements of the present time ...

The NLP protests were more successful. On 28 March 4 further NLP members and 4 women (2 SPD, 1 CDU, 1 FDP) were added, increasing the number of councillors to 56 - a figure which appeared to some observers, to be far too large to carry out sensible local politics. However, according to British intentions the important work was to be done in the smaller, more specialist committees the recommendations of which would be discussed and decided upon at the far less frequent full Council sessions. The practice in Hanover shows that this is what happened. Between 29.1.46 and 8.10.46 (when it was replaced by the newly elected Council), there were 128 committees but only 9 full Council meetings. (15)

There were 10 committees set up, including the most important Executive and Finance Committee. The latter in turn formed a sub committee for 'Standing Orders' and it was this which had the unenviable task of working out a new town constitution. (16) The basis for its work were Military Government guidelines as well as the Hannoversche Städteordnung (Hanoverian Town Charter) which had been in force up to 1933. (17) It is revealing for the political preoccupations of local politicians that the first question the committee discussed was whether its findings needed the approval of the Regierungspresident. They also used this wider forum to protest again against the limitations imposed on the political activities of civil servants.

A second problem relating to the nature of local democracy was that of the accessibility of the Local Council to the public and whether in the course of a Council session deputations and petitions could be received. This was strongly advocated by the communists but equally strongly rejected by members of the CDU who feared that it might act as a device by which effective local government could be undermined - the recent past acted as a powerful example, when the Nazis had used this device to their great advantage. It was decided that petitions had to be handed in at least 10 days before the next council meeting and that deputations of not more than three were admissible if the Council approved. The speaker of the deputation was allowed to address the house for a maximum of 10 minutes. (18) Most proposals for changes in the constitution were made by the communist councillors. They had advocated the greater openness of the Council to deputations and petitions. They pleaded unsuccessfully for the removal of a law degree as qualification for the post of Oberstadtdirektor. They objected to the appointment of the Ostdir for life and got Military Government to reduce the term to a more flexible 12 years. They also introduced into the constitution a clause which allowed the city to take over Nazi property.

One of the last tasks of the Standing Order Commission before putting the Draft Constitution to the full Council was to decide the party political composition of the various committees. (19) It transpired that the KPD's activities did not result in a better representation in the system: the distribution key was SDP - 5; CDU - 3; FDP - 1; NLP - 1; KPD - 1. This was of course, unfair to the communists but on their protestations '... the representatives of the SPD stated that they thought 5 seats for their party was fair. An agreement could not be reached ...'. When it came to forming a Denazification Chamber, the KPD again demanded that the Chamber should be made up of 'recognised anti-fascists'. There were to be 16 members: 5 SPD, 3 KPD, 3 CDU, 3 FDP, 2 NLP. On paper there was a balance between 'left' and 'non-left' but as the debates on the constitution showed, in practice the KPD and SPD would only occasionally be allies.

In the course of the deliberations on the local statutes there were few serious disagreements between the German experts and their British counterparts but for one clause by which the Germans wished to keep the door open for sympathisers with the previous regime to return to political life after the lapse of a suitable period of time. There seemed little point in writing into the constitution the permanent ostracism of those who made up a sizeable part of the most active population. However, on this point the British were adamant.

The new Gemeindeordnung had come into force on 1 April 1946 by Military Government Ordinance No 21; it was voted on by Hanover Town Council on 8 October. It was passed unanimously but OB Henkel expressed a telling reservation:

> In order to bring to an end the long drawn-out deliberations on the Statutes and the Standing Orders, the main Committee decided ... to recommend to the Council the wording laid down by Military Government for the Statutes, especially since it is obvious that Military Government will not alter its decision. I assume that there is no objection to this and that the Council therefore agrees but that at the same time it expresses the hope that in a later version of the Statutes (the Council's) at present unfulfilled wishes ... will be born in mind ... (20)

Together with the changes in the institutions of local government the British had planned to reform the German civil service. The Directive of September 1945 contained a number of measures by which the German civil service, like local government, was to become more like its British counterpart. It was to be dissolved into a number of different 'civil services' according to which public body it was to work for. In this way the unified, monolithic and, because of its numerical strength, extremely powerful civil service was to be fragmented and made more accountable. As in Britain only immediate government servants were to be called 'civil servants'. They were moreover to be clearly subordinate to elected representatives of the people and were themselves not to take part in politics. On the other hand civil servants were to develop a new understanding as counsellors and servants and for this reason social privileges were to be removed by eliminating the academic qualifications previously required for entry into the service. This was to remove the 'Kastendünkel', the class snobbery which the British believed to have existed in Germany. This was of course

> a rather selective way of looking at things which ignored the social exclusivity of the Civil Service (in Britain) where membership of the Administrative Class was almost exclusively reserved for Oxbridge graduates. (21)

As has already been noted the new Hanover local constitution reintroduced the old academic qualifications for executive office against the wishes of the communists whose ideas were very close to original British intentions. German opposition was particularly stiff - and successful - against the British proposal that civil servants should abstain from political activity and turn into public servants 'above party politics'. Naturally, German opposition was notably vociferous among all the political parties. It was feared that all those civil servants whom the parties had carefully placed in civil service posts so as to make the service more politically reliable would be lost to party work. This would have been a particularly disastrous blow to the Social Democrats who were short of qualified people in any case and who, in times of political powerlessness, had pursued Personalpolitik particularly vigorously. However, the British saw in their proposal another cornerstone of their long term policy in Germany.

> This again is an essential part of our policy. The restriction on the political activity of the public official will be clearly defined in the second part of the Directive on Administration, Local Government ... which is shortly to be issued. This will make our reasons clear and the restrictions must be maintained. We

regard this matter as fundamental to the introduction of true democracy. (22)

In spite of the declared importance of the policy for British long term objectives in Germany the second part of the Directive was slow in coming, and when it came in June the restrictions on civil servants' political activities had been removed. The British themselves admitted that their proposals had been based on assumptions which could not as easily be transferred to other countries as, say, the institutional changes in local government. (23) The British were once again caught in the dilemma of having to introduce democracy with dictatorial means.

If they were to affect long term change in Germany by democratic means they could achieve this only by getting the co-operation of the Germans - an approach practiced also in the field of educational reform. Unlike the measures taken in education, however, a reform of the civil service was attempted which then failed rather ignominiously. This revealed on the one hand

> an amateurish reformatory zeal which was often the product of far reaching ignorance or misunderstanding of German history and (of Germany's) administrative traditions. (24)

On the other hand, despite the enormous numerical strength in the first two years of the occupation of CCG when a reform might have worked not enough experts with the necessary knowledge were available to carry the policy out.

Decentralisation

If local politicians had at best 'mixed' feelings about the British proposals for local government reform, they were much more enthusiastic about the second set of proposals which was to complement the first: the decentralisation of the political system with more autonomy for the cities and country communities. Greater powers for the localities had been a long standing objective of local politicians; during the Weimar Republic their pressure group, the Deutsche Städtetag, had made strenuous albeit not very successful efforts to improve the situation. This reached a nadir during the Third Reich. Not only did the introduction of the

Führerprinzip at local level reduce the communities to mere executive organs of higher authority, but during the war the most stringent central direction of the economy led to ever increasing central interference in local affairs. The British proposals which, if implemented, would have gone beyond what the cities had achieved under Weimar, were therefore met with great hopes by local politicians.

The general circumstances seemed to favour a complete reorganisation of the system. As the end of the war approached the cities were more and more cut off from communication with the outside world and had to cope, as best they could, with bomb damage, problems of law and order as well as the supply of basic necessities. Hanover's position was special in that it became the headquarters of the Military Government Region (25) and later, in August 1946, the capital of the newly created Land Niedersachsen. It therefore had a large number of soldiers and their families, civil servants and white collar workers whose needs under the existing post-war conditions could only be met if Hanover was given special status such as the Ruhr area or a city such as Hamburg.

For these various reasons local politicians were determined to fight for greater autonomy. Gustav Bratke with his long history of working for greater local self determination was a formidable advocate of the cities - their pressure group, the 'Städtetag' was soon revived - and notably of Hanover's case. He clearly hoped that Military Government would be a most valuable ally in his cause.

The most immediate obstacle to local autonomy was the institution of the Regierungspresident (RPr), the lowest echelon of the state administration and in the past, having controlling power over local government. The retention of this office therefore became the battle ground of all concerned. In spite of their declared intention to decentralise the system, the British had unwittingly done much to reintroduce the old administrative order which at the end of the war had effectively disappeared. As noted above, they were reintroduced as a temporary co-ordinating body but on the ground in a city such as Hanover there was obvious contradiction between strengthening local government and the instituting of the office of Regierungspresident. Moreover, many of their functions overlapped such as the collection and distribution of food which the city had been ordered to carry out by Military Government; there were also problems of reconstruction, where Military Government instructed the city's building department to take on the business for the whole district. (26)

The extra administrative layer in one and the same city was simply inefficient. It was claimed that the RPr was slowing down business unnecessarily, that urgent letters sent by officials had taken over 20 days to receive a response. (27) But how well the Regierungspresident was in fact already established in the administrative system was illustrated by the fact that the copies of the city's new Statutes had been handed by the British to the higher authority from where Bratke had to obtain them.

The issue was openly tackled by Bratke in a letter to the RPr of 8 April 1946, shortly after the new City statutes had come into force. Bratke outlined the anomalous position in which the cities found themselves; National Socialist legislation had not been formally lifted but simply replaced by Military Government directives; 'Higher Authorities' behaved accordingly and obviously thought they could still give orders to those 'below'. This also applied to the OP who was interfering with the city's traditional right to look after its roads, and who was now dictating to the city even the composition of refuge committees. The Council of Hanover city had in fact formed its own committees - in accordance with the new statutes - and only they were entitled to carry out official business. Interference from above were the 'remains of centralist legislation'.

If Bratke's attitude was supported by the declaration of British intentions to decentralise the German system, in reality the position of both RPr and OP was by now so consolidated that Bratke's initiatives made no impact.

In August 1946 Hanover's OB therefore complained quite rightly to Military Government that its own principles on which their local Government Reform was based, were eroded. There were two particularly disturbing developments: the fragmentation of public administration by the interference of central agencies in local affairs and the undermining of local autonomy by local responsibilities being discharged by higher authority. He submitted a detailed plan for the distribution of functions and duties between the institutions involved, the implementation of which would give the city that degree of autonomy on which 'truly democratic self-administration' must be based to be effective. As with previous initiatives, so this one achieved nothing.

In December 1946 a further combined attempt by Hanover's Ostdir to use the establishment of Regional Economic offices to obtain the desired status for the city was equally unsuccessful. The city's constitutional position was by now of course very much weaker than at the time when its demands were first expressed. In January 1947 Bizonia came into operation and with it the British had handed over much of the running of their zone to the Germans and their complete withdrawal in the not too distant future was a real possibility. The proponents of greater local autonomy had lost their potentially most effective support. The shift in power had become so obvious that in June 1947 the Rpr launched a vociferous counter-offensive, bombarding all with lengthy letters. She won easily, the law being on her side, although some British observers could see no purpose in the retention of the office of Rpr other than that it provided 'jobs for the boys'. The German people themselves did not care either way. The matter was officially settled later in 1947 and announced the in 'Official Journal of Lower Saxony' in January 1948. The office of Rpr survived. There was naturally considerable disappointment at the local level. At the first meeting of the elected Council on 26 October 1946 the OB had reported:

> ... In April of this year the Council welcomed the fact that with the introduction of the new statutes local self government was being revived. In the meantime we have had the painful experience that the hopes which we attached to it have not been fulfilled in the execution of many an important task ...

The situation - from Hanover's point of view - only got worse from then on.

REFORMS TESTED: LOCAL POLITICS 1945/46

To many British observers the concept of local self determination under allied occupation was a contradiction in itself. The British fell between two stools of wishing to exercise as tight control over local developments as possible, thus frustrating German parties and unions, while having to honour the provisions of Potsdam and depriving the Soviets of the propaganda weapon of allowing Germans to run organisations whereas the western allies did not.

It is therefore not really possible to speak of 'local politics' as such. Allied constraints and the higher German administrative echelons on the one hand were matched by the dependency of the localities on supplies from outside. What can be done here is to examine whether the institutions created by the British stood the test of the time. Did the Council show itself responsible for the administration, was it the mouthpiece of the population or was it just decoration leaving public opinion to find other outlets?

The records of Council and committee meetings suggest that the institutions were established easily enough as was to be expected of a city with a long tradition of local government, albeit in a different form from that which the British were introducing. There were some protests over the party political composition, as we have seen, but the system quickly settled down, once the constitution was accepted. The bulk of the deliberations was in fact carried out in the committees, as intended by the British. A consequence of this was that the Council developed expertise in different fields which could be called upon to give Council pronouncements greater weight. Thus when Military Government announced in July 1946 that Hanover would have to take in 103,880 refugees, a figure which was subsequently reduced to between 32-36,000, the Council debated the impact on living conditions in Hanover. The speakers of each Council committee demonstrated convincingly the disastrous effect such an influx would have. (28)

Another important function of the Council and its committees was that of pressurising the executive into taking more effective action and that of exposing inefficiencies. In a time of acute shortages it provided an essential pressure valve to be able to show where the responsibility for the state of affairs really lay. The communists were particularly active in demanding the setting up of special commissions to negotiate with Military Government or to investigate the town administration. In the case of the enormous flood of 6/7 February 1946 it gave the administration the opportunity to demonstrate that it was not to blame in spite of allegations to the contrary by local inhabitants. On the other hand, in the question of lack of heating materials it could be shown that the executive had failed to address itself vigorously and in good time to this problem which culminated in the city's intolerable dependence on rapacious private coal dealers. (29) This emerged only gradually and would undoubtedly have been covered up had it not been for the insistent search of Council representatives.

There were no 'Rathausparteien' in Hanover, no local pressure groups. The largest group, the refugees, were absorbed into the SPD with their speaker in the Council rising to become a member of the party's district executive committee in 1947. It was the problem of the influx of refugees, however, which brought about one of the few 'political' debates because having to take in refugees at a time when resources were already stretched raised fundamental questions about the nature of the society people wished to live in. How deeply the city was affected is indicated by the fact that between August and December 1946 alone no fewer than six big debates took place in the Council on this matter. Indeed in the debate on 8 August party political differences broke through. But this was the only time that a local issue was used close up to make standard speeches for party political purposes. The temptation to do so was particularly great as the first local elections, to be held in September, were approaching. But it also shows that by mid-1946 the Council members were able to speak with increasing confidence and that the Council although not yet elected had grown into the only forum in which conflicting German opinions could express themselves. Thus, in the autumn of 1946 with food and heating material desperately short, it responded as best it could under the circumstances by rapidly setting up a network of Consumer Councils which consisted of one Council member, one trade unionist and one housewife; this was in response to a proposal made by the SPD.

It was seen as a forum also by the population. Of course, the Council's limited powers were recognised but it remained the addressee of many a protest or petition until the situation deteriorated to such an extent in late 1947 and early 1948 that more dramatic gestures were necessary, such as the 'hunger strikes' between 29 April and 18 May 1948. The general frustration found expression in a general strike in November of that year.

Hanover Council emerged as a responsible and increasingly confident body which refused to panic into resigning even in the appalling circumstances of 1947 as the Council of nearby Brunswick had done. (30) Such maturity of conduct cannot be ascribed solely to Military Government local government reform but indicates rather that there was a greater tradition of local self government which the British chose to belittle. As we have seen, the local politicians in Hanover were not overwhelmed by the demands made on them by British changes but on the contrary, were frustrated that the changes fell far short of what the British had intended and the Germans had hoped for.

British Local Government Reform has always been considered the most successful aspect of British occupation policy and the local evidence in Hanover suggests that this interpretation is correct. In many areas of the former British Zone the system as introduced after the war is still in operation today. On the other hand, the reform did not contribute to wider political activity among the inhabitants. In Hanover and throughout the zone observers agreed that in the immediate post-war period the population showed little interest in 'democracy' but persisted in apathy and that its main preoccupation was with the provision of daily needs. In this respect therefore the reform policy appears as a rather futile effort. (31)

NOTES

1. They had written a book together on 'The Town Councillor' in 1925.

2. W. Rudzio, <u>Die Neuordnung des Kommunalwesens in der Britischen Zone. Zur Demokratisierung und Dezentralisierung der politischen Struktur: eine britische Reform und ihr Ausgang</u>, Stuttgart 1968, p.45 passim and W.A. Robson, 'Local Government in Occupied Germany', in: <u>Political Quarterly</u>, vol. 16, 1945.

3. Loc. cit., p.283.

4. STAH NdS Z 50 Acc 32/63 No 93 229(P) Mil Gov Circular 18.10.1945.

5. Loc. cit. Circular 24.10.1945.

6. SAH NB 11 722(k) Mil Gov Detachment - <u>Oberbürgermeister</u> 8.11.1945.

7. FO 371/55610/C1322. Brigadier Bridges, Director of the Administration and Local Government Branch, Internal Affairs and Communications Division, CCG to <u>Regierungspresidents</u> of the British Zone, 4.2.1946.

8. AsD <u>Sammlung</u> Schumacher. Schumacher-Bratke

27.11.1945. How difficult Schumacher found the proposals is illustrated by the fact that he tried to talk Bratke into accepting the post of elected OB while the (existing old-style) OB of nearby Hamelin was to become the new executive head of the Hanover administration. The rationale behind this curious proposal may have been that this would have been an opportunity to move the vastly experienced but by now rather difficult Bratke to a decorous post. Schumacher tried to sweeten the matter for the latter by pointing out, that there was no one other than Bratke in the Hanover SPD who could fill the post of OB adequately - not exactly a tactful remark about his host local party.

    9.   WO 171/7990 HS/WD/NWE 1859/3 Monthly Report of Mil Gov 504/720 Det. for October 1945. Appendix C (Civil Administration).

    10.   SAH-L-40a, op.cit., 10.10.1945.

    11.   SAH Niederschriften über Besprechungen mit den Dezernenten und dem Stadtbeirat, 16.10.1945.

    12.   In September 1945 there were 10,700. The situation was compounded by the new Mil. Gov. instruction which allowed only extremely low payments. Bratke thought them quite unworkable:

> I do not believe that this instruction can be carried out. I have proposed that the rates of payments fixed in the directive should be given a certain lump sum. This has so far not been done. This can be attributed to the fact that the directive was issued at Bad Oeynhausen and that all subordinate Military Government offices have to follow suit. Loc.cit.

    13.   STAH Z 50/Acc 32/63 No. 92 a II Lingham - Kopf, 13.2.1946.

    14.   SAH Unsignierter Bestand, 53/1 Ratssitzungen. 29.1.46.

    15.   Loc. cit. 8.10.46.

    16.   SAH Unsignierter Bestand, Fach 53/1 'Niederschriften über die Sitzungen des Ratspräsidiums und der Geschäftsordnungskommission' for the following.

    17.   Loc. cit., 4.2.1946.

    18.   Loc. cit., 28.2.46.

    19.   Loc.cit., 25.3.46.

    20.   SAH Unsignierter Bestand. Fach 53/1. Niederschriften über die Sitzungen des Ratspräsidiums und der Geschäftsorndungskommission 8.10.46.

21. U. Reusch, Versuche zur Neuordnung des Berufsbeamtentums, in: Foschepoth/Steininger (eds), op.cit., p.171 passim.

22. Brigadier Bridges, op.cit., 4.2.1946.

23. R. Ebsworth, op.cit., p.140.

24. U. Reusch, op.cit., p.176.

25. This redressed the balance in Hanover's traditional competition with the nearby city of Brunswick which under the Nazis had overtaken her rival. See war-time correspondence in: STAH Nds Z 50 ACC 32/68 No. 113 I.

26. SAH Protokolle des Bauausschusses 10.4.1946.

27. STAH Nds 120 Hann Acc 58/65 No. 153 City of Hanover - OP 11.12.1946.

28. Special session of Town Council 8.8.1946. The committees consulted were Health, Education, Welfare, Accommodation, Food and Economics.

29. SAH Nachlass Lindemann. Dezernat des Stadtdirektors Lindemann - An den Oberbürgermeister, 3.10.46.

30. C.W. Zöllner, Aspekte kommunalpolitischer Entscheidungsprozesse, dargestellt an der Entwicklung der Stadt Braunschweig nach 1945, Phil Diss, Braunschweig 1971, p.36. The city was temporarily run by a 'Commissioner for the Affairs of the City of Brunswick'.

31. For similar conclusions for the cities in the Ruhr area: Pietsch, op.cit. p.42.

Chapter Five

THE ORGANISATIONAL FRAMEWORK

WORKS COUNCILS

Although during the 'Interregnum' Works Councils continued their operations where required, their official activities started up again only with the announcement by British Military Government, on 18 August 1945 that shortly elections to Works Councils were to take place. This announcement appeared in the form of posters in all Hanover factories ('To the Workers of this plant') and contained as noted above the most detailed application of British electoral practices. The elections were either to confirm old or produce new workers representatives.

We have already seen that there was close contact between Works Councils and trade unions at this early stage with experienced Works Councillors often active and leading in the union movement. Conversely trade unionists took a keen interest in the developments at the factory level. After all

the democratisation of the economy is (now) largely the task of the Works Councils. We can talk about co-determination as long as we like, if we do not tackle this problem at the bottom, at the place of production, we all will not reach our goal ... (1)

On the other hand workers in individual factories needed the support of the stronger trade union movement to push through demands against recalcitrant employers, in particular by providing protection for those activists in the factories who were threatened with dismissal for their actions.

> I expect from you (the trade unions) that you will
> support our cause, because in the last analysis it was us
> who have always represented the cause. I ask you now
> to support us ... (2)

This did not of course preclude a measure of distrust
between the workers in the factories and the union officials,
particularly later when, with the organisational framework
reconstructed, economic life returned to more 'normal'
channels and workers feared that the unions might make
deals with management over their heads. (3)

From the autumn of 1945 Works Councils and Trade
Unions alike pursued a common aim: to have their
organisations recognised by Military Government and to
achieve for them a specific role within the factories and the
economy at large.

As far as the workers' influence at factory level was
concerned its increase depended of course to a large extent
on the plant's size and structure. In small family run firms
such as that of F Benecke in the north of Hanover which had
a workforce of about 300 there was a strong paternalistic
atmosphere which defused potential workers' militancy. On
the one hand, management re-arranged working hours and
the annual leave to suit workers to attend to the harvest on
their smallholdings - of vital importance at a time of food
shortages. But when the Works Council sought the removal
of a politically undesirable manager the director simply did
not find the time to attend the meetings at which the
matter was to be discussed. This situation continued for
over six months and although the workers eventually
prevailed, it was a pyrrhic victory with management making
all kinds of difficulties later on over Christmas bonus
payments etc.

If progress in workers' rights was to be achieved, the
large factories had to act as trail blazers whose examples
could be followed in smaller plants. The workers themselves
were of course well aware of this and in Hanover's largest
plant, the Continental Rubber Works, certain moves were
made. All three sites combined in September 1945 to set up
a 'Production Committee' of special delegates of the whole
workforce who had to present themselves for re-election
every year. Its rights and duties were: to take part in all
discussions of factory matters, including those with Military

Government; to gain access to all production and financial records; to examine, together with the Works Council and with management, all work norms in order to prevent unfair pressure on some workers at the time of production increases; to supervise the remaining politically unacceptable experts and their replacement in time by other skilled labour. In exchange the Production Committee undertook to guarantee peaceful labour relations, highest possible productivity, optimum use of the hours of work and the fulfilment of all production obligations towards Military Government. This was the most far reaching list of demands as well as promises for co-operation by any workforce in Hanover. It guaranteed the smooth running of the plant in return for detailed rights for the workers. To the chairman of the committee they represented 'the safeguard against Conti becoming a fascist armament or a big capitalist concern again which would be hostile to the people.' (4) The directors had given their verbal agreement to these proposals at a joint meeting between them and the Works Council. But there were prolonged and bitter controversies about some of the proposals in subsequent months.

In another larger firm, HANOMAG, with 3000 workers and employees in September 1945, the Works Council was convened through the initiative of the directorate. The workers demanded and obtained the right to co-determination in matters of personnel. They apparently did not make any further reaching economic demands. (5)

A similar pattern emerges for most factories. There were no determined efforts to achieve greater workers' say. One of the reasons for this must be seen in the party political composition of the Works Councils which had a strong preponderance of the SPD. (Of the 33 chairmen of Works Councils in the larger Hanover firms 22 were members of the SPD, 9 of the KPD, 1 of the CDU and 1 of the DVP (6)). The SPD was, as we have seen, committed to using the parliamentary path, which ruled out grassroot direct action.

From September 1945 onwards elections duly took place in the larger Hanover factories. After successful pleading with Military Government from as diverse quarters as the World Trade Union Congress, Oberpresident Kopf and Kurt Schumacher, the British had removed the voting restrictions, thus enabling all workers in the plants over the age of 18 to participate. It was a laborious process with entirely predictable results: an almost complete endorsement of the officials of the 'first hour', except in individual cases such as that of E Paats in the Continental Works who had only recently returned from concentration camp and had therefore not been available when the Works Council was first set up. It appears that the insistence by the British on the confirmation of the officials 'from the bottom' in formal British style elections was somewhat futile. On the other hand there is evidence that the trade union leaders and notably A. Karl were anxious that the Works Councils should not develop too much of an independent existence at a time when the unions themselves had not reached the stage of organisation of their colleagues on the factory floor. A. Karl for example circulated a note in Hanover factories advising the workers to delay the elections to the Works Councils until such time when, with the licensing of unions achieved, Works Council elections would make more sense. This was approved by most of the Works Councils approached but, as was to be expected, some of the more militant workers in HANOMAG protested to the British who forced Karl to send out a second circular in which he implored the workers to follow British instructions most scrupulously, and to hold the elections at once.

The election process could on the other hand not silence ongoing workers' demands for a settlement of their rights in the factories. It was clear that Military Government had to make the decision, but the latter was unwilling to take unilateral action in this matter. It was not until 10 April 1946 that the Control Council Law No. 22 was announced. It was short, consisting only of 15 clauses and came as a severe disappointment to the German workers. Law No. 22 did not even provide the Works Councils with the rights they had enjoyed under the Works Council Law of 1920. (7) On the other hand the Germans quickly saw that the very shortcomings of Law 22 were also an advantage in that it allowed the Germans to fill the frame provided by the allies with concrete Works Agreements. In subsequent months a well organised campaign was mounted in support of the demand for Works Agreements with the unions devising specimen agreements, based on which WCs in individual factories could pressurise their employers. The latter found WC demands unacceptable particularly in the areas of personnel, wages and business transactions, and this in particular as '... (the WCs) do not wish to commit themselves to absolute secrecy ...' (8)

The matter came to a head in Hanover in two 'test'

cases which won significance far beyond the local level: two strikes in the metal industry, in the firm Bode-Panzer (19.11-13.12.46) and in the Schmedding Works (10.6.-11.11.47). The owner of Bode-Panzer was the chairman of the metal industries in Lower Saxony and therefore a proponent of employers' attitudes. The metal union was led by Otto Brenner, one of the few younger union officials who was already prominent not only in the union movement but also in the Lower Saxonian SPD. (He was to become leader of the DGB in later years). The chairman of the WC at Bode-Panzer was a communist. The conflict in the firm therefore had the hallmarks of a 'struggle of principle'. The firm had 320 employees, about 90% were organised in the General Union. They went on strike on 19 November in order to force the employer to accept a Works Agreement. Because of the strong unionisation and the good organisation of the strike it was entirely successful in spite of the employer's appeal to Military Government and to the government of Lower Saxony for support. On 13 December a Works Agreement was concluded which allowed the WC co-determination in the areas of personnel and wages (Pt 3), of production targets and new work techniques as well as the closing down or expansion of the plant (Pt 8). The WC had access to full information including finance and personal records (Pt 9).

The strike was significant in several respects. It demonstrated that where their own interests and public order were not affected Military Government did not interfere. (9) It also showed that determination and good organisation at plant level had achieved the success. The union's Hanover branch was also supportive, but not the union at zone level. The latter was too far removed from the scene of action and had other priorities. (This had of course always been the suspicion voiced against the General Union, but the subsequent evidence suggests that a different union structure did not produce a more vigorous leadership).

The 'Bode-Panzer Agreement' also served its wider purpose of becoming the specimen towards which Works Councils in most plants could strive. The employers however fought a prolonged and in most cases successful delaying battle according to the evidence of the factories which have been investigated. But hostility to Works Agreements also existed in more unexpected quarters, such as in the plants which were working directly for Military Government and in the office of the OP which was headed by the prominent

Social Democrat H. Kopf. He apparently could see 'no point' in having such an agreement in his organisation. (10)

The most striking feature of the Bode-Panzer dispute was the great reluctance by the higher union echelons to endorse it which led to the battlecry in Hanover that the struggle had to be waged 'without' support from above. A similar pattern emerges from the second strike in Hanover in the firm Schmedding which was due to be dismantled because it had been involved in the production of war material. Here too the workers were eventually successful with very late support from the union which came only after a court of law had declared the strike to be lawful. It was one of the few examples where Military Government did in fact intervene not to support the workers' cause but because the strike seriously interfered with the dismantling programme.

> During the last six months the Industrial Relations staff successfully mediated and ended a six months old strike on an internal basis in the Schmedding Works. This mediation was only carried out so that dismantling could continue. (11)

To the workers it seemed however that progress could only be achieved by direct action from below after the settlement and in subsequent years there was ongoing tension between those union leaders who based their expectations on co-operation with parliaments and Military Government and the younger men who hoped for more immediate progress. (12)

TRADE UNIONS

Organisation

Although on 5 July 1945 the imminent formation of Trade Unions was again announced it was not before 1 September that Bratke was informed that through him applications could be put forward to British Military Government for meetings in preparation for the establishment of trade unions. Phase I of British plans for the organisation of German trade unions, the licensing of unions at the local level, was reached. It was a very cumbersome procedure, designed, it appeared, to maintain maximum British control and to enable them to determine the speed with which trade unions were to be set up. The only explanation which the Germans could find for this approach was that 'Military Government fears the trade unions ...' (13) Up to November all applications had to be submitted in eight copies (4 in English, 4 in German with a detailed report on each meeting at the end). Not even smaller meetings were allowed to take place without official approval.

Between 7 September and 14 October, 49 meetings were held in different Hanover factories which were well attended and at the end of which a vote was taken on the kind of union the workers wanted, or rather, given the massive presence of Albin Karl and his helpers, whether they approved of the proposed GU. (14) As Karl was also able to supplement these meetings with circulars in the factories and by use of the only newspaper, the 'Neue Hannoversche Kurier', the outcome of these votes was almost a foregone conclusion. In all 18,156 votes were cast, of which 17,166 or 94.6% were in favour of the GU. On 18 October the application for a license for the GU of the city and urban district of Hanover was made which was granted on 7 November. Immediately, the collection of membership fees was begun in the different branches and further finance came from taking up loans and from using those Labour Front funds which individual firms - against Military Government instructions - put at the GU's disposal.

By 27 October the statutes of the GU were worked out. There were to be 15 different economic branches (Wirtschaftsgruppen) with one for white collar workers and one for civil servants. The overall structure was centralised with the centre having the final decision-making power. In the central body all branches were to have equal power, irrespective of the number of their members; this body was to be elected not by grassroot membership but by a 'district advisory council'.

It was clear that in spite of the massive vote in favour of the general principle of the GU these statutes would arouse disputes which would have to be overcome in subsequent months. In the meantime the impressive support for the GU manifested itself in a dramatic growth of the membership: From 10,600 on 30 November 1945, to 24,895 by 31 December 1945, to 46,667 by 31 March 1946, to 52,024 by 31 May 1946, to 58,640 by 30 September 1946. By 1 July 1947 there were 91,894 members although in mid-1947 the General Union in Hanover was in the process of

transforming itself into industry based unions (see below) -
an impressive achievement if compared to the figure of
70,000, the membership of the Socialist Trade Union
organisation (ADGB) in 1928/29 which recruited from a
much larger number of workers. Obviously, the concept of a
GU had been successful in overcoming the divisions of the
past and members now came from all different political and
ideological backgrounds.

Among union officials however the uneasiness
concerning the union structure remained. This was
particularly pronounced among the leaders of the strongest
individual branch of the GU, the Metal Workers Union. From
the beginning one of the questions raised was that of
finance. How would the GU intervene in a strike? How much
financial autonomy was left to the individual unions? In
Hanover Otto Brenner also objected to the existence of
separate branches for civil servants and white collar
workers. In the metal industry he had built up industry
unions which automatically comprised the whole workforce
of specific plants. But it was not intended to ignore the
sensitivities of the employees

> ... we do not want to pull down the white collar workers
> from the level which they have achieved years ago; on
> the contrary we want to push up the workers to the
> level of white collar workers. (15)

Another uncertainty was the top-heaviness of the
centralised GU structure which must affect union
responsiveness and flexibility. Indeed, leaders of the Metal
Workers Union in the Rhineland were reported as referring
to the 'Einheitsgewerkschaft' as the 'Eintopfgewerkschaft'
(the 'all-in-one-stew union') in order to ridicule the attempt
to create unity where clearly diversity was more practical.
(16) It was therefore not surprising that when the British put
forward their proposals for a different union structure this
found some support among German unionists notably in the
west, in North-Rhine-Westphalia, although the majority
were, as we have noted, firmly committed to the GU.

A further area of potential dispute was the question of
the GU's political orientation. We have seen that the
original proposal was for a union above political parties, and
the statutes refer to this explicitly when stating that the
union would seek to represent the economic and social
interests of its members 'excluding all political, religious

and racial questions.' One of A. Karl's closest associates demanded in the first meeting in the firm HANOMAG at which the statutes were introduced to the workers, that

> politics has nothing to do with the reconstruction of trade unions ... Those who are honest will agree with me that trade union questions have nothing to do with politics. (17)

But from the beginning there was also the view that the unions whether they wanted to be or not were political in their activities.

> It goes without saying that as long as there is an occupation power in Germany we will not be able to discuss any problems. We have therefore decided, and these principles existed already in the old union, that it is not the union's business to concern itself with whether someone is catholic, protestant etc ... We need not discuss the racial question. This was part of the misery ... and no sensible person will want to discuss the religion of a member. On the other hand it will be impossible for the union to do without politics. Only those can become members who recognise the democratic order. Strictly speaking, politics can not be excluded from unions, and this is also not forbidden ... (18)

There were thus already in 1945 fundamental differences about the political orientation and role of the trade union movement. On the other hand, the political composition of the GU leadership in Hanover was moderate: 15 out of 18 were members of the SPD, two were CDU and only one was a communist.

As far as the union's long term objectives were concerned these were expressed in the General Guidelines of May 1945 which demanded co-determination not only in the economy but also in the institutions of the state, the communities, industry, agriculture, trade, crafts and the professions. 'Our work must concentrate on co-operation in all official bodies, because reconstruction without the co-operation of the workers is impossible.'

These demands were scaled down later in 1945, presumably in order to pacify Military Government, to the 'safeguarding of the right of co-determination in all

121

economic and social questions' and 'equal representation of workers in existing or future bodies of the economy.' (19) This was all rather general but probably unavoidably so in the circumstances of the time. The lack of concrete guidelines however, became particularly noticeable in connection with the co-determination demands of the Works Councils. When the situation arose that individual Works Councils set about fighting for Works Agreements they did not receive much help from the unions, which to some extent must have been due to the lack of clarity on this matter in the union leadership. Some union leaders, on the other hand, did have an idea of the union's role at the factory level:

> It matters that we do not only appear as peacemakers in the factories, but our task consists also of determining (with the workers and management) the planning of production. (20)

But this was not the accepted union line.

While in the Rhineland the principle of the GU had been abandoned by the end of 1945 the leadership in Hanover continued the build-up of their structure in Lower Saxony. On 11 January a first meeting was held of Lower Saxonian union officials in Hanover-Linden which elected a committee of nine to draft the statutes for the province. These were more or less identical with those for Hanover city, but required minor adjustments from some other towns. There were 42 delegates from different towns and regions. 'In the discussions it emerged that they all were followers of the concept of the General Union.' (21)

The important question of which form of organisation the trade unions in Lower Saxony should adopt was discussed again at the first full Lower Saxony trade union conference in Hanover on 28 February 1946. Military Government officers were present; they congratulated the Germans on the 'great progress' which they had made in building up their organisation and stressed that 'Military Government is neutral on the question of (trade union) organisation.' (sic!) An executive committee for Lower Saxony was elected. Its members were unanimous in their intention to continue the build-up of the union organisation along the principles of the GU. In subsequent months the secretariat worked towards the acceptance of the statutes for the whole of Lower Saxony - the precondition for recognition by Military

Government of the union having reached Phase III. After long negotiations this was achieved and adopted as union policy on 4 July in Hanover. Lower Saxony had placed itself under a different union system from that prevailing in the rest of the British Zone. When challenged that they were blocking the emergence of zone wide unions, Karl defended 'his' system by pointing to the lack of clarity in union matters within Military Government itself.

> Only when there is clarity about the kind and the structure of the future union system in the different areas of the British Zone would the time have come for mutual concessions (in the question of organisation). (22)

In a way the union leaders in Lower Saxony were just wasting their time. It was true that Military Government had promised them freedom of choice in the question of union structure, and that they had won the support of the local representatives of Military Government. But they overestimated the power which these local representatives had within the hierarchy of Military Government. They must also have realised that if they could not win over the rest of the unionists in the west and north of the zone to their form of GU, the Lower Saxonians would have to come round to accepting the union structure existing elsewhere. It was a matter of efficiency alone which required one and not several different systems.

These matters were discussed at a number of zonal trade union conferences. At the first, in Hanover-Kirchrode in March 1946, no agreement was achieved. The decisive meeting took place in Bielefeld from 21 to 23 August 1946. As the region with the highest number of union members, Rhineland-Westphalia had already gone over to the industry union concept by the end of 1945; it was their view which also prevailed at Bielefeld, by 267 votes to 78.

In determining their response to this defeat the Lower Saxonian union leaders were guided by one desire; to get for their organisation recognition by Military Government as the precondition for any official work. When therefore the Lower Saxony committee convened in November it decided to 'speed up the creation of a union organisation for Lower Saxony irrespective of its name.' (23) The reorganisation of the GU into individual trade unions according to industries took place in late 1946 and in the course of 1947. By this stage the unions' energies were taken up by different concerns: the appalling living conditions, workers' apathy and the struggle to gain more say in the economy had superceded the preoccupation with organisational questions.

Trade Unions and Chambers of Industry and Commerce

It has already been noted that the Chamber of Commerce in Hanover continued in operation practically without interruption. It had changed its name to 'Economics Chamber' and rendered important services to British and Germans alike. It did this to the former by providing information and by mediating between Military Government and German industry: the Chamber had the expertise, the contacts and the men who spoke English fluently. All Chamber reports mention the 'good terms' on which they soon were with the Economic Branch of Military Government. For the Germans the Chamber was useful in that it could help with papers and petitions and exercise in general a 'buffer' function towards the 'men in the Town Hall', i.e. the Reconstruction Committee. (24) The Chamber had from the beginning declared itself to be the successor organisation of the National Socialist Gauwirtschafts-kammer with all the contractual obligations this implied. This had, according to their own report, a 'calming influence' on the business community. Hanover was spared the bitter disputes which existed in other cities.

Into this cosy set up broke Military Government on 19 July 1945 with a wave of arrests of leading and politically compromised managers. But subsequent developments were to show again the two factors which characterised British Military Government as a whole: the divisions among the British themselves on the one hand and their preparedness to allow organisations and individuals to operate where this appeared justified by expediency on the other.

Thus the Public Safety Branch of Military Government carried out the arrests mentioned. On 18 August a Control Council Directive officially banned Chambers of Commerce. In the subsequent discussions between the Oberpresident of the province and the Military Governor, the German put forward precisely the arguments which were convincing to the British: the efficient running of the economy required the continued existence of the Chambers.

The OP said that instructions had been received that Chambers of Commerce could only be constituted at the Land- or Stadtkreis (urban or rural district) level. This was suitable in the Rhine province where there was a density of industry but was not suitable for most parts of the province of Hanover where the representatives of agriculture and industry should be on Regierungspresident level at least ... If the existing arrangement were not allowed to continue, in order not to lose the great value of their advice, might the existing chamber although closed, be left constituted to act in an advisory capacity to the OP? (25)

Military Government's Economic Branch allowed the Chamber to operate 'as if' it was still officially recognised. Oberpresident Hagemann concurred and lent his office for the Chamber to carry on as 'The Oberpresident of Hanover Province's Office for Industry, Commerce and Crafts for the Province of Hanover'. By 30 October permission was given by Military Government for the Chambers to operate again openly with the proviso that membership had to be voluntary, that they had only advisory functions and that members and officials had to be politically vetted. In the words of the acting chairman of the Chamber 'As long as there is no uniform central legislation the work of the Chamber will continue as before on the basis of districts and provinces.' (26) The Chamber in Hanover was proud to have obtained official recognition at such an early date, the earliest licence in the whole of the British Zone. (27)

Two aspects of the Chambers remained controversial: their function within the economy and their composition. Should they remain loose, advisory bodies with voluntary membership or should they actively involve themselves in economic planning and, based on compulsory membership, become an important element in economic life? Clearly, it was the latter position to which the Chambers aspired, because this was the function they had fulfilled before and during the Third Reich, until during the war they had become mere executive organs in a tightly controlled war economy. However if the Chambers were granted such an influential position it was only logical that now, under the changed circumstances of the post-war period, trade unions should also be represented in an organisation which was to help formulate economic policy.

This was the objective pursued by the trade unions.

Already early in 1946 the General Union presented a long and detailed paper to the Chamber with the reasons why union membership was now called for. (28) Three arguments were put forward: economic, political and organisational. Economically, Germany had collapsed completely and only a concerted effort by all could overcome the disaster; politically everything must be done to remove social tension by co-operation - if this failed political extremism would benefit. Organisationally the union proposed 'economic self-determination' in order to dismantle the bureaucracy which the previous regimes had erected and which seemed not only to have survived but to be flourishing under the occupation.

The union's proposal to form a provincial Economic Chamber was not welcomed by the Chamber. It touched on a number of fundamental principles, in particular it was considered the thin edge of a wedge which would lead to greater workers' influence in general. At a meeting of Chamber representatives from the whole British Zone in February 1946 at Bad Nenndorf, specimen statutes were worked out which specifically excluded the unions. (29) The question of union participation was brought into the open at the next zone wide Chamber meeting in Stadthagen near Hanover on 18 July 1946. Here the so-called 'Ölkrug Resolution' (after the inn in which the meeting took place) was passed which, while stressing that the workers had an important role to play in formulating economic policy, said that this should take place in a more elevated body to which both Chambers and Unions could send representatives. The Chambers themselves had the task of mediating between different economic interests in their own areas. (30) This position remained unchanged in the subsequent negotiations with the Economic Central Office of the Zone at Minden on 19 July and also when Military Government applied pressure.

If the unions had relied on Military Government support they were going to be disappointed. A paper drawn up in October 1946 revealed that Military Government, yet again, was divided on the issue. (31) The Economic sub-commission of the Zonal Executive Office and the Political Division of CCG (BE) were in favour of trade union participation, the Commerce Branch of the Trade and Industry Division and the Manpower Division were opposed. In view of the outcome - the trade unions did not achieve their objectives in spite of a long battle in the Länder parliaments (32) - the two arguments put forward by the opponents are of some interest: (a) that employers as well as workers were entitled

126

to their own respective associations. This ignored the fact that, of course, the employers had their own associations outside the Chamber; (b) the views of the Americans who were opposed to unions in the Chambers. With economic fusion of the two zones approaching, and in view of British economic weakness, it was almost inevitable that the American approach prevailed. In the Friedmann Directive of 27 November 1946 the British removed compulsory membership and barred trade union membership and thus officially fell in line with American thinking.

The Trade Unions and Living Conditions

After the end of the war food supplies were precarious. The harvest was disappointing not only in Germany but in other European countries as well. A city like Hanover to a large extent depended on food deliveries from areas which were now cut off by the zonal boundary in the east; indeed very little food came from the other food surplus area, Bavaria, although it was under the control of a friendly ally, the Americans. The problem of supplying the German population with adequate food was rapidly turning into the most important and difficult task of the British (and American) authorities in Germany. The full extent of the emergency was revealed at the beginning of 1946, after the much publicised 'battle of the winter' had seemingly been won. At the beginning of March the British suddenly announced the cutting of the food rations to 1015 calories a day. (33) It is not clear whether this had become necessary due to a lack of precise and early information within the British Military Government or whether a combination of factors outside British control was responsible for this state of affairs (shortage of shipping, shortage of Canadian and American wheat). The effects in the German population were compared to a 'bombshell'. (34) Urban industrial workers were naturally particularly hit.

On 6 March a mass meeting took place between workers of Hanover firms and Military Government officers, speakers for the Chamber of Agriculture and leading officials of the Hanover General Union. (35) The meeting agreed that 'the present terribly low level of rations in the British Zone naturally leads to physical weakness and a decrease in the capacity for work.'

The main reasons for this predicament were identified

127

as 'the Hitler regime and the total war for which the Nazis were responsible'. The question was what could be done to alleviate the hardship? A number of proposals were put forward: 1. Reduction of the number of hours worked, with the exception of vital industries, for the duration of the current food situation; 2. In spite of the reduction in the hours worked, guarantee of additional rations for workers in heavy and very heavy industry; 3. Partial compensation for the drop in wages caused by this reduction; 4. A comparatively sharp reduction in the rations of the self supporters (Selbstversorger) and the addition of food so obtained to that of the normal working consumers and in the first instance to those in full employment; 5. Promotion of the fishing industry; 6. The strictest control of the food producers and traders by the authorities and the Agricultural Inspection Committees with the participation of trade union representatives; 7. Very severe penalties for the non-fulfillment of the delivery obligations, for illegal slaughtering and for trading on the Black Market. Severe offenses to be punished by expropriation and immediate transfer of the business or farm to Trustees; 8. The cleansing of the economy, including agriculture, as quickly as possible, of Nazi officials since these posed a constant danger of sabotage.

The German workers found themselves in an intolerable catch 22 situation. Reduced intake of food over a prolonged period had weakened them already and the new reduction of rations made the continuation of full working days impossible. This in turn would lead to a reduction in wages which would lower their standard of living even further. The task of the trade unions was simple: to help workers survive. The remedies proposed however, were as predictable as they were ineffectual: appeals to the authorities to introduce more controls of producers, distributors and of those with their own food supplies (i.e. allotments). There was little hope of enforcing these demands. Although the Nazis had demonstrated that a considerable degree of control over food production and distribution could be achieved (albeit not total), this kind of system was impossible in the post-war situation. Only the British could have provided the massive force required to put such a policy into effect; this they were unable and unwilling to do. (36) The suspicion that shortages of all kinds were due to sabotage by National Socialist employees in the different organisations, and notably in the Food Estate, was widespread, hence the

repeated demands for thorough political purges. Denazification was of course the one political demand put forward
permanently by the trade unions (and they co-operated
vigorously in the system of denazification boards set up in
1946). Although there was no direct evidence of sabotage by
National Socialist employees of the Food Estate, the
presence of a great number of Nazi officials became
increasingly intolerable, and their removal was demanded
more and more forcefully. But ultimately even the most
committed anti-fascist official could not produce sufficient
quantities of food where there was none. Ultimately
Military Government would have to provide if the disaster
of starvation was to be averted. This it did, and the Hanover
workers acknowledged it.

> Those assembled recognise the efforts of and the
> measures taken by Military Government up to now to
> relieve want in the area occupied by the English. They
> are particularly thankful to Field Marshal Montgomery
> ... (37)

This was a more realistic appraisal of the causes of the
German predicament than British observers found in other
sections of the German population where British
malevolence was blamed. (38)
    After a temporary improvement in the food supplies the
situation deteriorated once more by the beginning of July to
the level of March. On 13 July Works Councils and Trade
Unions met again in the HANOMAG firm. They considered
that the consequences of reducing the food rations were
again incalculable.

> It will lead inevitably to even more severe damage to
> health and to the ability to work. The ever increasing
> hunger and fear of winter cold will increase the
> population's despair to such a level that the trade
> unions, like all other organisations working for
> reconstruction, will not be able to make Germany into a
> reasonable community again. (39)

This time the demands were made with greater urgency for
the removal of the barrier between the western and the
Soviet zones to facilitate food deliveries and for the
suspension of coal reparations.

The coal obtained from this moratorium should be used above all for the production of agricultural equipment and the production of artificial fertilisers. It should also be used to provide the population of the towns with heating materials, in order to diminish their special hardship caused by the food situation.

As already in March the system of collection and distribution of food was heavily criticised. Now a purge of personnel was no longer sufficient. Instead, 'the trade unions will be charged with working out a new form of organisation for the whole zone ...' there was an urgent appeal to trade unionists in other countries not to stand idly by while the Germans suffered.

Until it is possible for the Germans to help themselves, the German trade unions issue an urgent appeal to trade unions in all countries to make their influence felt, not only to guarantee the physical existence of the German workers, but also to guarantee a standard of living which will not destroy again the tender beginnings of a free and democratic Germany.

It was not only the wretchedness of their situation which caused misery among German workers but the unfairness of it: on the one had there were many Nazis either still in their jobs or else able to make an obviously good living by other means. On the other hand, the allies made no attempt to distinguish between German anti-fascists and the rest of the population. When therefore German emigrants began to organise the sending of parcels to German workers from the United States it was this aspect which was often singled out by the German recipients.

We see in the parcels a sign of solidarity which proves to us that there are people abroad who want to help so that we anti-fascists are not punished in the same way as the Nazis. Unfortunately, there is little evidence of that here. Everyone is treated alike and so we see the workers among whom are many anti-fascists go hungry while the many party members and followers as a result of their possessions, and because they still help each other, have a much better life ... (40)

At a meeting of the workforce of HANOMAG in November

1946 the general living conditions were summarised. (41) Everyone had expected that Germany's reconstruction would be slow but few had anticipated a deterioriation. For months the workers had been depressed by the news of the reduction of sickness pay and in the pensions of war victims.

In addition there is the totally inadequate provision of works clothing and of all the other supplies for daily needs. Because of rising prices in all sectors the low payments of social security are insufficient for the purchase of (even) small food and heating material rations. In the factories it is more and more common for sick people to continue work to complete exhaustion because the meagre sickness pay is insufficient to keep a family. Because of the wages stop and the increase in prices the real income of workers is low. This situation is made worse by the reduction in working hours as a result of the food shortages. Workshops ... are left unheated by order of Military Government in order to save coal ... The workers today stand in unheated rooms with torn shoes, without warm underwear and with totally inadequate clothing. These people are hungry, live in overcrowded flats, live practically without the intake of fats. The food situation is becoming more difficult from week to week ... Colleagues in the factories state again and again how easy it is for many people to live well without work ...

The meeting ended with an open warning to Military Government not to go beyond what was endurable for German workers. This was followed by the by now usual demands for the removal of zonal boundaries, the punishment of saboteurs etc.

The worst was of course still to come, the longest and most severe winter in living memory. By April 1947 there were widespread protest demonstrations such as that on 4 April when over 50,000 congregated in Hanover's main square, the Klagesmarkt, to vent their indignation: 'We do not want calories; we want food!' They were addressed by trade union leaders who again demanded the participation of trade unions in official bodies at all levels such as the administration of Bizonia, created in January 1947 by the amalgamated US and UK zones. (42)

Not only were the trade unions unable to obtain a more influential position in the food collecting and distribution organisations, they also failed to win better conditions for workers who, as a result of the general economic decline - even now most factories had not returned to full length working days because of repeated power cuts - were either on reduced wages or even unemployed. At a rather acrimonious meeting between Albin Karl and Military Government officers on 2 June 1947 the latter refused to give the German unions credit for their restraining influence on the mounting critical mood among the German workers. (43) The latter, on the other hand grew increasingly frustrated with what they perceived as a lack of forcefulness in the way the unions represented the workers' plight.

> ..the trade unions are accused by their members of not pursuing their demands with sufficient rigour and of showing too little tenacity in the fight for a general improvement. (44)

On 17 June there was the first of a series of 'hunger strikes' in Hanover factories (45) and, as already mentioned in the previous chapter, these recurred frequently. By January 1948 the situation had further deteriorated and the Hanover trade union leaders called a 24 hour strike as a 'clear and unmistakable warning'. But even this strike was called only in support of the Trade Union Council of the American and British Zones rather than independently in response to local grievances. The strike took place on 3 February with ovewhelming support but the demands put forward for how to avert a 'hunger catastrophe' were almost identical to those made on previous occasions with an equal lack of success. (46)

Throughout the year 1948 the strike movement did not abate. The trade unions, and in the factories the Works Council officials, found it increasingly difficult to restrain the radicalism of their members on the workforce. In April in a series of ballots the large factories decided on a general strike with the approval of their Works Councils. This took place from 28 April in a series of 'individual actions', with the metal workers coming out on 29 April, being joined by Continental and the chemical works on 4 May and by public transport on 10 May. A tidal wave of discontent seemed to be rising which was given new impetus by the effects of the Currency Reform in June which lowered workers' living conditions still further. 'The housewife can no longer make ends meet' was one of the more restrained comments in the communist newspaper, the <u>Volksstimme</u>. (47) The development culminated in a General Strike throughout the British Zone on 12 November 1948 which the occupation powers allowed to take place. (48)

In all these demonstrations the trade unions tried to act as moderating influence and were only reluctantly pushed into action by their more radical members. The material conditions of the workers were not substantially improved by these activities, as the unions rightly predicted; this came about only gradually. The unions were not given much credit for their moderation, neither by Military Government nor the German employers nor by their own members. Moreover, the preoccupation with daily worries took on a disproportionate importance at the expense of long term perspectives and strategies. According to Otto Brenner, there was

> no position on any important problem ... Today the daily worries (food, accommodation, clothing and heating) stand in the foreground of our political and trade union work. In this respect our work is radically different from that before 1933. But we must not forget our (long term) aims ... Everyone wants to save first himself and his possessions. Over that everything is forgotten - the past, the causes! Only the present counts! But we should also care about the future. We as socialists ought to think beyond the present and prepare already now ideologically for the future form of not only Germany but also of Europe and the world.

This was of course wishful thinking by a frustrated individual. But according to Brenner it was not only Germany's predicament which prevented a longer term view. There was the additional problem for German socialists that they were operating in a vacuum.

> Clarity about the political and economic intentions of the allies is of the utmost necessity, so that we can gauge from them the economic and political perspectives. The undefined political and economic situation has a paralysing effect on any positive concept of the socialist parties and trade unions. (49)

How much daily worries preoccupied the workers was

illustrated again in October 1947 at a meeting which Otto Brenner called of the Metal Workers Union to decide finally the question of the union organisation. Only 123 men attended.

> It is obvious that we have to start ... our work at the beginning again (after the dissolution of the GU). The tasks of the trade union movement have changed radically, not only in the objectives but also as a result of the conditions. The worry about the daily misery is the activating factor which determines our work. If we today had called for a demonstration rather than a meeting, more would have followed the call. (50)

But of course the questions of organisation were important.

> We need the organisation so that with it we can use the unions as a power political factor. This is why I want to stress that we have to start at the beginning again and that this beginning must be an obligation for us to rebuild with the same idealism which we had when we (first) founded the unions.

The practical difficulties would be enormous, not least because there was a dearth of functionaries in the age group between the old pre-1933 officials on the one hand and the very young ones who, under National Socialism, had had no opportunity to gain experience in union matters. It was up to the forty year old age bracket to work particularly hard to fill the gap.

It emerges that the delayed start of union work based on a definite union structure coincided with a shift in union work to the short term defense of workers' livelihood. The unions' position was thus weak in their struggle for a greater say in the running of the economy, as we have seen.

In conclusion, the uneven developments of the main economic pressure groups is obvious. From the beginning the employers and the Chambers continued to operate. On the other hand, the attempts by the workers to get their organisations licensed was made difficult with long delays and the resulting frustrations. Their attempts to gain more influence in the decision making process in the factories or in the economy at large failed, because they came up against the distrust of individual members of British Military Government, and later against the very clear views

134

of the Americans. Nevertheless, it has been argued that given greater determination on the part of the German workers more could have been achieved, more 'socialism' could have been introduced at least in the British Zone. (51) Examples for this view could be the two successful strikes in Hanover in which the British either did not interfere (Bode-Panzer) or mediated (Schmidding) because their own security was not endangered. Indeed, Brigadier Lingham, the Commander of Hanover Province singled out the determination of the German communists positively, compared with the rest of the German politicians (and by implication: unionists). This seems to imply that the Germans had more room for manoeuvre than they cared to explore and use. On the other hand British Military Government would have been the first to suppress wide spread German strikes or a general 'flexing of muscle' as illustrated in Bevin's letter to Robertson in November 1948. (See Footnote 48). As always, individual Military Government officers are not representative of Military Government as such. The overall evidence suggests that 'safety first' was the priority. This was as we have seen certainly the view of the British Government and particularly that of Foreign Secretary, E. Bevin.

There were two reasons why the unions did not achieve more: the commitment of the vast majority to democratic socialism and the physical conditions of the time. There are numerous instances testifying to the former. Alfred Dannenberg, the deputy leader of Hanover's metal worker union made it clear: the unions had no intention of jeopardising the SPD's struggle by extra-parliamentary methods. (52) Once parliaments had been set up and elected, socialism would be introduced by democratic means. To men who had survived a totalitarian dictatorship parliamentary means signified decency, fairness and legality - values which their later critics often dismiss as unrealistic and naive.

The conditions of the time were such that apathy spread rather than decreased. The minutes of the IG Metal illustrate this vividly. The union leadership would not have acted in the interests of their members had they called strikes for political ends in a situation where the place of work was often the life line. Moreover, only about 40% of the workforce were unionised so that a strike call would not automatically have been followed even had all union members been loyal.

The local evidence in Hanover seems overwhelming in putting responsibility for many of the developments in the zone on British Military Government. Certainly, there were individual officers who wanted early trade union organisation and greater influence for them. But they did not have the decisive say as the controversy over trade union representation in the Chambers of Commerce illustrates. It was also more than just the limited question of trade unions or Works Councils. This had to be seen in the context of the failure to remove known Nazis from influential positions and the stifling of German initiatives in that direction. The problem was that in order to minimise British involvement in Germany the British favoured as few changes as possible (except for Local Government). This meant maintaining continuity even at the expense of political consistency and credibility. This status quo was endangered by the German left, however moderate. It therefore had to be discouraged and it was.

NOTES

1. Protokoll der Gewerkschaftskonferenz der Britischen Zone, Bielefeld 21-23.8.1946, p.20.
2. Günther Wagner, Pelikan Works Archive. Minutes of Works Council meeting 30.5.1945.
3. Loc. cit., Minutes of various meetings 1945/46.
4. Material Hartmann Continental Works Archive, Bericht Paats in 'Die Wirtschaft'. Monatzeitschrift für Fragen der deutschen Wirtschaft, Mai 1946. Hartmann, op.cit., p.113 passim.
5. Hartmann, op.cit., p.117 passim for details on developments in other Hanover plants.
6. Hartmann, op.cit., p.129/30.
7. Protokoll der niedersächsischen Gewerkschaftskonferenz 11/12.9.1946 in Hanover-Kirchrode.
8. Die Gewerkschaftsbewegung in der Britischen Zone. Geschäftsbericht des DGB, Britische Besatzungszone, Köln, 1949, p.82. Rundbrief der Unternehmer vom 21.10.1946.
9. Although some very nervous officers appeared in the plant 'who discussed excitedly what was going to happen'. Minutes of Interview Hartmann - Dannenberg 28.9.1974.
10. Material Hartmann, p.97.

11.   STAH Nds Z 50 Acc 32/63 No. 93 Monthly Report of the CCG (BE) May 1948.

12.   see also Pietsch op.cit., for the different approaches in different cities of the Ruhr area.

13.   Protokoll der Gewerkschaftskonferenz der Britischen Zone, Bielefeld 21-23.8.46.

14.   Hartmann, op.cit., p.99 passim.

15.   Bericht über die Delegiertenkonferenz der Wirtschaftsgruppe Metall in der Allgemeinen Gewerkschaft Hannover, 8.4.1946, in: Material Hartmann.

16.   Minutes of Interview Hartmann - A. Dannenberg, 28.9.1974.

17.   Hartmann, op.cit., p.103 Erste Betriebsversammlung bei HANOMAG, 7.9.1945.

18.   Loc. cit., Zweite Betriebsversammlung der HANOMAG Belegschaft, 6.11.1945.

19.   Hartmann, op.cit., p.106, Statut der Allgemeinen Gewerkschaft Hannover.

20.   Material Hartmann. Bericht über die Delegiertenkonferenz der Wirtschaftsgruppe Metall in der 'Allgemeinen Gewerkschaft', 8.4.1946 in Hannover.

21.   Hartmann, op.cit., p.260.

22.   Hartmann, op.cit., p.266.

23.   Hartmann, op.cit. p.273.

24.   A. Lefevre, 100 Jahre Industrie- u.Handelskammer zu Hannover, p.158 passim.

25.   WO 171/7879 Military Governor, (P) Detachment. Diary 21.8.1945.

26.   Lefevre, op.cit. p.226. Circular letter 1.11.45 to all Chambers of Commerce in the area of Hanover-Province, Copies to: C of C Bremen, Hamburg, Münster, Köln, Essen.

27.   Op.cit., p.159.

28.   SAH, NB 2. Allgemeine Gewerkschaft. Kommission für Einschaltung der Gewerkschaften in die Wirtschaftskammern - An den Präsidenten der Industrie- und Handels-zu Hannover, 14.2.1946.

29.   Op.cit., p.160.

30.   Op.cit., p.161.

31.   FO 371/55620/C 12203. Appendix 'A' to GOVSC/P(46)71.

32.   The SPD motion in the Landtag of Lower Saxony on 25.3.1947 for trade union representation in the Chambers was defeated 43:41 (SPD and KPD - against CDU, FDP, NLP and Centre).

33. The average consumer required a minimum of 2000 calories a day; manual or heavy workers a daily ration of over 3000 calories.

34. FO 371/55798/07690 ISC Report for the period ending 8 April 1946. 'The gravity of the situation was not realised and ... the scaling down of the rations came as a thunderbolt.' Soon a new version of the Nazi 'Horst Wessel Lied' circulated:

'Die Preise hoch!
Die Zonen fest geschlossen!
Die Kalorien sinken Schritt für Schritt!
Es hungern jedes Mal dieselben Volksgenossen.
Die andern hungern nur im Geiste mit.'
(The prices high!
The zones are firmly closed.
The calories are sinking step by step.
The same people are hungry every time.
The others are hungry only in 'spirit').

from: T. Grabe ao, op.cit., p.112.

35. SAH N B 2.

36. The following year however they were prepared to bomb German cities should the hardship suffered by the population lead to further unrest which might endanger British security. (Regional Commissioner G. Macready - Minister President Kopf. 17.6.1947. In: STAH Nds Z 50 Acc 32/68 No. 41 I).

37. SAH N B 2. Resolution of Trade Unions representatives, 8.3.1946.

38. FO 371/55800/07690. See also: B. Marshall, German Reaction to Military Defeat 1945-47, in V. Berghahn and M. Kitchen (eds), Germany in the Age of Total War, 1981.

39. SAH N B 2 Resolution of Hanover Works Councils, 13.7.1946.

40. Fritz Treu, Plumber, Hanover-Ricklingen - To the Solidarity Fund, New York, 22.9.1946, in: H. Grebing, B. Klemm, op.cit.

41. AsD, Sammlung Schumacher J. 44, Betriebsrat Hanomag - Vorsitzender der SPD K. Schumacher, 27.11.1946.

42. H P 5.4.1947.

43. DGB Archiv Düsseldorf, A. Karl, Schriftverkehr 1947-48. Protokoll der Sitzung vom 2.6.1947.

44.   STAH Nds Z 50 Acc 32/65 No 15 IV <u>Chef der</u> Polizei Hannover - An die Militärregierung 18.7.1947 Betr: <u>Verhalten und öffentliche Meinung.</u>

45.   H P 20.6.1947.

46.   DGB Archive, A. Karl, <u>Schriftverkehr 1947-48.</u> Deutsche Gewerkschaftsbund. <u>Kreisausschuss Hannover,</u> <u>Streikentschliessung 30.1.1948.</u>

47.   <u>13.8.1948.</u>

48.   A list of the various strikes is in <u>Material</u> Hartmann. British Military Government had, unsuccessfully, tried to avert it. The British (and Americans) let it go ahead because the strike was not directed against them and because 'the right to strike is a principle which we have admitted since we first came into this country.'

This was however not the view of Foreign Secretary Bevin who reprimanded General Robertson; it so incensed the latter that he offered his resignation. In his reply Bevin gave some insight into the government's thoughts on Germany. These seemed to have changed little since the end of the war.

> The first point is that the recent strike in Germany was a general strike ... and as such objectionable ... It was a demonstration against the authorities of the state ... In the present conditions in the world a general strike in Germany is a serious matter ... The French who are now the target of concentrated Soviet action against the Marshallplan, are in the throes of a struggle against strikes fomented by the Cominform ... The Germans at this moment mount a general strike against their own authorities ... The time may come when they will take action by general strike against the occupation powers ... The sense of power may go to their heads as it has so often done before. There are already signs that they are becoming arrogant ... the time may come when these (moderate) trade union leaders would be ousted to give place to others of more extreme views, and we may pay the penalty for our forebearance on the present occasion ... In saying this Secretary of State asks you to believe that he is speaking from a long and extensive experience of political and industrial affairs ... (FO 371/70603/C10729/71G Correspondence General Robertson - FO 18.11.1948; W. Strang (for Secretary of State) - Robertson 24.11.1948).

49.   Otto Brenner - Joseph Lang, 15.8.1947. In: H. Grebing, B. Klemm, op.cit.

50.   Protokoll der Delegiertenkonferenz am 11. Oktober 1947, in Material Hartmann, op.cit.

51.   These views were expressed in a number of German publications in the 1970s which investigated the reasons for the restoration of a capitalist system in the Federal Republic such as Huster op.cit.; Schmidt, op.cit.; Pirker a.o.

52.   Interview Dannenberg - Hartmann.

Chapter Six

THE POLITICAL PARTIES

The mistrust with which Military Government officials viewed the trade unions also applied to the political parties; in particular it was the apparent overlap between the General Union and the SPD which caused concern.

> The German still persists in regarding trade unions primarily as a political ... force. Although this outlook is based on experiences in Imperial Germany and under Weimar it receives strong reinforcement at this time when political parties are limited to Kreis level whilst the Trade Unions have no similar limitations. The danger of the parties going 'underground' by amalgamation with Trade Unions is causing K Detachments considerable concern and will need constant watching. The problem is particularly difficult in such a broad organisation as the General Union. The latter is in effect virtually an alias for the Social Democratic Party. (1)

These sentiments, expressed as late as November 1945, are a good illustration of the general atmosphere in which the licensing of the political parties took place. Much of what was said in the last chapter about the difficulties encountered by the trade unions also applies to the parties.

Their enforced inactivity between the beginning of June until after the conclusion of the Potsdam Conference in mid-August 1945 did not produce the 'time of reflection' the British obviously hoped for; no new political forces emerged as a result of it. On the contrary, it strengthened the position of the old pre-1933 leadership. No new political

141

formation appeared in the autumn of 1945 which had not come into existence already earlier.

On 30 August Field Marshal Montgomery announced the imminent granting of permission for political parties to operate at local and district level. In transmitting this information to the German politicians, Bratke made it clear that this political activity was not to infringe the orderly running of the local administration. 'There must be no doubt that politics must not interfere with the present German administration'. (2) German and British administrators alike were unanimous in their priorities. Any such action would be considered by Military Government as directed against itself.

The Germans did however have the right to hold meetings provided the name of the organiser and the time and place of the meeting were communicated to Military Government in good time. These meetings took place but on the whole the German public remained aloof. (3)

The process of obtaining a licence for the operation of the parties got under way. According to the Directives No. 10 and 12 of 15 September the applications should be made in six copies, one in German and five in English; the programme of the parties must be included, again in German and English. But the German activists should not be too enthusiastic too soon: 'The decision about these applications will take a long time, as all applications have to go to headquarters at Bad Oeynhausen.' (4) It was only from 20 December onwards that the parties were able to operate at the lowest level.

THE SPD

The Licensing Process and the State of the Party

Through Bratke, Schumacher had made a number of earlier attempts at getting the local branch licensed, the last as late as 23 August. (5) On 29 August he filed a new application, this time for the publication of posters also in Oldenburg and Brunswick which were 'to give the population a first impression of how the social democratic party views the situation and how it wishes to shape the future.' In a memorandum to Bratke of the same day Schumacher informed the OB:

Basically the SPD wishes to obtain a licence for the entire area of British Military Government with the application in order to minimise the difficulties and confusion which must arise from a great number of local applications.

He enclosed copies 'in order to inform local branches of Military Government of his step.' (6) If Schumacher thus studiously ignored British regulations, Bratke did not. He only forwarded Schumacher's request on 10 September which was duly turned down.

On 1 October Schumacher made another attempt, this time in the correct form. The difficulty which arose from the requirement of producing documentation in English is illustrated by the original English version of the SPD-statutes.

A first mass meeting was granted by Military Government for 13 October; Schumacher was to address an estimated 10,000 on 'For a new Germany in peace, democracy and social justice'. Although Military Government had limited the audience to 5,000 it was a great success. (7) Encouraged by it Schumacher filed another application to obtain a licence for the 'local branch Hanover of the SPD in Germany'. At last, on 18 December the licence arrived with the following restrictions: no members under 18 years of age, only inhabitants of Hanover could become members, every elected official had to submit a questionnaire with personal details to Military Government which could moreover withhold approval of the election. (8)

As soon as official permission was obtained, membership lists which had been secretly drawn up could be published and subscriptions collected. On 20 January 1946 the Ortsverein of the local SPD branch was ceremonially refounded, in the style of the old pre-1933 party with the 'Arbeiter-Sängerbund' performing Beethoven. Schumacher used the opportunity to expound his views to a wider public (see below). (9)

At a first glance the party's development appeared healthy. Party membership was almost immediately as high as it had been before 1933. At the end of 1945 the local branch had 10,164; on 31 January 1947 there were 14,224 members. However, over half of these members had already been members before 1933, and the share of women was actually down compared to 1932. (26.6% in 1947 as against 28.4% in 1932). 5.1% of the population had been recruited: a higher percentage than in other comparable towns. (10) Particularly worrying was that only 5.3% of all members were between 18 and 25 years old. (11)

> Looking at the faces in any meeting, one is forced to conclude that the best age groups are missing. The old comrades who have remained true to their cause are back in place and the age-groups which are capable of putting ideas into effect and contributing to success are nowhere to be seen. The discharged soldier back from the front simply does not want to know ... (12)

At the end of 1946 the increase in membership was less than the party had hoped for in 1945. Indeed, the growth was so disappointing particularly in working class areas and compared so unfavourably with cities such as Düsseldorf and Frankfurt that Schumacher in the summer of 1946 threatened to remove the party's zonal headquarters from Hanover if the party could not display greater dynamism. (13)

In spite of Schumacher's presence in the town, and that of a growing number of leading party officials, the local branch does not appear to have derived greater dynamism from this. On the contrary, it performed worse than other cities. The SPD as a whole of course suffered particularly from the prolonged impact of National Socialism and the poor living conditions of the working class. Thus women would be doubly affected by the lingering nazi propaganda banning them into the kitchen and by the struggle to provide for their families. Many youngsters had never known a working parliamentary system; here again the nazi slogan of parliament as a time wasting talking shop had long term effects. Many young men were of course still away as prisoners of war or indeed were dead. However, if the party was to succeed, many more young would have to be won over.

More worrying in the short run was the apathy amongst the SPD grassroots, the industrial workers. This emerged from the elections to local councils held in December 1945 in the nearby district of Gifhorn which comprised besides rural areas also four industrial voting districts, including the town of Wolfsburg. According to SPD observers (14) the outcome of these elections was 'alarming' for the party. Although it had to be taken into account that the elections were held without proper campaigning and candidates did not stand as representatives of parties but as independent 'personalities', it appeared that the bourgeois voters had shown far greater involvement and responsibility in casting their votes than the working class. Thus while the average vote had been 61%, that in the cities was much lower. In a town such as Wolfsburg it was as low as 20%. Politically, the SPD had always been weak in the area, but the particularly bad performance in urban electoral districts had additional reasons:

> ... our comrades are mainly responsible for the results. They are aiming at creating again 'Workers' Associations' and not a political party. We are meeting in smokey rooms, we do not have the agility and confidence of the middle class, such as when they invite all local groups, including us, to discussions. This ability to take on a leadership role, when one does not really have one, is something our friends still have to learn.

While the bourgeois voters had elected independent candidates of the right, the workers had voted only for those put up by the party. Other candidates, however much they supported workers' interests, had failed, because of workers' distrust:

> Our friends keep to the old principle: anyone with a stiff collar cannot be a socialist! it will be difficult to carry out enough political education by May or June next year for us to appear more mobile and clever. So far we have been neither of these things. The practical result of this is: ... we must hold a lot of meetings ...

Although these observations were made in an area with its own specific problems there is no reason to doubt the characterisation of the political attitudes of the workers. It was only natural that they would want to start up where they had left off in 1933 - it was the only form of political activity which they knew. But it also underlined the magnitude of the task which Schumacher faced in his attempt to rebuild the SDP as a 'new party'.

A great deal of hard work was indeed necessary and we have already mentioned the factors which made this so arduous. In addition there was the chronic shortage of suitable party functionaries and it was relatively easy to analyse the reasons for the party's weakness as lying in

145

'yesterday's men' but much more difficult to ameliorate the situation. Thus a few activists carried a heavy burden.

> Everything here has to be done in terrible haste, because we do not have enough people. Qualified people are extraordinarily hard to come by and even leading officials, who can really fill a position are not to be found. (15)

This problem was to plague the party throughout the period under investigation and is well illustrated by the way the successor for Schumacher was chosen, once the latter resigned from the local party in July 1946 to devote himself to the build-up of the party in the Zone. There were few suitable candidates. Eventually August Holweg was chosen. A solid, hard working and dependable man, he was already heavily involved in the affairs of the Town Council. He was now also to take on the task of stirring the lethargic local party to greater dynamism, for which he was hardly ideal. From Schumacher's point of view the choice was a safe one: a loyal man who was committed to following Schumacher's line. He was also well suited to bridge the continuing divisions in the party. This emerges from the fact that for the first (and last) time in the history of the Hanover party there were two deputy party leaders: a representative of the right, in charge of the town's accommodation service, and a member of the party's left wing who had become quite unpopular because of his vigorous participation in the denazification process in the course of which he even co-operated with communists. (It is noteworthy that by 1947 he was not re-elected and that the party reverted to its traditional system of one deputy).

The new party leader, August Holweg, true to expectations, launched an energetic but somewhat aimless recruitment drive in response to Schumacher's strictures. This was not very successful, as 'no-one seemed to know how to recruit members.' (16) Apart from the difficulties already mentioned - the effects of N.S. propaganda, the living conditions, general apathy, there were a number of practical problems which made party work so difficult: there was a chronic paper shortage which meant the lack of a party newspaper and a very small number of posters - which moreover had to be suitably dull so as not to provoke Military Government intervention. (17) Often also they were too close to the style used by the Nazis to be satisfactory. (18)

The paper shortage was such that as late as 26 July 1947 the party's education committee published an appeal in the 'Hannoversche Presse' (19) 'for the donation or sale of privately owned socialist books, magazines, periodicals and other (suitable) publications.' The party's dearth of such material was of course only one aspect of the general shortage of reading material, but it hit the SPD particularly hard because of the party's need to recapture attention and kindle interest in its ideas and policies. This was particularly keenly felt in the party's Karl-Marx-Schule which was opened ceremonially on 14 October 1946: the school was intended as a training centre in law, economics and politics for a new Social Democratic elite but from the beginning was bedeviled by shortages of staff, materials and, worst of all, of students. The conditions of the time left little energy for 'continuing education'.

Schumacher's Vision of a 'New Party': a Summary

From the beginning of his political activities in Hanover Schumacher's sights were raised beyond the local level. The city provided him with a party machine and back-up and, owing to its geographical situation in the centre of Germany, it might prove ideal for setting up a central headquarters which however would eventually move to where the future German Government was located.

Earlier than other branches local officials were exposed to and familiarised with Schumacher's ideas. We have already noted that these did not really make much impact on the 'converted'. One of the reasons was of course the strict control under which meetings and publications were held by Military Government. In fact, Schumacher only issued two major communications in the summer and autumn of 1945 to Hanover and the surrounding districts: the 'Politische Richtlinien' (Political Guidelines) of 28 August 1945, and an appeal, written in the second half of August 'For a new, better Germany'. The guidelines were conceived as 'tactics to be followed' and not as a new party programme which was to be devised later. Indeed, local branches and individuals were discouraged from formulating new ideas which would make a future synthesis of ideas all the more difficult.

147

Unintentionally Schumacher reinforced the disinclination of many of the functionaries who were quickly devoted to him, to think for themselves about new ideas, aims and concepts of Social Democratic policy. (20)

As well as the 'guidelines' the appeal 'For a new, better Germany' was widely distributed at the time and although Schumacher stressed its provisional nature its influence was considerable not only because there were few other ideas to go by but also because of the ideas themselves: no one would take issue with Schumacher's analysis of the criminal Nazi dictatorship, and the sacrifices made particularly by Social Democrats. The SPD was indeed the only party whose 'policy of democracy and peace can bear examination in the court of history'. The guilty on the other hand were preparing a new stab-in-the-back legend and, worst of all, were allowed to survive in the guise of administrative and economic 'experts'. Schumacher's reference to the unsatisfactory way in which denazification was being conducted found open ears among the working class as has already been shown. The implicit criticism of Military Government becomes even clearer in the statement 'suddenly there is only to be democracy' - it was this equal treatment of all parties and groups which seemed to discriminate against those in Germany who had been democrats long before the British arrived. There was a call for national unity and a reference to Germany having to be a republic (against proposals by the NLP to link Lower Saxony with the UK and establish a monarchy!)

All ideas put forward were welcomed by (and were rousing for) old party faithfuls but the document did not provide concrete proposals. 'The great principles of socialism' against 'irresponsible big capitalists' and 'agrarian exploitation' were proposed. But there should be independent crafts and trade. Reconstruction must take place under planned control. Democracy in politics must be supplemented by that in the economy where workers must realise the right of co-determination. And although all this was to be achieved by the working class, the vision must be wider. '... the ideals of their class struggle are now the ideals of the nation and of the whole humanity ...' All the weak and suffering needed the party's help, and a list with proposals to achieve greater social justice followed. There must be hard work, and honesty to gain for Germany the trust of the United Nations.

Although not meant as a programme, the document in fact sets important yardsticks which were to be reflected in the conduct of the party's Hanover branch: the fact that as the only truly democratic party in Germany they ought to be treated differently even if they were not, may have contributed to a certain over confidence that their 'hour' of power would somehow come about, without giving much thought on how this was to happen. The proposals for 'socialism' did not go much beyond demands for greater social justice - a programme which could be endorsed by the great majority of Germans at the time. In particular, the idea that the working class struggle was that of the whole nation and even that of 'humanity' went well beyond any more narrowly defined 'socialism'.

Here was the sense of responsibility for the whole community, for the sake of which one must strive for co-operation with other parties and even when it appeared necessary for 'the sake of peace' surrender positions in Government or administration. Indeed, the document lacks 'socialist' vigour and militancy. On the other hand, it was written under special circumstances, with Military Government keeping a watchful eye on 'democratic' behaviour. It also seems to reflect that groundswell of German opinion which we have already noted when examining the formation of trade unions. There was a sense of 'togetherness' of the decent Germans against two enemies: the (capitalist) Nazis and the (foreign) occupiers who were depriving the Germans of the one achievement most believed in passionately: national unity. If those two could be removed, the Germans could well look after themselves. Only then would the moment come in which class divisions would assume their old importance.

Such a wide approach to politics which left the decisions on crucial matters to the future was also useful in that it could unite many internal factions in the SPD. We have already noted that Schumacher's 'magnet' theory according to which the SPD should become the political home of a wide spectrum of left groups worked in that the SAP and JSK joined the party. Within it Schumacher's position now quickly became unassailable. On 20 August 1945 14 out of the 19 party districts which were already in operation authorised Schumacher to prepare for a Reich conference. (21) On 9 September he was elected chairman of the Hanover district, and on 5-7 October a 'Reich' conference of the SPD was held at Wennigsen near Hanover which was attended not only by the members still in emigration in London (Ollenhauer a.o.), but also by those of Berlin (O Grotewohl) who, because of their geographic situation in the former capital, could lay considerable claim to the party's national leadership.

But it was far too early to consider 'national' leadership questions. The British when learning of the planned conference has insisted on the word 'Reich' being dropped, and on the conference being divided into two: one for members of the British Zone (surreptitiously joined by the 'Londoners') and the other for those from outside, notably the Berliners. In the course of the conference Schumacher emerged as the leader in the western zones, if not undisputed then at least strong enough (22) to prevent an open challenge to his leadership. In his main speech he again referred to an economy planned according to the needs of all the people (Allgemeinheit), leaving to the future the precise nature of his proposal and echoing ideas first put forward as early as May.

Shortly after the Wennigsen conference the SPD sent out 'Principles (Leitsätze) of an Economic Programme of the SPD' to the districts. Written by the party's economics expert Dr E. Nölting who had already co-operated in drafting the 1925 Heidelberg programme. It was interpreted by Schumacher specifically as not 'carrying programmatic obligations'. Essentially 'economic democracy' was a question of power, of law and of educating people to operate the system. The working class should be the vanguard in this process of change, although 'socialism' was not stressed. On the other hand, Schumacher talked of a 'radical agrarian reform' which would break up large agrarian estates. Compensation for the owners could not be taken for granted, as neither the state nor the new owners could be expected to take on economic hardship to satisfy the former. These themes were expounded in public on two occasions, once, as we have seen on 13 October at a mass rally in Hanover and during the public reconstitution of the party in Hanover, on 20 January 1946. According to the newspaper report of the latter event two aspects were again given prominence: the distortion of democracy by Military Government and that 'democracy and socialism' were the demands of the hour. British Military Government reinforced the German anti-democratic tradition by introducing a Ständestaat in the guise of its Nominated

Representative Councils (NRCs) which were composed of interest groups rather than parties. As for the second: '... democracy and socialism are the demands of this hour, but bureaucracy and economic experts are the masters of the situation ...' (23) This was of course rousingly put and was widely applauded but it did not enlighten this captive audience.

Already this short summary of some of the SPD's views suggests that in the winter of 1945/46 the SPD around Schumacher emerged with many old ideas. One central concept was that the party had to come to power by democratic means and that in order to do so it needed a wider appeal to sections other than the working class. Thus, the aspects of 'greater social justice' and the work for the 'general good' were stressed, but on the other hand concepts such as 'socialism' based on the class struggle were not abandoned. Events in the Diet of Lower Saxony illustrate this point. (24) When Minister President Kopf (SPD) in December 1946 announced cautious measures to remove certain basic industries from private control this was attacked by a leading member of the SPD in the Diet as being insufficient. 'We want nothing more or less than complete socialism'. The speaker, Kriedemann, one of Schumacher's close aides, based his analysis of the situation on the fact 'that we are in a stage of acute revolution'. To most observers this assumption derived from wishful thinking which ignored the reality of an apathetic population in desperate need of basic supplies and the presence of Military Government which was intent on preventing any disturbance.

As after 1918 the party appeared divided. Even worse, now there were the moderate pragmatists in positions of some authority notably in local and regional administration who, faced with enormous practical tasks, would accept help and co-operation often regardless of the political quarter from where it came - as against the party 'ideologues' who by the circumstances of the time were kept out of power but who also never seriously considered how to obtain it. Schumacher seemed to straddle the two, very aware of the difficulties and responsibilities of power and the problems of achieving it but he was unable to give realistic and comprehensive political leadership which would have given the internal party debate direction and purpose. The SPD emerged contradictory and confused and often negative where people were desperately seeking answers and clarity.

151

This obscured from the eyes of the majority of the general public the very considerable and beneficial contribution which many individual Social Democrats had made towards the reconstruction of their devastated country.

The Reception of Schumacher's Ideas at the Local Level

There was little debate of Schumacher's basic principles. On the one hand more urgent practical tasks stretched the physical resources of the party activists to the utmost. (1) On the other, the situation under Military Government was so confused that it seemed useless to speculate about the future; indeed the party leadership discouraged it. This limitation was openly endorsed by the local party leadership as illustrated by the statutes of Hanover's SPD at the beginning of 1947. These read:

> ... The organisation has the purpose of clarifying and making known in speech and writing the principles and objectives of the Social Democratic Party, as well as of working towards the election of Social Democratic candidates to all legislative and administrative bodies ... (25)

It was only in the following year, at the local SPD's annual general meeting in February 1948, that a lively debate on various aspects of party doctrine and policy ensued and this took place against the wishes of the chairman. According to him '... the Ortsverein has direct influence only on the work of the party in the local Council ...' (26) This view was strongly opposed by one member of the executive committee who subsequently resigned: '... The Executive Committee (of the local party) is not an organisational 'apparat' but a living political institution ...' He referred particularly to the unsatisfactory treatment of the question of youth: '... The Ortsverein must be the forum of serious intellectual disputes ...'

In February 1949 Holweg again stated

> ... that the decisions about the party's attitude and position in Questions of Bizonia and international reconciliation do not need the support of the local party. These important decisions are made by other bodies of the main party. The party here has one task:

the conduct of local politics ... (27)

These statements indicate firstly the rather limited vision of the local leadership which loyally executed orders from above but was devoid of constructive proposals, indeed which strove hard to discourage them. One of the reasons for this was of course to prevent internal divisions in the party from becoming too apparent. Those who wanted debates tended to be activists of the left whereas the mass of the membership succumbed increasingly to lassitude which affected the party as a whole. They also reveal however by the very fact that they had to be repeated every year that some functionaries in the wards were not happy with this state of affairs. Indeed a considerable number of ward motions were tabled at the annual general party meetings but as far as can be ascertained none was ever adopted. It seemed that Schumacher was caught in the dilemma that in order to maintain control the activities of the most dynamic members needed to be stifled while on the other hand those who supported his policies were often dull, or, according to one witness seemed at times even unaware of the meaning of his words.

> You (Schumacher) and other leading comrades speak in Hanover and other towns ... but you are speaking to at least 80% of the same people who are nearly all exclusively party members, and the most frightening thing is, as I saw clearly at the founding meeting, most of the people who attend the meetings are not able to follow your arguments. Otherwise your statements would have been interrupted by applause when you made your most salient points, which would have brought down the walls and carried your words to the ears of the leading men of the democracy which is occupying us ... (28)

Another aspect of this problem was that Military Government's insistence on party political neutrality of organisations such as Workers' Welfare, Youth, Trade Unions, Workers' Music Societies and Sports Clubs deprived the local party of a whole network of supportive organisations which in the past had created a separate identity, a working class culture, and while many functionaries behaved as though it still existed, the base on which to refound the SPD had in fact shrunk considerably.

153

What therefore needs to be examined more closely is the reception within the local party machine of certain key issues such as 'democratic socialism', the relationship with other parties, notably the communists, the 'widening' of the party towards women, youth and the Mittelstand and lastly, the attitude towards Military Government.

Democratic Socialism. To the majority of party members in Hanover the acceptance of 'democratic socialism' was axiomatic. It was the logical and morally acceptable answer to the totalitarian system of the Nazis. Socialism in the sense of 'greater social justice' (particularly for the workers) but to be achieved by legal, parliamentary means was the objective of the majority of party functionaries. (29)

By the local SPD's own definition the one area where it felt direct responsibility was the SPD in the local Council. If 'democratic socialism' was to be introduced at the local level this would be where it could happen. The analysis of the Council's activities showed that there was little scope for constructive policies. However, there was one instance in which this was attempted, the Bill for Reconstruction which the Council passed by 23:19 votes on 28 March 1946. This bill had been tabled by the SPD and contained a 'socialist' principle in that property owners could be forced to sell if their property obstructed the reconstruction process. Moreover, the actual plans for the rebuilding of the city with the building of broad thoroughfares and department stores to provide the people with as cheap goods as possible, also had a 'left' flavour and was opposed particularly vociferously by the NLP which stood up for private property and the small retail trade. (All bourgeois parties voted against the proposals). In the event the bill, although passed locally, came to nothing because the Lower Saxonian Government took over control of the entire building sector in the province, as was shown above. Once again a 'socialist' initiative had been frustrated by lack of power.

The local Social Democrats therefore needed little convincing that Schumacher was right when he insisted that 'democratic socialism' was possible only after obtaining power, by hanging on to it and making good use of it. For the time being with little prospect of direct power, one way of achieving it was Personalpolitik, i.e. to place as many Social Democrats in influential posts as possible. This would ensure that all possible scope for socialist policies would be used and that once a real power base had been created at the polls Social Democracy would not be subverted from within as had been the case during the Weimar Republic. Even now the traditional civil service was a bastion of political reactionaries.

'Personalpolitik' is another example of the dichotomy in the SPD between its pragmatic and its ideological wings. Thus the Hanover party's AGMs in successive years castigated Bratke for having placed Social Democrats at the head of only six out of ten departments of the town administration, and that this did not even include the important Finance Department. Bratke always refuted the allegations of political compromising: for him the main objective was that the administration was working efficiently. Indeed, it is difficult to see more than long term objectives in 'Personalpolitik'. It was of limited usefulness in the immediate political struggle. This is well illustrated by the SPD's 'Cologne Resolution' of 26.9.1946 in which the zonal party leadership threatened to withdraw all SPD members working in local and regional administrations if the party's political demands were not fulfilled. That the resolution was never carried out is symptomatic of its impracticability which was made worse by the impending creation of the American/British Bizonia; it would have placed men like Bratke and Kopf in an intolerable situation of conflict of loyalty, and might have rebounded on the party. Another example of the fact that the 'withdrawal of social democratic labour' was a blunt political weapon is that of the resignation of local Councils as the ultimate protest against the intolerable conditions of the time. The local SPD in Hanover in fact debated a motion put forward by an urban district at the AGM in February 1947; this was defeated, and the Hanover Council did not resign. In nearby Brunswick it did so, as we have seen, in May 1947. It achieved nothing concrete, except possibly some propaganda value. (30)

'Democratic Socialism' in the economy was equally elusive. The attempts to introduce more economic democracy into a number of Hanover firms have already been traced. They failed in the first surge of anti-fascist activities; they failed in negotiations between employers and unions, and between the Chambers and the unions. They failed by using the strike weapon in individual firms. At the SPD's AGM on 21 February 1948 it was stated that '... the subjective preconditions for socialism are absent ...'.

Although the meaning of this statement is somewhat obscure it seems to reiterate Schumacher's definition that socialism needed 'power', 'people' and 'education' to succeed. In the conditions of 1945-46 only Military Government could have provided a consistent political framework and the power, and this was not forthcoming.

Relations with other Parties. In his early pronouncements during the summer and autumn of 1945 Schumacher had recommended that SPD members should co-operate with other parties; only together could the enormous task of reconstruction be tackled. In Hanover this did not present a problem because good relations with the other parties had been established during the Third Reich, and the SPD in the city was so strong that it did not need to fear closer contacts. There were therefore a number of joint appeals and actions by all the parties like that for the establishment of a 'Land Niedersachsen' in the summer of 1945. Their co-operation first in the Advisory, then in the Nominated Representative Council was always good. Here the SPD had no serious rival, with the CDU only gradually emerging.

The real problem lay in the relationship between SPD and KPD. It has already been noted that Schumacher never wavered in his assessment of the KPD as being controlled from abroad and being as undemocratic after the war as it had ever been. This view was not generally accepted after the war with a strong tendency to create a united working class movement not only in the trade unions but also in the SPD and KPD. Initially it had been the KPD which opposed these unifying tendencies, and the behaviour of Hanover's communists in the Reconstruction Committee was a good illustration of this. In subsequent months, as the SPD organisation was gradually revived the attitude towards the KPD became an important issue in the emerging conflict between the SPD in the western zones, led by Schumacher, and the 'Zentrale' in Berlin led by O. Grotewohl, who claimed to lead a 'Reichspartei' (and had been given a license by the Soviets for it) but effectively only led the SPD in the eastern zone. (31) In Berlin an 'anti-fascist bloc' of SPD and KPD with bourgeois anti-fascist parties had been set up in July and a number of local SPD branches in the western zones such as Hamburg, Bremen or Brunswick were actively considering whether to introduce such blocs which would have meant the recognition of the Grotewohl-style SPD in the west. The situation was clarified at the conference in Wennigsen in October, with the division of responsibilities between Schumacher and Grotewohl for west and east respectively. However, from mid October pressure by the KPD on the SPD in Berlin and in the Soviet zone grew in an attempt to bring about a united front type of organisation - this time the KPD was to be the leading force. A circular sent out from Hanover after the Wennigsen conference to the districts in the Hanover area illustrates the continuing worry of the SPD leadership, including Schumacher, while also reflecting the poor state of party organisation generally. The SPD in the west was in no position to counteract a communist propaganda offensive, lacking a functioning organisational structure and with a desperate shortage of paper and party activities. (32) Schumacher now faced two obstacles: elements in the SPD who favoured a link with the KPD on the lines of the 'Zentrale' in Berlin, and the pressure from the KPD in the west. However, the proposed fusion with the KPD was less popular than expected in the west; on the contrary the more obvious communist pressure on the Berlin SPD became, the less support in the west became. Indeed, as western opposition to fusion hardened so communist attacks on the SPD increased. The communists claimed that western obstruction reinforced SPD opposition to the fusion in the east. Schumacher therefore sent out a warning to all districts of expected communist propaganda tactics in their all out attempt to overcome the SPD's resistance.

In Hanover the SPD leadership had no problems in isolating the KPD. (33) In a letter to the SPD secretary of 26 September 1945 the KPD in Hanover demanded the creation of a joint Action Committee because 'today the will to unity must become the guiding idea'. The Action Committee should be a first step on the road of the 'melting together into a unified party of the working class'. A second letter of 10 October repeated this appeal.

Schumacher side-stepped these demands by inviting members of the (tiny) Centre Party to join the Action Committee and by turning it into a committee of the local Council. No joint public meetings took place. The KPD however continued its activities particularly in the Hanover factories after the SED had been formally set up in April 1946. It had far more propaganda material at its disposal but in spite of this did not make much impact.

There was strong agitation by the KPD in the factories, but so far with some success only in the Conti Main Works. For (our) work in the factories a special Factory Organisation (of the party) has been created which grows stronger every month and which is being developed systematically. The importance of the Factory Organisation for the work of the party particularly with regard to the political activities of the communists has been clearly recognised. But we lack the necessary materials. The 1500 copies of the SPD weekly are almost torn from our hands in the factories ... (34)

At a crowded meeting of the party's ward and factory organisations on 8 February 1946 Schumacher gave a detailed account of the situation. According to the newspaper report Schumacher explained that the last elections (in Hungary and Austria) had shown up the importance of maintaining an independent party against the communists. It was a Milchmädchenrechnung (35) simply to add the votes of KPD and SPD. The SPD did not want an anti-Soviet or anti-French policy. Peace should realise the objectives for which war had been waged. This could not be achieved by replacing German capitalists by foreign capitalism but by transferring the means of production from the hands of big capital to that of the people, the 'Allgemeinheit'. There was only one vote against the resolution 'to stand unshakeably loyal to the idea of independence and autonomy of (our) party and to activate all political forces in Germany in this direction ... (36)

The KPD nevertheless continued its efforts. On 26 May 1946 the ceremony for the foundation of a local branch of the FDJ (the communist youth organisation in the Soviet Zone) took place in Hanover. (37) On the other hand the leading SED officials Fechner and Ulbricht from the Soviet Zone were not given permission to enter the British Zone. This made their appearance at a rally in Hanover impossible. The 'Socialist Committee' of Hanover communists which had formed itself to prepare the meeting announced its dissolution

because of the withdrawal of the entry permit of the above gentlemen the rally could not take place and thereby the existence of the committee has become irrelevant. (38)

As far as the Hanover SPD's attitude to other parties was concerned it followed Schumacher's line very closely and the temporary uncertainties as to the forming of a united workers' party that had existed in cities such as Brunswick or Hamburg were avoided. It is unlikely that there would have been substantially more support in Hanover but with Schumacher actually involved in the local scene at that time other tendencies had no chance.

The Position of the Mittelstand, (39) Women and the Youth.

One recurrent theme of Schumacher's publications on the new Social Democratic Party was that in order to come to power democratically it needed to widen its appeal from its traditional working-class base to the Mittelstand. In preparation of the elections in October 1946 the Hanover SPD therefore devoted special attention to refuting the accusation by other parties that it pursued policies 'hostile to the Mittelstand.'

In a special leaflet (40) the SPD advocated 'A Healthy Mittelstand': even in a socialist planned economy independent craftsmen, traders and artisans had an important role to play. It was the aim of a socialist economy to prevent periodic economic crises with their mass unemployment and the collapse of the system from inflicting undeserved hardship on all. These were the hallmark of an unprincipled profit economy which resulted in giant concerns, price cartellisations and a desperate search for new markets culminating in international conflicts. These factors would be excluded from the new economy which did however need real, personal enterprise but this enterprise should not be in a position of suppressing the interest of other social classes.

This was a rather sophisticated argument and, as the voting figures suggest, few businessmen were prepared to accept vague promises. Moreover, developments in the SPD indicated that this aspect of Schumacher's ideas was more controversial among party members. Thus, during 1946 and 1947 attempts had been made to build up within the local party a 'Working Group of independent Businessmen, 'Arbeitsgemeinschaft Selbständig Schaffender) in accordance with the guidelines issued by the party leadership'. At the AGM on 21 February 1948 it was at last possible to put a motion that such a Working Group should be officially formed and that it should be given representation on the party's executive committee. (41) The debate was lively but the motion was turned down (no voting figures were given). The arguments put forward for and against the motion reveal some of the reasons why Schumacher was unable to create a 'new party'. The division was clearly between 'right' and 'left' or between the 'pragmatic' and the 'ideological' wings. Thus the proponents of the motion argued that as only 35% of SPD members were factory workers it was important for the party to learn to speak the language of the middle class; it would enable the party to exercise greater influence on economic policy; besides it was what the leadership wanted the local party to do. (The reference to the fact that Marx and Engels themselves had been members of the Mittelstand met with vigorous protest!) The arguments against the creation of a Mittelstand group were that the acceptance of this motion would turn the SPD into a 'liberal-democratic' party (W. Wendt) and that special interest groups inside the party were undesirable (O. Brenner). The dilemma for the SPD was clear: the majority of the local party followed the arguments in favour of preserving the SPD as a working class party, if possible making it more radically 'socialist'. While this was ideologically pure and intellectually consistent, it nevertheless precluded substantial gains in elections. It was not until after the party had succeeded in widening its platform at the conference in Bad Godesberg in 1959 that it was able to win more votes.

A similar discrepancy between party programme and political reality on the ground existed in the treatment of women and youth. In order to grow the party would have to mobilise support in these two categories. Women made up over 50% of the population and of the voters. However when the election of autumn 1946 was prepared the special attention given to women consisted of an appeal to women in general which referred to their 'guilt' in the past when they had helped Hitler to power. '... They, more than men succumbed to propaganda, because they were emotional, because they let themselves be guided more by sentiment than by reason ...' (42) They should at least this time listen to the Social Democrats. After all, Social Democracy had always fought for equal rights for women.

It was not surprising that such a mixture of schoolmasterly reckoning and patronising advice was not very successful with women. The poll of 80% suggests that women voted, and indeed voted for the SPD, but far more revealing was the fact which has already been mentioned that by the beginning of 1947 there were fewer women in the SPD than there had been in 1932. Very little more than paying lipservice to the importance of women was actually done to recruit them. Thus at the AGM on 22 February 1947 a motion was tabled to ensure that out of the ten members of the Executive Committee four should be women. This was turned down; there seems to have been no debate, nor any offer of a concession (1 or 2 women perhaps?). No specialist secretary for women was employed by the local party.

The problem of how to attract the young was particularly intractable.

> (It) causes us particular concern as much in the political as in the trade union organisations. Whereas after 1918 a special type of youth grew up which attempted to cope with the difficulties of the post-war period in its own way, we are now dealing with a young generation which is getting back to orderly conditions only reluctantly. In parts they also do not want to. To a large extent the young are still infected by National Socialism and there is no movement which could provide the all embracing idea which could carry the young with it (and which) would be necessary to make them into active helpers in the construction of a new democratic state ... We must not leave the young in their passivity, because we cannot renew our movement without exerting influence and attraction on wide circles among the young; we also need the revolutionary élan ... of youth ... (43)

The local party, however, found it very difficult to put such ideas into practice. One of the traditional avenues for recruiting young men into the party, through sports, was of course closed because of Military Government's ban on 'political' sport organisations. Indeed, the party was not even allowed to run its own youth organisation, but had to ensure that those groups such as the Falken (10-16 years) and the Jungsozialisten worked as closely with the party as possible. (44) At the AGM in February 1948 it was reported that the Falken had twice as many members as in 1945 and that it had been possible to send 650 of them to summer camp where they had put on weight and generally benefited from the experience. But there was a desperate need for more helpers and officials. Youth in general showed little stomach for organised activities.

Moreover, a speaker for the Jungsozialisten revealed another cause for their weakness: as they were not able to operate as the party's youth organisation and with the 12 year gap of the Third Reich they had 'no tradition on which to build'. Youth were repelled by many organisational questions, they were often absent from meetings. He appealed to party ward organisers to show more understanding for the young. Perhaps the most revealing aspect of this report was that so far the party had failed to explain to the young concepts such as 'solidarity', 'socialism' and 'democracy'. The young did not dislike politics but they wanted to know what will be 'sozialisiert' and what the party means by Bodenreform (Agrarian reform).

What party functionaries had to offer in tackling the problem showed little imagination. This is illustrated well by the vaporous appeal to 'youth' in the autumn of 1946 to support the party in the forthcoming elections: (45) 'The young had been made to suffer for the mistaken policies of the bourgeoisie which had made them believe that it was the highest honour to die for one's fatherland. Now millions of them were dead, crippled or prisoners of war.' This was, of course, the sad reality of many young men in 1946, but what hope did the party hold out for the future? There seemed little more than platitudes.

> Dr K. Schumacher, the chairman of the SPD had often raised his voice to speak up for the young. Youth must not let the chances which are offered to them go by unused. We want to help the young, and the young must help us. They must take their place in the frontline of those who want to build from our devastated fatherland a new and more beautiful world in which all who work productively can live with dignity: in a socialist community.

These were pretty empty phrases and developments in the local party organisation confirm the impression that youth was not given the kind of backup which their officially professed importance would have warranted. In 1946 a youth secretary was appointed, but he was given only 'advisory' status on the Executive Committee. In the course of 1947 attempts were made to include this secretary on the

Executive Committee. At the AGM this was pushed through by a motion from the floor, whereas the chairman had intended to transfer the work for youth to another secretary which would have allowed the abolition of the office of 'youth secretary', as 'youth work had decreased to such an extent'. This, one member felt, was acting 'irresponsibly'. (46)

Although the sources do not permit a closer examination, the limited information available seems to confirm the general impression of the local party: dominated by old functionaries they were unable to respond to new demands. Where they tried to do so, they were caught in the strictures of the ideological wing. Either way they seemed to have failed.

The Relationship with Military Government. From early May 1945 onwards, Schumacher criticised the allies in general for a variety of reasons, for their ban on political activity or the blanket imposition of 'democracy' on the political landscape in which the allies did not distinguish between 'good' or 'bad' Germans. (47) In particular he repeatedly castigated the allies for dividing the country and stood up with determination for German 'national' interests. (48) The attitude of the British came as a particular disappointment; after all they had a Labour Government which according to Schumacher had 'some socialist tendencies'. Whereas no support for the SPD's aims could be expected from the Americans, Schumacher believed in the will to help among some members of the Labour Party and even the Labour Government itself but that this was obscured by circumstances. (49)

Closer to the ground the SPD leadership for district Hanover thought the 'attitude of several English officers ... at times completely incomprehensible.' (50) This applied to the long drawn out licensing process of the party and Military Government's ban on the publication of an SPD information sheet in January 1946. Although this ban was lifted two months later, the fact that almost ten months had passed since the end of hostilities and the party was only just beginning to operate properly, caused considerable frustration. (51)

These views were also partially reflected in the local party. On the one hand local attitudes were far more positive. Thus while Schumacher expressed criticism of the allies in the early summer of 1945, local meetings in Hanover specifically refer to the debt of gratitude which the Germans owe to the allies, for liberating them from the tyranny of National Socialism. (52) The speaker at the biggest of these meetings was the trade unionist A. Karl and it is noteworthy that trade unionists in the SPD often refer to this aspect of the occupation. As late as February 1948 when Military Government came under considerable attack at the SPD's AGM Otto Brenner of IG Metall pointed to the decisive fact which had determined public life in Germany over the last three years: 'that it was not us who removed the Nazi dictatorship but the allies'. (53) Local party functionaries still recall with admiration the tremendous effort by the British to get basic services going. (54)

On the other hand local criticism of Military Government was more specific than the sweeping attacks by the party leadership. Here it was the ban on all political activity of 2 June which SPD activists thought was unfair and shortsighted because the British rejected co-operation with democratic elements in the town. This was linked to the wider criticism which Military Government incurred over the following months and years: because it refused political co-operation with German anti-fascists it was unable to come up with a political solution of the problem of denazification. The 'legal' approach to denazification as practised by the western allies was criticised repeatedly, in motions put forward at SPD meetings and also in the factories and trade union meetings.

Having at last received their license on 18 December, the next bone of contention was the composition of NRCs by occupation rather than on the basis of parties which has already been mentioned. This was condemned by the SPD district organisation which expressed 'very strong criticism' on 3 January 1946. (55) The SPD - OV Hanover repeated this at its founding meeting on 20 January.

> The attempt to create the first beginnings of democracy in Germany by making a tranche through economic and cultural life is a danger. Such attempts have an anti-democratic tradition in Germany. (56)

The SPD in the NRC repeated these criticisms at the latter's first meeting on 26 January and again at the first meeting of the elected Council in October. The hope of individual party members using special links with the Labour

Party came to noticeable fruition only once, in the context of denazification of the Hanover police.

But neither at the level of leadership nor local party level was there ever a suggestion of rebellion: K. Schumacher made some attempt to simply ignore the sillier instructions issued by Military Government but when this did not succeed he exhorted his followers to adhere strictly to Military Government regulations. On the contrary, some Social Democrats believed that the Germans slipped too easily in the role of utter obedience. They accused the German authorities of continuing the old 'Untertanengeist': ('underling', subject mentality); they often based their actions on the pretext of carrying out Military Government instructions. 'The language and attitudes of many offices betray clearly their origins in the empire and their blossoming under the Nazis.'

> ... (the citizen) has noted with displeasure that in pursuing his justified interests he is often confronted with 'Military Government'. (This too has tradition - only two years ago it was the NSDAP local branch leader) ... it is our impression that the pointing to Military Government is in the majority of cases only a reliance on the fear of authority which unfortunately has not died out in Germany yet ... (57)

A change of behaviour among local party members occurred gradually after their organisations had obtained their license and, particularly, with the growing shortages of all kinds. It was the despair over their living conditions which drove many to articulate their opinions more freely: there was little more to lose. On the other hand, there was also growing confidence that the British would not penalise critical opinions.

The local SPD discussed the overall problem of the impact of Military Government on German politics at its AGM in February 1948; this was done in the light of the defeat of social democratic aspirations in the Lower Saxonian Diet where the two bills on trade union representation in the Chambers of Industry and Commerce, and on the socialisation of basic industries had been defeated. What had gone wrong? How much blame was to be put on Military Government? There was a noticeable division of opinion between those such as the editor of the paper 'Hannoversche Presse', Korspeter, who was also a member of the Lower Saxonian Diet and close to Schumacher and two other speakers and, on the other side, O. Brenner. The former three thought 'all our demands ... are overshadowed by occupation policies'. It was useless to pass laws in the Diets if these were subsequently suspended by Military Government. (58) 'We only play act democracy'. Korspeter thought that local politics ought to draw on the experiences of world politics. The situation in 1945 had certainly been revolutionary '... but this revolution was prevented ...'. Otto Brenner did not blame Military Government but the Germans themselves for their misfortunes. As noted above he was fully aware of the failure of the Germans to overcome National Socialism by their own resources. From this he drew the conclusion that 'the socialist revolution has not been prevented. It was not possible'. (59) The reasons for the failure after 1945 lay with the weakness of the German left itself. The conditions of the times made any coherent policy impossible.

In conclusion it emerges that local SPD members were less sweeping in their criticism of Military Government than the party leadership around Schumacher. This was due partly to the experience of the end of the war on the ground with the allies' massive effort to help the Germans get their services going again. Schumacher rarely refers to this; his criticism was more general. Also, at the local level greater prudence towards Military Government was advisable; it was here that possible reprisals might be felt. Anti-Military Government attitudes really surfaced once the initial post-war period was over and parties and other organisations were allowed to function. With living standards declining anti-British sentiments increased generally, (60) but protests about this went far beyond the confines of the SPD and were expressed by all sectors of public life. As far as Military Government's impact on the fortunes of the left in general was concerned, a wider approach than through the eyes of the SPD alone will be required to come to a definite answer.

The SPD in the Town Council

As we have seen the local leadership of the SPD refused to allow a debate on the party's principles or programme by stressing its limited power. The only area for which it felt responsible was the work of the party in the Town Council. From the beginning of some kind of 'parliamentary' activity, the party had pressed for stronger representation on the basis of its strength before 1933. It was for this reason and also because the first election after 14 years had almost a plebiscitery character that the SPD displayed great energy in fighting the town council election campaign of summer and autumn 1946. Between 10.9 and 13.10.1946 90 meetings were held in Hanover alone. (61) All the well known personalities spoke, and with the help of the other parties, one major success was achieved: to stir the electorate out of its apathy. In the event 80% voted even though the voting system was new to them, as each voter had six votes to cast. Although the SPD on this basis gained over 50% of the vote, it has been calculated that on the basis of the Weimar elections or that used later in the diet and <u>Bundestag</u> election the result was far less positive, namely only 37%. Nevertheless, the SPD celebrated the result as a massive victory (62) and 30 out of 48 seats in the Council were taken up by party members.

How seriously the party in general began to take its work in these councils is indicated by the installation at party headquarters of a <u>Kommunalpolitische Ausschuss</u> (Committee for Local Politics) later in 1946 on the basis of a 'local political resolution' passed at a meeting of local SPD-politicians at Bad Gandersheim on 15 and 16 October. This local politics department tried to establish a common approach and in particular to mediate between the 'strong divisions of opinion' which still existed 'particularly between our civil servant comrades and those in purely honorary positions'. (63) A list of 'guidelines for social democratic local politics' was published and sent to all party districts which in 28 'basic principles' outlined the party's position. (64) Many of these were already being fought for by Hanover's Town Council and notably the SPD members in it such as Bratke (see above). For example Point 3 refers to 'decentralisation' which necessitated the 'extreme limitation of supervision by state authorities'; this controlling function was indispensable only in areas where planning on a wide scale was necessary such as in the economy or in cultural life. How sensitive the question of control of local government was is illustrated by the fact that it is referred to again under 20 (co-ordination of local and central economic planning with as much power as possible), and 27 (the 'control' function of higher government echelons was to be one of mediation and co-ordination).

How these principles were to be applied at the local

level emerges from 'guidelines on the practical work of local parliaments' circulated early in 1947. (65) As local councils were the only mouthpieces of the party the motions tabled and the justification for them 'must at all times express the objectives of the SPD clearly and unambiguously'. (Point 1) The document is revealing about the aspirations of the SPD at local level at the time. Co-operation with other parties should be sought (3), and all sessions should be held in public (4). Particularly noteworthy were: the SPD in the Council represents the sovereign people and therefore has the right and the duty to criticise measures of the administration (5). Specifically it was to concentrate on (6): corruption, elimination of Nazis from local administration, fair treatment of all citizens, decent behaviour of all employees towards the needy public and a shortening of the public's waiting time. Refugees should be given particular attention by avoiding every injustice to them and 'avoiding labelling all refugees as Nazi activists and workshy elements' (sic!). 'Never lose sight of the fact: refugees are (often) 50% of the electorate ... They must not be pushed into a-social ways'. (7) The rest of the document is devoted to internal party procedure in preparation for and during Council sessions.

There was no hint in this document of the party's overall objectives such as 'socialism'. As expressed by A. Holweg in Hanover, the party was to work efficiently 'for the sovereign people' and to win votes. Within these confines the Hanover party on the Council was quite successful. At the AGM of the OV in February 1947 the Council party listed the following achievements: (66) it had won the rights of a 'Mittelinstanz' (i.e. exclusion of the control by the Regierungspresident) in the construction sector: (67) In direct negotiations with Minister President Kopf the numbers of refugees pouring into the city had been reduced; the newly elected social democratic Oberbürgermeister had stood up to Military Government and reaffirmed, after the elections in October, 'now democracy stands or falls with Military Government's readiness to give the elected Council the right to democratic self government'; in all branches of the Economics Office which were responsible for the issuing of ration cards Consumer Councils had been established; it had introduced Works Agreements with blue and white collar workers in municipal employment and had provided heating material for them; it had undertaken a variety of social measures such as the opening of a children's sanatorium to replace those now inaccessible in the Russian zone. In short:

In spite of the unfavourable conditions of the times and burdened with the terrible inheritance of a devastated city the social democratic Fraktion in the Town Council hopes to continue its constructive work for the benefit of Hanover's working population.

In general the AGM accepted this report, asking only for further branches of the Economics Office to be opened to ease the burdens of the consumers. The town administration should also endeavour to introduce a general price freeze to alleviate the effects of ever rising prices on notably the working class.

More serious was perhaps the criticism by some urban districts, that the party in the Council lacked commitment to overall party aims. Thus it had not resigned, despite the Cologne Resolution of 26.9.46, once it had failed to stop the flood of refugees. As we have noted above, the Fraktion believed that to reduce the flow of refugees was already an achievement, and in this it gained the support of the majority of the local party.

However the rumblings at the party's grassroots continued and were more clearly articulated at the AGM in 1948. We have already noted that this was the AGM with the most vigorous soul-searching so far. The activities of the SPD in the Council were subjected to such extensive scrutiny that an additional session of the AGM had to be held on 3 April 1948. There were three main criticisms of the Fraktion: Personalpolitik, lack of active involvement by Council members in the affairs of the local party and the reconstruction of the city. These points had been made before in a slightly different form but came down again to the differing interpretations of the party's role at local level between those who were tackling real problems and those who took a more narrowly 'socialist' line.

As far as Personalpolitik was conerned, by 1948 the SPD councillors had to admit that, owing to the educational preconditions for entry into the civil service, the party did not possess enough people to fill the posts and that there had been examples where SPD policies had not been carried out by civil servants unsympathetic to them. Here was a clear repetition of the situation after 1918 when the civil service had been a bulwark of reactionary forces. Schumacher had fought energetically to have the civil service opened up but it had been the British who insisted on the introduction in their zone of the politically neutral 'public servant' who in the German tradition turned out to be indistinguishable from his anti-republican ancestor during the Weimar Republic. (68) In addition there was a problem in the Fraktion itself where 32 out of 35 members were new to parliamentary work and needed to learn the 'ropes of Council work' (the wording in the minutes was 'the most primitive ropes ...'; but the qualification was crossed out).

The problem of involving SPD councillors in the local party was one of practicability for the councillors. For local party activists however it represented the fundamental question of accountability to the party and political awareness of social democratic Council members. The AGM accepted the councillors' declaration of theoretical good will. Their numerous other commitments prevented them from playing a greater part in party activities.

It seemed to SPD Town Councillors that the party's criticisms were often based on 'principles' which sounded impressive but which were not touched by the facts of reality. This emerged from the debate on the city's building activity. The SPD Fraktion was bitterly criticised, notably by one of the few articulate younger party members, for their approval of the reconstruction of a cinema and of an office complex as well as that of the Cafe Kröpke - a traditional landmark in the centre of Hanover. Instead, more flats and some youth centres should have been built. Too much of the city's resources were also going into the mounting of the Hannover Messe, (69) not enough into accommodation for the youth organisations.

The whole debate reveals the contradictions in which the SPD found itself at the local level in a time of economic hardship. On the one hand, the party demanded as much decentralisation from central control as possible and power for the local institutions. This implied that the city would have to try and generate as much income for itself as possible and only after it had done so could it progress to distribute the income for the benefit of the most needy or for clearly defined socialist measures. This was the argument put forward by Bratke. By letting the Cafe Kröpke the town would raise more capital than was available from tax and other income. The Hannover Messe - largely financed by the British and industry - would have an enormous beneficial effect on the city's service industries. In this respect Hanover was the envy of her peers. But it was true, that these were 'capitalist' ventures, supported by private initiative. (70) The problem with the town's own building ventures was that they were dependent on the production of building material which in turn depended on the output of coal which was out of the city's control. Moreover, locally, the city lacked one vital means of attracting scarce material and labour in 1948: it was not able to compensate. In other words, it could not use the means of the black economy, although, in desperation, this was precisely what some party functionaries suggested. (71) No legislation would be able to get to grips with the situation. One answer seemed to lie in building co-operatives and, particularly after the expected currency reform, this would be the only way out of the dilemma.

In summing up the debate the SPD's deputy chairman came to the following assessment of the party's performance:

> Opinions and counter-opinions have been expressed in comradely fashion. There was a need for debate. There are positive successes to be noted; the same membership figure as in 1933. As a party of Bizonia we can hold our heads high ('Können wir uns sehen lassen'). We have no cause for despondency. We cannot reach the great goal within one or two years, for that we need a generation. We should be glad and proud to be able to contribute to it. (72)

THE OTHER PARTIES

None of the other political parties could rival the strength of the SPD's position in Hanover, and the source material does not allow a more detailed analysis of how they attempted to counteract their weakness.

The KPD

A short reference has already been made to the active co-operation of the communists in the Reconstruction Committee and in the numerous anti-fascist organisations in the different areas of the town. After the failure of the anti-fascist movement, however, and after the return of leading functionaries from prisoner of war camps, the local party switched to the political line of the Central Committee in Berlin. (73)

171

A first application to the British for a license of 8 August 1945 contained an 'Action Programme' which was identical with an appeal by the Central Committee of 11 June. At the same time, and equally unsuccessfully, they applied for a license for their own newspaper, the <u>Hannoversche Volksstimme</u>. (74) After two leading functionaries had gone to Berlin at the beginning of September a new application for a license was sent to Military Government on 20 September in response to the latter's directive of the 15th. It carried the signature of the five leading local communists. No doubt in order to impress on Military Government by their commitment to the anti-fascist cause the length of the prison sentences and how much of them they had actually served was appended (58 and 47 years between them respectively). It did not achieve the desired result of obtaining a license more quickly. The short version of the party programme which was also contained in the letter, however showed in which direction the party was moving when it stressed

> the creation of the active unity of all antifascist forces for the realisation of democratic rights and freedoms of the people ('<u>des Volkes</u>'). Organisation of the active participation of all anti-fascist and honest Germans in the creation of the bases of a democratic people's republic. (75)

The local and district leadership of the Hanover KPD offered the SPD the creation of a joint 'Working Party' to prepare the setting up of a 'Committee of Democratic Parties'. As a joint platform they presented the SPD with an 'Emergency Programme for the City of Hanover' with a catalogue of measures to be taken in the areas of housing, food, heating, social services, the provision of clothing and shoes.

We have already noted that Schumacher had no difficulty in declining this offer although the fact that he in turn offered a Working Party which was to include non-socialists may indicate more grassroot support for a closer unity between the two working class parties than he was prepared to admit. The KPD therefore stressed this aspect repeatedly: 'Today the will to unity must be made the all embracing leading principle.'

This unity should find expression in joint KPD/SPD activities because the unity of action between the two brotherly parties with the aim of fusion ('Verschmelzung') should develop to the creation of one unified party of the working class.

This appeal was repeated again on 10 October in a letter to K. Schumacher:

In the process of reconstruction and of the creation of a new and democratic state a united workers' party must develop through the unification of the SPD and KPD. (76)

But these appeals fell on deaf ears among the SPD leadership who moreover were in full control of the membership. This was the interpretation by the KPD leadership of the situation in a report of 9 November 1945:

They (the leading functionaries around Schumacher) enter into negotiations with us now, after the Wennigsen Conference. But they refuse any concrete practical joint action. There is even the fact that they apply the party whip to lower party levels if they enter into a united action front with our units ... There is certainly turmoil in the SPD organisation but as this clique is well represented in all leading positions we shall have a more difficult stand with regard to the united front than in other areas. (77)

The KPD leadership probably overestimated the degree of support for unity between the two parties under their auspices. This was indicated by the moderate success which the communists scored at subsequent elections. Their lack of growth especially in those factories where their position had always been good was particularly disappointing. Only in the larger plants such as Hanomag or the main works of Continental was there sizeable support for the party, although as we have noted communists occupied only a few of the leading positions in the Works Councils there. Only in the Works Council of Continental's main works could the KPD maintain a majority. In 1949 they still held 12 to the SPD's five seats. But this did not dampen the party's drive. Its organisation, once it had obtained a license in the course of a protracted process which was similar to that of the SPD, was second only to that of the SPD. In February 1946 the SPD was operating in 49 districts, the KPD in 33 but the NLP only in 22, with the CDU in 15 and the FDP in only 5. (78)

The party's dynamism was displayed as we have seen in persistent demands for a greater democratisation of the local constitution for example when they insisted on the opening of the civil service to formally less well qualified candidates. They were also the most uncompromising party in their attempts to apply the denazification procedure rigorously. Here again, however the party tried to project itself only as the vanguard of a political force in which the other parties should join:

> It is clear to everyone of good will that denazification must not be left to any one party alone ... not that there should be fundamentally different criteria if the representatives of the parties are to come to fruitful work. (79)

They also protested most vehemently against the sentences passed at the Nüremberg Trials on Schacht and von Papen. Their press was unanimous: 'Nuremberg - a mockery!' (80) It was a slap in the face for the anti-fascist Germans. The party organised a strike in protest against it but there was only modest support. Only in the firms Hanomag and Hackethal did the workers down tools for ten minutes. (81)

By this stage, October 1946, the KPD in the west was widely seen in the context of what was happening in the Soviet Zone; for example the forced fusion of SPD and KPD there into the SED and the increasingly uncompromising imposition of a Soviet style political system. Lack of support for the KPD was therefore to be expected. But all the party's dynamism could not disguise its isolation even earlier, when they were unable to obtain the number of seats which they felt they were entitled to on bodies such as the Advisory Council. In the autumn of 1945 they were also particularly incensed by and powerless against Military Government's decision to fill the NRC in January 1946 on the basis of estates, rather than as a result of a political approach which, it was felt, would guarantee fairer representation. The question arose therefore for the KPD of how it could overcome these handicaps. The answer seems to have been to appear as similar to the Social Democrats as possible, make almost identical demands - only pursue them with greater determination. This is borne out by the first public pronouncements of KPD leaders in October 1945 when addressing mass meetings on themes such as 'The struggle for a democratic Germany' or 'For Democracy and Freedom'. It was particularly noticeable from a long newspaper article in January 1946 in a series run by the Neuer Hannoversche Kurier on the political parties as they presented themselves after having obtained their license. The KPD called for a genuine people's initiative which alone could create a truely democratic Germany. The instrument for achieving this should be the united strength of all anti-fascist democratic parties. No Social Democrat would object to the following demand or, if so, it would be on the grounds of 'lack of socialism':

> We support the completely unhindered development of free trade and of the private initiative of the entrepreneur (Unternehmer) on the basis of private property and we are of the opinion that in Germany there is no place for any sort of socialist experiment. This could only bring the high socialist objective into low esteem ... We have our own German conditions and tasks. The precondition for a democratic system in Germany is the complete eradication of Nazism ... Also the power of the Junker and of aggressive monopoly capitalism must be broken by a Bodenreform and by the transfer of concerns into ownership of the self governing bodies ... (82)

These demands like the many made before and later, remained on paper; no concrete progress was achieved. The KPD's proposals prior to the elections in the autumn of 1946, that they and the SPD form a 'United Party' list were turned down by the latter. (83) Nevertheless, the result in these elections of 6.4% for the KPD was the best the party achieved in Hanover. Looked at another way it again demonstrated its weakness.

The CDU

This was the only new party which emerged after 1945. Whereas all other parties talked about the lessons learned from the past only to settle down in their previous organisations and with often similar ideas, the CDU did make an attempt to overcome the religious divisions which had led catholics to form their own party, in the Centre, and which had dispersed the protestants among a number of parties which had collapsed ignominiously under the onslaught of the Depression and National Socialism. The disaster which had befallen Germany made religious divisions irrelevant in the political sphere. Their common value was Christianity and this was to be the party's basis on which it could embrace all social classes and create a 'true Volksgemeinschaft'. (84)

While it was easy to agree on the principle the problem was to reconcile widely different social classes and political interests ranging from catholic workers in the Ruhrgebiet to protestant landowners in Sleswig-Holstein; it was hardly credible that a united party could emerge. Thus perhaps realistically, the Statutes of the CDU in Hanover had a detailed section on how the party should dispose of remaining assets when it came to dissolve itself. Schumacher did not take it seriously, suspecting it to be the disguise in which the capitalist bourgeoisie hoped to survive until less hostile times. He scorned those who claimed to represent Christian values in politics, a preposterous suggestion, implying that everyone else lacked Christian beliefs. (85)

In any event, the formation of such a party would take time. In Hanover the situation was complicated by the existence of the Niedersächsische Landespartei which had old links with the protestant church and which in the past as the Guelph party had been particularly close to the Centre Party: their common hostility to the Prussian state had provided the joint platform. There was thus initially some confusion, and the leader of the pre-1933 Centre Party in Hanover B. Pfad established links with the emerging Centre in Westphalia where he attended a meeting outside Münster on 15 September 1945. (86) On the other hand, a prominent member of the NLP, the former Oberbürgermeister Arthur Menge, also attempted a 'co-ordination of all non-socialist forces'. (87) The situation was such that a visit by Adenauer to Hanover in August ended in failure. He seems to have had few illusions about the prospects of a CDU in Hanover. (88)

But it was precisely the emergence of figures such as Menge whose relations with the Nazis had been more than ambiguous, and greater attempts by the Centre from Westphalia to build up its organisation in Hanover which led to greater pressure by CDU circles from Sleswig-Holstein to build up a CDU branch in Hanover. The CDU leader in

<u>Sleswig-Holstein</u>, Schlange-Schöningen, contacted protestant circles in Hanover. Substantial opposition to the revival of the Centre party emerged, and this move away from the Centre gained the important support of two catholic trade unionists: Anton Storch who had already been active in the Reconstruction Committee, in the formation of the General Union and in the Town Council, and Hans Wellman who as a student had been influenced by Carl Sonnenschein in Berlin, the creator of the catholic-social student movement. Pfad eventually joined this group and a first meeting to set up the CDU in Hanover in fact took place in his house, on 14 November 1945. Pfad made the main speech on 'Duties and limits of a democratic State and the role of a Christian in such a State'. A businessman addressed the meeting on 'A Market Economy with social obligations' and Anton Storch on the 'Social responsibility and the position of the workers in a new state to be created on the basis of Christian responsibility'. On 18 November 1945 a CDU local branch was set up which on 14 December held its first mass meeting. (89) Like the other parties, a number of applications for a licence from Military Government were turned down but on 31 December 1945 this was obtained, although not 'for the merger of two or more (local) parties'. (90) If the British suspected a surreptitious concentration of potentially hostile, undemocratic forces they were wrong. The CDU in Lower Saxony was considered the biggest but worst organised regional party; only in May 1946 did it begin to employ a full-time secretary. (91) The party in Hanover was bitter about the attitude of Military Government which ever since the victory of the Labour Party in Britain put 'everyone who was not a member of the SPD or KPD as a 'conservative' under a magnifying glass'. (92) With this confused start it was not surprising that at the end of February the CDU had only 15 district organisations. However, by April it was represented in all 59 districts. But only in June 1947 was there a CDU Lower Saxony. (93)

In spite of its bad organisation the CDU emerged as the strongest bourgeois party at the elections in October 1946, beating the NLP into second place and, of course, emerging in subsequent years as the strongest party in the western zones. Much of its programme and the projection of it must therefore have expressed ideas and emotions shared by a majority of Germans. For the CDU in Hanover there are three illustrations of this: the <u>Kölner Leitsätze</u> as distributed in the summer and autumn of 1945; the speech made by (protestant) Pastor Cillien at the founding meeting of the party in Hanover, and the party statutes as submitted to the British.

The 'Cologne Guidelines' were written in stirring and emotional language.

> National Socialism has plunged Germany into a misfortune which is without parallel in her long history .. This would not have come over us if wide circles in our people had not let themselves be seduced by rapacious materialism.

Against this the German people should seek salvation in an honest return to Christian and 'abendländisch' values.

This was not a political language but that used by the catholic church: (94) implying that National Socialism had come over the German people like a disease. It had been seduced but was not actively responsible. Dictatorship, tyranny, Herrenmenschentum ('Master Race' mentality) and militarism had to be eradicated to make room for a free people based on the respect for human dignity. Not all had been bad under National Socialism: the concept of Volksgemeinschaft was worth preserving, only it must be new, and protected by social justice and charity which reconciled the freedom of the individual with the demands made by the general good. The party-to-be stood for 'true, Christian socialism which has nothing in common with wrong, collectivist objectives which profoundly contradict the essence of human beings.' In the 20 points which followed these general principles, more precise and far reaching political aims were set out which in many respects came close to those of the SPD, notably those for the breaking up of private monopolies and concerns, work creation schemes, settlement of wage and working conditions by collective bargaining, the preservation of a social insurance scheme, the formation of trade unions, the distribution of war damage relief among rich and poor. Already here the concept of a 'militant democracy' emerged. The document however stressed the right to property and not surprisingly was silent on agrarian reform, preferring instead the vague formulation 'a generous internal settlement policy should increase the number of independent farmers' (13).

By the time the Hanover CDU submitted its Statutes to Military Government all references to National Socialism had disappeared from them, except for the membership qualification whereby only the 'politically uncompromised (unbelastet)' could join. There were only 10 points, three of which were taken from the preamble to the Cologne guidelines and two from the 20 points. Thus in paragraph 3 of the Statutes 'social justice and charity' as guarantors of a new Volksgemeinschaft and in paragraph 4 true 'Christian socialism which has nothing in common with mistaken collectivist objectives' were mentioned. Paragraph 5 referred to '... our firm will to erect a social order which responds to the democratic traditions of our German past as well as the breadth and spirit of our Christian natural law ...'

Paragraphs 7 and 8 refer to the role of the family (Cologne Pt 2) and to the rule of law (Cologne Pt 3). Both the Cologne and Hanover documents in foreign policy envisaged peaceful co-operation in recognition of concluded treaties, but whereas Cologne still talked of 'Germany' as an international agent the Hanover document refers to 'peoples' in recognition of the fact that a German nation state was an unrealistic concept at this stage. There were only two divergent points in the Hanover document: the demand for an education system 'based on real Christianity and the democratic idea' (Para 6) and 'maintenance and widening of the independence and the rights of the churches and religious communities' (Para 9). In all the Hanover document was far less specific than that of Cologne. Indeed, the economy was not even mentioned. Urgent questions such as agrarian reform, the role of the industrial concerns or the position of all those who had suffered in the war were ignored. This not only reflected the social basis of the CDU in Hanover which despite the collaboration of two prominent catholic trade unionists was predominantly protestant - conservative. It also represented a fragile modus vivendi on the basis of the lowest common denominator between protestants and catholics. For in spite (or because) of the fact that the first instigators and the party leader in Hanover were catholics, (95) the protestant churches were much stronger in the city, and it was the protestants who needed convincing that co-operation with the catholics was a necessity. This was done very successfully by Pastor Cillien who not only was an early supporter of the idea of a CDU, but also became a prominent member for the party of the Lower Saxonian and later of the federal parliament, rising to deputy Fraktionsleiter (whip). (96)

Cillien in a significant speech at the CDU's foundation ceremony in Hanover justified this new venture for the protestant church which, so he claimed, was for the first time involving itself openly in politics (sic!), and this time together with the 'enemy', the catholic church. There were two sets of reasons: all Christians formed one large community because they all had suffered together in the past (Leidensgemeinschaft), they had fought together (Kampfgemeinschaft), they had altogether become guilty (Schuldgemeinschaft), they were united in their present misery (Notgemeinschaft) and together they lived in the grace of God (Segensgemeinschaft). Turning to the future all Christians must be aware that the struggle between Christ and anti-Christ was reaching its climax and this was the justification - a hint against Schumacher here - for a 'Christian' party. In these times of distress there was very little the churches could do help materially, but they could provide help and comfort for the soul. (97)

There is no reason to doubt the sincerity of the speaker and of the many who later worked and voted for the CDU. In particular taking the western zones as a whole the CDU did succeed in catering for a 'Volksgemeinschaft' of (however vaguely) Christians, which did attract the support of workers as well as of the middle class. This was a party of a 'new type', a people's party. The possibility of such a venture being successful in the long run was of course, quite inconceivable to men such as Schumacher who continued to see in the CDU a body 'whose giant size says nothing about its strength and the qualities of its muscles'. (98)

But subsequent election results, and particularly those in the North-Rhine Westphalia elections to the Diet on 20.4.1947 where the SPD polled 32% to the CDU's 37.5%, (99) confirmed that, given the commitment to 'social justice' in both parties the CDU had more to offer to a greater number of people: where the SPD preached a militant reckoning with National Socialism the CDU stood for reconciliation and 'bygones be bygones'. It mattered little to contemporaries that the CDU's conciliatory position on National Socialism obscured the necessary for a 'reckoning' with leading National Socialist elements and for a restructuring of political power. Nor surprisingly there were a high number of former Nazis among the CDU's membership. (100)

In the economy the SPD advocated change, notably in agriculture, and a planned economy with an ambiguous position on private property. The CDU's 'Property and prosperity with responsibility' had the great advantage for a majority of Germans of dealing with known quantities. A tired people had little stomach for change. Above all, it seems the stress on the traditions of a 'better Germany' could be made more credibly by the CDU because it could be linked with a vague non-political and all embracing concept such as Christianity which conjured up the possibility of a 'new beginning' which was comparatively painless; as against the SPD who could not free its public image from the experience of Weimar and whose new Germany was to be achieved at the price of new suffering (however well deserved in individual cases) and struggles.

In Hanover itself the position of the SPD was unassailable. But it has already been noted that the CDU became immediately the strongest non-left party. Its voting figures were better than those of the Centre and DNVP together in the Weimar Republic and suggests that it attracted some liberal and working class votes. The CDU's main representatives in the Council were Dr Pfad (until his promotion to Minister of Interior of Lower Saxony) and Anton Storch (until his rise into the zonal trade union organisation). Although the creation of religious schools was demanded in the party statutes, the dispute over their introduction did not arise during the period under examination. On the contrary, A. Storch in particular excelled in Council debates with many a sensible and constructive contribution, and partisan disputes were noticeably absent.

The FDP

The revival of a liberal party after 1945 was more difficult than that of the other parties for a number of reasons. During the Weimar Republic there had of course been two liberal parties but both had declined in the early 30s. In Hanover, in November 1932, they, the DDP and DVP, had polled 3% between them. Their representatives in the Reichstag had voted for the Enabling Act. This record did not predestine the liberals for vigorous resistance activities during the Third Reich.

Illegal work would have contradicted the character of these parties; in addition there was agreement with

> many of Hitler's policies. Liberalism which had essentially been devalued already before Hitler's advent to power, did not provide an ideological basis for a fighting opposition against Fascism. In the best case loyal indifference was the hallmark of the political attitude of liberals towards the Nazi state. Personally decent behaviour towards one's fellow human beings, a critical word among friends ... that was all ... (101)

There were always individual exceptions, as the case of Franz Henkel demonstrated who kept in more active touch with the underground opposition network. It was Henkel who, having been a member of the Reconstruction Committee, first started reconstituting a liberal party. Initially this was undertaken in terms of reviving the old DDP.

> The Weimar of Coalition of 1919 ... began the great work of the reconstruction of Germany after World War I ... These policies would also today form the most purposeful basis for a parliamentary system ... (102)

It remained to be seen to what extent a simple revival of the DDP would attract support in Germany after 1945. Locally, Henkel was not accepted in those business circles who previously had supported the DVP. (103) In the different zones the different attitudes of the allies as well as the different political backgrounds played an important part in the long and painful process which eventually culminated in the emergence of the FDP. Over the next years, indeed throughout its existence in the Federal Republic, the party was beset by divisions, arguments and even splits which derive from its origins.

Lack of source material obscures the precise process by which the FDP came into existence in Hanover. Together with the other parties it received its licence in December 1945. On 14 February 1946 it obtained its licence for the whole Zone. A list of the party's executive committee in Hanover of January 1946 showed six names of which five were businessmen and one a lawyer - the FDP was thus recruiting from traditionally liberal circles. Its organisation remained weak. At the end of February 1946 it had the smallest number of district organisations, only five as against the SPD with 49. In 1947 the party saw the reasons for its bad performance as follows:

> Despite our biggest propaganda efforts the FDP so far
> has failed to attract a greater number of members or to
> achieve success at elections. The main reasons for this
> are:
> 1. lack of support from Military Government
> 2. preferred treatment of the SPD by Military
>   Government
> 3. the fact that the SPD as well as the KPD and the
>   CDU can make use of an organisational structure
>   which existed before 1933.
> ... A (further) reason for the lack of growth of the
> liberal idea is the bad support by the German
> authorities. The administration is staffed by people who
> are members of the SPD or CDU ... (104)

In terms of votes the FDP in Hanover failed to poll more
than on average 10%, which was lower than the vote of the
DVP and DDP combined in the Weimar Republic up to 1930.

The main weakness of the liberal party was that it
lacked a central idea around which its thoughts, propaganda
and activities could be organised. In its early phase, almost
as if to compensate for its sometimes close proximity to
National Socialism in the past, the party advocated a strict
reckoning with the Nazis. In a leaflet which circulated in
Hanover in the summer and autumn of 1945 the
Demokratische Union (later the FDP in Hanover) advocated
its determination.

> in clear recognition of the crimes committed by the
> Hitler regime and the obligations which arise from
> them for the German people to work for an honest
> reconciliation and compensation ('Wiedergutmachung').
> (105)

Apart form this, the party defined itself essentially in
negative terms. It opposed the SPD's proposals for a planned
economy as well as any form of socialism. Indeed in its
vehemence it did not refrain from using slander such as
when, in January 1946, it advocated opposition to socialism
in all its manifestations, 'be it as National Socialism or
Inter-National Socialism'. (106) It also opposed the CDU for
bringing religion into politics. While recognising religious
ethics, and committing itself to 'absolute tolerance towards
other creeds' it rejected 'the claim by the Church to
political power and considers it for the church itself an

unacceptable link with political parties.' (107)

At the same time it was committed to the reconstruction of a German state ('deutsches Staatswesen') and the fight against despair, withdrawal, lassitude and hesitancy 'which are about to paralyse every political initiative.' In this early phase the only positive allegiance was that to private property and to free private initiative in the economy. This implied a limit to the size of concerns and capital concentration where this was required by 'the needs of the overall economy'. There was no mention of those who had suffered most in the war, and the party's professed concern for the refugees seemed to owe more to their voting potential. Particularly striking was the absence of any reference to 'social justice' in the sense of giving more rights to the workers in their factories or in the economy at large. This was due to the fact that the FDP's support came from non-working class elements; it also demonstrated the general ideological unease. The party's position on these issues emerged only gradually in the course of 1947 when, as we have seen the SPD put two decisive motions to the Lower Saxonian Diet, concerning the nationalisation of basic industries and the role of trade unions in the economy, and more specifically in the Chambers of Industry and Commerce. It was clear that an acceptance of the SPD's proposals was impossible for the FDP.

> If this proposal (to democratise the Chambers) was accepted there would be a danger that these purely economic and regionally useful activities would be prevented and that the Chambers would become political debating clubs with the external appearance of an 'Economic Parliament' ... (108)

The only concession the FDP made to the 'new era' was that workers should have more say in the running of their factories, at least that they should be given their rights granted by the Works Council Law of 1920. But the motives for this proposal were clear from a party which exclusively represented employers interests; such concession would ensure a greater degree of industrial peace by deflating worker's frustrations.

It can be seen that the social and electoral base of the FDP was small, notably in Hanover where it had to contend with another party which also recruited from the same, bourgeois circles. It was closest to the NLP and it was with the NLP that it allied itself in the subsequent elections.

The NLP

By September the NLP leadership in Hanover had worked out new 'Guiding Principles' which it submitted to Military Government as the basis for its eventual licence. (109) They stated in greater detail the party's position on the following: Lower Saxony, Germany, the Relationship with Britain and other states, Political Aims, Economic Principles, Demands in social matters and Cultural demands. The most salient features of these principles were - besides the obvious objectives of autonomy for Lower Saxony in a federal German state - the reference to the 'rule of law'. This implied that the NLP was, like the CDU and FDP, averse to political change. Indeed, National Socialism simply had to be removed in order to achieve equal rights for Germany internationally; its removal from school books would bring about the teaching of non-Nazi values. There was also the rather lofty demand

> ... that the lust for power, military ambition and race hatred revealed by National Socialism (was) to be replaced by the spirit of love of freedom in the service of economic recovery and true morality ...

Britain had a special importance for the party. Thus the 'closest connections with the British Empire' were demanded which led to attacks on the NLP for alleged separatist tendencies. Subsequently, these 'special links' were explicitly repudiated in internal instructions to party speakers in February 1946 as the Labour Government made any prospect of realising the connection futile and opened the party to ridicule.

The aspirations in the party to bring back the monarchy were also played down for the same reasons. Like all parties the NLP suffered from an acute shortage of active younger members. Moreover, owing to the dated concepts of the old leaders, those who did tackle organisational tasks such as a protestant pastor, not only had to battle with great practical problems but he also had to face the criticism of the younger members. (11) This tense relationship between old and young was to be a constant problem of the NLP in

Hanover. One way of overcoming the organisational weakness was to establish from above party secretaries who would be responsible for several districts 'and who could also keep an eye on developments on the local level'.

> From among those secretaries our next leaders will emerge and to ignore them would therefore not only be foolish, it would also make simultaneous action impossible ... several districts should form Working Groups and send representatives to the provincial headquarters ... In this way the special wishes of the people can be taken into account. (111)

The organisation was still weak in February (112) and the party in Hanover finally obtained a licence for the town and the surrounding districts on 14 February 1946. The appropriate letter from Military Government contained the revealing phrase that 'this license is not to be considered as an approval. Military Government does not support the ideas or the objectives of this party or of any other.' (113)

There were a number of reasons why Military Government should be suspicious of the NLP. In the first instance there seem to have been some uncertainties among the British as to the objectives and distinguishing features between the non-socialist parties. (114) Secondly, there were noticeably more politically compromised figures in the NLP than in any of the other parties. We have already noted the prominent role which the former OB Menge tried to play in the summer of 1945. Then he had not been successful. Later he tried to become the head of a 'Central Bureau for the Search for Missing Persons' but his application was turned down by Military Government. (115) He nevertheless continued as the NLP's main speaker in public and its negotiator behind the scenes. Another member of the NLP's executive committee had to resign from his post in May 1946 because of his membership in the NSDAP. (116) But the party continued to use known Nazis by employing a specialist in housing who had been sacked by the city administration in 1945 for political reasons. (117) As one of the most popular figures, the journalist and member of the Diet for the NLP, Kwiecinsky, put it 'we cannot afford to ignore the expertise of the Nazis but we must use it secretly'.

In a letter to His Majesty Duke Ernst August of Braunschweig, Kwiecinsky gives a good survey of the state of the NLP in February 1946. (118) According to this, the CDU's insistence on a republican form of state was a stumbling bloc for the NLP to have closer co-operation with it. On the other hand 'the idea of the monarchy is deferred under present circumstances with the Labour Party in control in England.'

However, if the party and its main objective, a future state of Lower Saxony, were to prosper in future it was essential that it unite all political forces on the right of the SPD. This was spelt out in a revealing circular to party officials of 7 March 1946. Written by Biester after consultation with Menge it bore the former's flowery style. The main points, how a united political movement could win over Social Democracy, were the following: 'Prussia' should no longer be fought as it had obviously ceased to exist, and such a fight would put off refugees. (How much the NLP was fighting the battles of the past was revealed by the recommendation that 'the incorporation of Hanover into Prussia of 1866' should no longer be mentioned as this might be too divisive!). Militarism must not be attacked as this might forfeit the support of many valiant and honourable soldiers; nor should any criticism be made of Bismarck.

In particular 'nothing should be said about the collective guilt of the German people. Under no circumstances should it be acknowledged that the German nation is guilty of the war'. In view of these recommendations it was not surprising that the Hanover leadership considered an electoral alliance with the Deutsche Reichspartei, a right-wing party which tried to gain recognition by Military Government in the summer of 1946. (119) Although the NLP decided against this its attitude to National Socialism remained unchanged. An election pamphlet (undated, August or September 1946) stated clearly: 'We do not ask where you once stood. We ask: who are you and where do you stand now?'

Although the NLP in this pamphlet committed itself to 'respect for the moral instructions of Christianity' its openly admitted objective of simply 'turning the clock back', of ignoring National Socialism and, particularly, its total lack of commitment to any concept such as 'social justice' made them unacceptable as coalition partners to the CDU. With this failure it became clear that the victory of the SPD in the October election was inevitable, although this was so in any case as the results were to reveal later. Nevertheless the whole wrath of the NLP leaders was reserved for the CDU's 'treachery'. In a pre-election speech of early autumn

1946 Kwiecinsky illustrates well the weight of the parties in Hanover on the eve of the elections, as seen from the bourgeois camp. (120) Where the SPD bemoaned the fact that its leaders had not been forceful enough in the local Personalpolitik, to the NLP the social democratic Oberbürgermeister held and had used all the available strings. Only one important department of the city's administration (finance) was not occupied by the SPD. 'Hundreds of their supporters (are) ... in important positions.' For employment, not expertise as in earlier days but 'the party card has become decisive. It is difficult not to think of Nazi methods'. A favourite tool of the SPD was denazification which was used to turn non-socialists out of their posts. This had led to the nasty slogan 'Pj rather than Pg' ('Postenjäger statt Parteigenosse' (job hunters instead of party members)). The amnesty for young Nazis was an act of particular hypocrisy, as this implied an admission of guilt. However, in the eyes of the NLP, '... there can be no question of guilt for our young people who were forced into the Hitler youth ...'

At the local level and in the prevailing physical conditions there was not much scope for party political differences. However, there were two areas where the NLP differed distinctly from the SPD: reconstruction and finance. In both cases the SPD was accused of pursuing a doctrinaire course. In the first case, the SPD planned 'large buildings ... and department stores ... . We decisively reject such development.' The NLP stood for variety, protecting the retail trade. Predictably it was the Regulation on Reconstruction of March 1946 (see above), which was met with indignation. A public protest meeting had been organised as early as 13 April 1946 (121) which had demanded 'extensive support for private initiative and the avoidance of all superfluous control of officialdom ... The public's voice must be heard.'

The NLP now claimed that the proposal had been stopped because of their protests to Minister President Kopf. But this was a nice piece of untrue electioneering. As to finance, Kwiecinsky resorted to irony, here was another example of how the SPD-controlled administration tried to 'protect' the small man.

With the creation of the Land Lower Saxony and the official abolition of Prussia on 25.2.1947 by the allies the NLP had achieved its most immediate objectives. These developments led to changes in the overall party organisation. From its second annual general meeting in Celle, on 4 June 1947 the NLP constituted itself as the <u>Deutsche Partei</u> which, committed to a federal German nation state, hoped to co-ordinate regional parties all over Germany (122). In particular it hoped to attract the refugees. But as we have already noted the latter were well aware of the lack of hospitality of the indigenous population and recognised the overtures towards them as tactical electioneering. Subsequently they set up their own organisations.

This was however not the only reason for the DP's steady decline. Basically there was no room for a regional party within the newly emerging political structure. Only in coalition with other bourgeois parties was there long term hope for the survival of local interest groups. More progressive elements in the NLP had realised this as early as 1945. (123) In those days the NLP enjoyed a short term advantage because of the temporary fragmentation of the political scene and could have joined one of the other emerging parties from a position of relative strength. This did not happen, however, because the majority of leading party members lacked this foresight and simply sought to re-establish the previously existing party. The Hanover group was particularly conservative and did not even play an important role in the party as it emerged. It was led from a small town north of Hanover, Stade. Tensions between the Stade and the Hanover groups continued with Hanover complaining that articles by their members were not being published in the party press and there was a lack of help from the leadership. (124)

The party's best result in Hanover was 13.6% in both elections of 1946 and 1947. This was slightly below the Guelph Party's best result during the Weimar Republic (16.1% in 1924). The NLP and FDP together polled 26.2% in 1946. Considering that no right wing party was licensed and that the poll was 80% the parties' approach, of playing down National Socialism and all forms of 'socialism', had paid off, in that they must have been able to attract the votes of many of the hard core Nazi sympathisers.

NOTES

1.   WO 171/7990 Monthly Report of Detachment 504(720) Nov 1945, Appendix 'A'.

2.   SAH, N B 22 OB Bratke - K. Schumacher 30.8.1945.
3.   WO 171/7990.

Activity by would be officials of the KPD and SPD continues to grow in all <u>Kreise</u> and many applications for their authorisation are known to be pending. The general public however remains aloof and seem to be awaiting a more practical approach than has hitherto emerged from party programmes to their urgent personal problems this winter. No party seems willing to commit itself to a practical line since opinion of all shades unites in placing the baby firmly in the arms of Military Government.

4.   SAH - II - L - 40a. <u>Ergebnis der 97. Besprechung zwischen dem Stadtkommandanten und mir am 27. September 1945.</u>
5.   SAH - II - L - 40a. op.cit., 78/23.8.1945.
6.   SAH N B (1).
7.   SAH N B Folder 'Verschiedenes 1945 - 49'.
8.   SAH N B Folder '<u>Politische Parteien</u>'.
9.   NHK 6/22.1.1946, p.4.
10.   For example <u>Braunschweig</u> with 2.8%. K. Franke, <u>Die niedersächsische SPD Führung im Wandel der Partei nach 1945</u>, 1980, p.30.
11.   <u>Protokoll der Delegiertenversammlung des Ortsvereins</u>, 1946, p.2 and 7 passim. According to A. Holweg Schumacher made mock of the local leadership whom he described as old 'fuddy duddies': '3 x 70 = 210 years old!' Interview with A. Holweg 11.5.81.
August Holweg 1905, leader of Socialist Workers Youth Hanover, worker in HANOMAG. Charged by Schumacher in 1945 with counteracting communist propaganda in Hanover's factories, forced to abandon this to work in Town Council. Schumacher's successor as leader of Hanover's SPD, 1946. <u>Oberbürgermeister</u> of Hanover 1956 - 1972.
12.   AsD, <u>Sammlung</u> Schumacher J 2 Bruno Sander, Hannover - Kurt Schumacher, 27.1.1946.
13.   <u>Universität Hannover, Politisches Seminar</u>, SPD Papers. K. Schumacher - <u>An die SPD, Ortsverein Hannover</u> 1.8.1946. '... it is pitiful that exclusively working class districts which have not been destroyed have a third or half the number of members of those in 1933 ... I would like to indicate the political consequences ... If Hanover falls back

and does not catch up, it will be impossible to keep headquarters here. Frankfurt ... is trying desperately hard ...'

14. AsD, <u>Sammlung</u>, Schumacher J 4, Fritz Sänger, Gifhorn - K. Schumacher, Hanover 17.12.1945.
15. AsD, <u>Sammlung</u> Schumacher J 4, Fritz Heine, Hanover - Richard Löwenthal, London 2.5.1946.
16. <u>Jahresversammlung des Ortsvereins</u> 1947.
17. Interview Hasselbring. These posters had to avoid all 'inciting', 'socialist' references.
18. AsD J 10, Scheibe, H. (Advertising Agent) - F. Heine 29.6.1946.
19. The H.P. was published for the first time on 17 July 1946.
20. Kaden, op.cit. p.71.
21. K. Klotzbach, <u>Der Weg zur Staatspartei. Programmatik, praktische Politik und Organisation der deutschen Sozialdemokratie 1945-65</u>, 1982, p.43.
22. Kaden, op.cit., p.137.
23. NHK 6/22.1.1946 p.4.
24. Franke, op.cit., p.128 passim.
25. Interviews Hasselbring, Holweg, '<u>Projekt Arbeiterbewegung Hannover</u>'.
26. <u>Jahreshauptversammlung des Ortsvereins Hann-over der SPD</u> 21.2./23.2./4.3.1948.
27. <u>Jahreshauptversammlung des Ortsvereins Hann-over der SPD</u> 26.2/27.2.1949.
28. Bruno Sander, op.cit.
29. Interviews Hasselbring, Holweg, '<u>Projekt Arbeiterbewegung Hannover</u>'.
30. This obsession with <u>Personalpolitik</u> struck British observers as distinctly odd:

> What was particularly striking in a conversation lasting over an hour was that Dr Schumacher never once spoke of Germany or the German people in connection with any particular problem, but always referred to the SPD. It would appear that his idea of a democratic Germany is one where all administrators, police, teachers, newspaper men, civil servants etc. are members of the SPD. In fact, democracy for him would appear to mean SPD domination under the undisputed leadership of himself.

(FO 371/55618/C9885 Ninth Monthly Report from HQ Mil

Gov Hanover Region for period 1-30 June 1946).

31. Kaden, op.cit. p.155 passim.
32. AsD, <u>Sammlung Schumacher</u>, J 10 Central Circular 1945/46. SPD of Germany, Hanover Area, To: District Committees of the SPD Hanover Area, 26.10.1945.
33. Kaden, op.cit., p.170.
34. <u>Universität Hannover, Politisches Seminar</u>, SPD Papers, Folder <u>'Bezirksarchiv'</u> SPD Hanover - <u>An den Bezirksvortstand der SPD</u>, Hanover, 15.8.1946.
35. Literally: bill based on the faulty mathematics of a milk(girl) man.
36. N H K 13/15.2.1946, p.4.
37. SAH, NB 1.
38. SAH, NB 11 Albert Hoff - <u>An die Englische Militärregierung</u>, Hannover 22.8.1946.
39. The term <u>Mittelstand</u> is most easily translated as 'middle class'. At the time it applied particularly to independent small business and craftsmen, farmers, etc.
40. AsD SPD - Beziek - Hannover.
41. <u>Jahresversammlung des Ortsvereins Hannover der SPD</u> 21.2.1948, p.24 passim.
42. <u>Wahlaufruf der SPD</u>, AsD, <u>SPD - Bezirk Hannover</u>.
43. Otto Brenner - Joseph Lang, 12.2.1947. In: Grebing/Klemm, op.cit.
44. <u>Jahreshauptversammlung des Ortsvereins Hannover der SPD</u>, 21.2.1948, p.11.
45. AsD, <u>SPD - Bezirk Hannover, Wahlaufruf der SPD</u>.
46. <u>Jahreshauptversammlung des Ortsvereins der SPD Hannover</u>, 21.2.1948, p.20.
47. 'For a better, new Germany', second half August 1945.
48. For example his fierce attack on the 'miserable whining' of those who 'for the favours of the East' recognise the Oder-Neisse border as definite. <u>Wahlaufruf 1946</u>.
49. AsD, J. 28 Schumacher - G. Seeger, 30.8.1946.
50. Franke, op.cit. p.112.
51. <u>Universität Hannover. SPD Bezirksvorstand. Protokoll</u> 29.8.1946.
52. A. Karl at meeting in the Capitol 24.5.1945.
53. <u>Jahreshauptversammlung des Ortsvereins der SPD Hannover</u>, 21.2.1948, p.7.
54. Interviews. This was in marked contrast to the town administration's official reports of the events in the

post-war period which did not mention the British contribution (see above Ch. II).

55. Franke, op.cit., p.112.

56. N H K 22.1.1946, p.4.

57. VSt 7.1.1947 'Der Schlendrian'.

58. This referred to a bill passed in the Diet of North-Rhine-Westphalia.

59. Jahreshauptversammlung des Ortsvereins der SPD Hannover, 21.2.1948, p.7.

60. B. Marshall, 'German Attitudes to British Military Government 1945-47', in: Journal of Contemporary History, vol. 15, 1980.

61. AsD, SPD - Bezirk Hannover. In the file is a 'Terminkalender' for activities of the party between October 45 - 31.12.47 based on announcements and reports in the NHK and HP.

62. HP 26/15.10.46, p.5.

63. SPD Kommunalpolitische Abteilung, Dr Diederichs - Genosse Ollenhauer, 27.12.1946.

64. Richtlinien Sozialdemokratischer Kommunalpolitik, no date, AsD, Sammlung Schumacher J. 44.

65. Richtlinien zur praktischen Arbeit in den Kommunalparlamenten, no date, SPD Bezirksverband Nordwest. A similar document would have been produced in all SPD districts.

66. Jahreshauptversammlung des Ortsvereins Hannover der SPD 21.2/23.2/4.3.1947 'Rückkehr zur Selbstverwaltung', p.14 passim; 'Socialist objectives' were only mentioned in connection with criticism of the 'Hannoversche Presse', the paper which was closest to the SPD. Unlike its predecessor of pre-1933 it lacked a clear commitment to 'socialism'. The editor's appeal that Military Government insisted on a more general approach and in addition, the fact that the new SPD wanted not only to speak to the already converted but to address itself to a wider general public and attract potential new voters, met with considerable criticism: this matter was brought up again at subsequent meetings.

67. We have seen already that legislation which the council introduced on this basis came to nothing owing to a concentration of the control of the building sector in the hands of the government of Lower Saxony (see above, V, 3a).

68. See R. Ebsworth, op.cit. for a recognition of British failure in this area.

69. This was an industrial show which was mounted,

with the help of the British for the first time in September 1947 as a showpiece of industrial achievements in the western zones, to counteract the traditional 'Leipzig Fair', now in the Soviet Zone.

70. Protokoll über die Fortsetzung der Generalversammlung am 3.4.1948, p.2.

71. op.cit. p.3, 'dass bei den Schwarzbauten von Wohnungen eventuell ein Auge zuzudrücken sei.'

72. op.cit., p.29.

73. Schröder, op.cit., p.502.

74. SAH, N B 22.

75. SAH; Zulassung von politischen Parteien, Vorbereitendes Kommittee des Parteiaufbaus der 'KPD', Bezirk Hannover - An die Britische Militärregierung, 20.9.1945.

76. Kaden, op.cit., p.171.

77 Schröder, op.cit., p.502.

78. STAH VVP 5/11 An den Parteivorstand der NLP, betr. Bericht über die Besprechung im Sterling House am 27.2.1946.

79. SAH N B 3 Bezirk Hannover der KPD - OB Bratke, 7.7.1946.

80. VSt 4.10.1946.

81. VSt 20.8.1946.

82. NHK 25.1.1946.

83. HV 11.10.1946.

84. SAH Die Zulassung der politischen Parteien, Kölner Leitsätze, June 1945.

85. NHK 22.1.1946.

86. A. Fratzscher, Die CDU in Niedersachsen. Demokratie der ersten Stunde. Hannover 1971, p.21. Fratzscher claims that there was some pressure from Catholics in the SPD to rebuild the Centre which could then form a coalition with the SPD and thus regain some of its former importance.

87. Fratzscher, loc. cit.

88. Loc. cit., According to Fratzscher, Adenauer reported to his friends in the Rhineland 'that the politically interested protestant circles thought of re-establishing a Guelph party and the catholics predominantly of the old Centre'.

89. K. Schütz, Parteien in der Bundesrepublik. Studien zur Entwicklung der deutschen Parteien bis zur Bundestagswahl 1953, Stuttgart/Düsseldorf 1955, p.62.

90. SAH, Zulassung von Politischen Parteien.

91. Fratzscher, op.cit., p.43.

92. Fratzscher, op.cit., p.25.

93. Schütz, op.cit., p.63; The jump from 15 district organisations on 27.2.46 to 59 on 1 April seems very large but it was not possible to check these figures.

94. B. Marshall, 'German Reactions to Military Defeat 1945-47: the British View.' in: V. Berghan, M. Kitchen (eds), Germany in the Age of Total War, 1981, p.218 passim.

In his first sermon after the end of the war on 31 May 1945 Kurt Groeber, the archbishop of Freiburg expressed the following view: 'They (the National Socialists) wished to make you (German people) great and more powerful than all other nations ... They knew only too well how to divide and disunite ... they attempted ... to bring to oblivion the nation's spiritual character ...'

95. Dr. Pfad, who was elected first chairman of the local and district party was also a conservative. He was a solicitor/barrister who specialised in representing clients in the denazification tribunals. He was on the board of a number of industrial concerns, notably of Continental. He was a member of the Advisory Council and was a candidate for the post of Oberbürgermeister in January 1946 a post which he declined. He subsequently became Minister of Interior in H. Kopf's first Lower Saxonian cabinet.

96. Fratzscher, op.cit., p.38.

97. Fratzscher, op.cit., p.34-37.

98. H. Klotzbach, op.cit., p.111, quotes SPD Parteitag Protokoll 1946, p.54.

99. In the western zones as a whole the CDU obtained 37.7% to the SPD's 35%. Klotzbach, op.cit., p.113.

100. Billerbeck, op.cit., p.105; Exact figures for Hanover are not available, but the example of Hamburg's CDU shows the following figures: up to 6.6.1946 of 1000 CDU members 528 had been in a political party before of which 254 had belonged to the NSDAP. This example also shows that the CDU was able to recruit previously non-political elements. Quoted from O. Flechtheim, Die deutschen Parteien seit 1945. Quellen und Auszüge, Köln 1957.

101. H.G. Marten, FDP in Niedersachsen, Demokratie der ersten Stunde, 1972, p.19.

102. SAH, Folder 'Neuzulassung der politischen Parteien' Denkschrift zur Begründung der Notwendigkeit der 'Demokratischen Union'. (undated).

103. Interview Pentzlin.
104. Marten, op.cit., p.31.
105. SAH, Zulassung von politischen Parteien.
106. N H K 25.1.1946 'Die Parteien stellen sich vor.'
107. Loc.cit.
108. H.G. Marten, op.cit., p.97.
109. SAH, Zulassung von politischen Parteien, 'Richtlinien der Niedersächsischen Landespartei'.
110. STAH, VVP 5/11 Lic theol A. Pommerien - K. Biester, 27.10.1945.
111. STAH, VVP 5/11 NLP Geschäftsstelle Hannover - 'Lieber Parteifreund Farke'.
112. STAH, VVP 5/11 An den Parteivorstand der NLP 28.2.1946.
113. SAH, Zulassung der politischen Parteien, Military Government (Ostdir) - NLP 23.2.1946.
114. STAH, VVP 5/11 An den Parteivorstand der NLP 28.2.1946.
115. SAH N B 1 Letter Bratke - Menge 5.1.1946.
116. SAH, 'Zulassung von politischen Parteien', Militärregierung - Dr. O. Nass 15.5.1946.
117. STAH, VVP 5/11 Letter F. Mock - NLP 28.8.1947.
118. STAH, VVP 5/11 W. Kwiecinsky - An Seine Königliche Hoheit Herzog Ernst-August zu Braunschweig und Lüneburg, Schloss Marienburg bei Nordstemmen, Hannover 10.2.1946.
119. The first documentary evidence of the DRP in Hanover is a protest by its secretary Count Westarp against the confiscation of a party owned house by the British. (29.7.46) The party applied for a postponement of the forthcoming elections because of 'obstruction in the conduct of its affairs'. (SAH N B 12) Military Government replied swiftly 'your protest cannot be recognised, and such protest can in no way invalidate the elections.' (Military Government - Deutsche Konservative Partei 31.7.1946. This was the provisional name, pending a licence as DRP. SAH, Zulassung der polit. Parteien). Bratke wrote to Military Government 'We have asked the party to address its protest against the elections to Military Government. We do not accept legal or moral responsibility for providing the party with premises for its headquarters.' He added 'is the DRP licensed as a political party?' (OB - Military Government 1.8.1946 SAH NB12). It was not. It received a licence on 12.2.1947. Its statutes made no reference to either democracy or a rejection of National Socialism. It

was banned later, in 1952.

120. STAH VVI 5/14. Undated manuscript.

121. This public appeal was signed 'Nass' who shortly afterwards resigned because of his membership of the NSDAP (see above) SAH, N B 32.

122. Loc. cit., NLP - Mil Gov Stadtkreis Hanover 13.4.1936.

123. R. Schulze, 'Bürgerliche Sammlung oder Welfenpartei? Ergänzungen zur Entstehungsgeschichte der Niedersächsischen Landespartei', 1945/46, in: Jahrbuch für Niedersächsische Landesgeschichte, 57/1985.

124. See correspondence Kwiecinski - Hellwege of summer 1947 in: STAH, VVP 5/11 and the report of an NLP meeting on 29.3.1947 in: loc. cit.

Chapter Seven

CONCLUSIONS

Of all the allies the British had been keenest during the war on getting inter-allied agreement on the treatment of Germany after the war. But differences in views, as we have seen, did not even produce a common approach between the closest allies, the British and the Americans as they moved into Germany. Nevertheless, to the British future allied co-operation was the basis on which to proceed. Up to the Potsdam Conference the western allies were careful not to make political decisions which might pre-empt this co-operation, in contrast to developments in the Soviet Zone. Britain's objectives in Germany were dictated by her economic and military weakness: she desired security against German or (later) Soviet threats but this security had to be achieved at least costs. Continued allied co-operation and Germany's joint political control on the one hand and the treatment of Germany as an economic unit on the other seemed to the British to promise best results. In this way a 'balance of power' would emerge whereby Germany ceased to be a menace and the Soviet Union would be 'framed' by inter-allied co-operation. The exchange of goods between the zones would relieve the burden on the British Treasury.

Allied co-operation however never worked satisfactorily. From the British point of view this hit them particularly hard: not only were they most dependent on food deliveries from the east which were not forthcoming. International limitations on industrial production, potentially the greatest asset of their zone, meant that the Zone could not pay for the import of the necessary food. The upward revision of these restrictions became the main

British policy aim over the next years.

Failing inter-allied co-operation the Zone itself had to be run as 'cost-effectively' as possible. The implications of treating the zone as a separate entity - the ultimate division of Germany - was seen early on and accepted as having possible advantages.

In the zone a system of 'indirect rule' was introduced not unlike what the British had done in their colonies: a body of dependable German officials were operating under British supervision. However, this underlying principle became distorted by security considerations and notions of 're-education': after all the Germans had just emerged from a barbaric totalitarian dictatorship and tight control was called for. British occupation policies in Germany were therefore characterised mainly by negative yardsticks; orientated more towards the past than the future. This was illustrated by the tight supervision of all German organisations and, even after their official operation was announced by the British, the slow process of getting trade unions, political parties etc off the ground.

Looked at from a different point of view the British treatment of the German problem was essentially 'technical', as against the 'political' approach of the Soviets. It was 'technical' in their efficiency in practical matters. But it was also technical or formal in the approach to political organisations. The notion that 'democracy' could grow from the bottom upwards without political content was either naive or else put forward by mainly conservative British soldiers in Germany to disguise the fact that the left was effectively being discouraged. The left was of course always a potential threat to the status quo, and thus to the British first objective, security.

The lack of a political dimension was particularly evident in the treatment of denazification with the reliance on a 'legal' approach and the outright refusal of the British to co-operate with German anti-fascists. British distrust of them has been illustrated in many instances, ranging from the treatment of ex-concentration camp inmates to that of trade unionists.

It could also be shown that the talk about 'British' approaches is in a sense misleading. Military Government was divided on all important issues but as policies were decided at the highest echelon, the political views there prevailed. Field Marshal Montgomery or General Roberts (a director of the Dunlop Works in his private life) were conservatives. To override them Foreign Secretary Bevin would have had to spend more energy on Germany herself than he was able and prepared to do. In any case, this would only have been possible during 1945/46 because growing US influence later made an independent British line less likely. Moreover, some Divisions within Military Government seem to have had more weight than others. Manpower for example seems to have been highly influential under its head R. Luce. Invariably it was these sections in Military Government who won the arguments and whose 'Germans' emerged strengthened. This could be shown in connection with the dispute over the composition of the Chambers of Commerce.

All these factors together provide at least a partial answer to why the British Labour Government failed to export socialism into their zone in Germany. The formal interpretation of 'democracy' as a game to be played according to certain rules led even more liberal Military Government officers to believe that support for the German left at an early stage of the occupation was interfering; it was in fact against the very principles which the British tried to instill in the Germans. Moreover, the argument runs that if the SPD had been seen to have been a favourite of the British, this would have operated against the party at later elections. Later election results are also cited in support of this theory, in that they demonstrate that had Military Government supported the SPD this would have been against the political wishes of a majority of Germans. It remains of course arguable whether better support earlier on would have created more popularity for the SPD later (according to the principle that nothing, particularly in Germany, is more successful than success).

More fundamental, and this criticism was voiced already at the time by an activist like O. Brenner, was that the 'revival' of yesterday's political forces was allowed and for this the blame has been put on the allies, but also and perhaps more so, on the German left itself. Its members were worn down by daily worries, they lacked any longterm political goals quite apart from a clear analysis of objectives and the tactics to achieve these. The Third Reich had taken a terrible toll of confidence and originality among the German Left. It was no accident that O. Brenner devoted most of his energies to trade union work rather than to politics; in the former more tangible results might be achieved. But even in the trade unions, it can be argued, there was excessive preoccupation with getting the organisational structure right, losing sight of the fact that organisation was only a precondition for action. Although the British had encouraged this preoccupation, in the long run there were other special conditions which prevented actions which more forceful men like Brenner advocated.

On the other hand, O. Brenner with the moral indignation of a committed anti-fascist was perhaps not representative of the majority of the German people of the time. In 1945 they had awaited a 'new beginning' of some kind with some trepidation and in their apathy were prepared for 'anything'. But they were relieved to find that it was possible to carry on where they had left off in 1933, and this included, as we have seen, even members of the SPD. This was one of the reasons why Schumacher failed in his attempt to create a 'new' party. After all, pre-1933 experiences were the only political forms which the majority of Germans knew.

It is in this respect that one feels the British failed to provide inspiration which - taking all their own arguments about the nature of 'democracy' into acccount - could have focused on a more positive reckoning with National Socialism. It was not only outrageous or simply demoralising for the ordinary German to see so many Nazis or their sympathisers 'get away with it', it also produced a profound cynicism in many would-be politicians and furthered the general 'ohne mich' (without me') stance. This left the stage to those activists who had been there before 1933.

Despite the visual evidence of the cities in ruins the hallmark of German politics and economics after 1945 was therefore continuity. There were few changes directly attributable to the occupation other than, say, the reform of local government. Even this remained incomplete for although it worked on the local level it failed in its wider objective, the decentralisation of the German administrative system. Other changes such as the creation of a unified trade union movement, were prevented by the British.

On the other hand a united 'Christian' party was allowed to emerge which undoubtedly strengthened the bourgeois camp and made the defeat of the SPD in future elections possible. It can of course be argued that a more flexible, industry based union structure was a contributory factor to Germany's later rapid economic recovery, and that support for the CDU rather than the SPD was what a majority of

Germans wanted; in other words, unwittingly the British had worked in the right direction in Germany. Indeed, as far as the success of the CDU is concerned the actual messages of the parties became more important than Military Government actions. The CDU which could build on the 'higher' values of Christianity and on this basis emphasise social justice and reconciliation struck a note in more Germans than the harsher, more austere SPD.

But despite the party programmes, and the trappings of parliamentary democracy German politics had an air of déjà-vu about it. This was attributable to a large extent to the fact that there had not been a clear enough break with National Socialism. This was of course not limited to the British Zone. The Americans had allowed denazification to deteriorate to a 'Mitläuferfabrik' (a production line for 'followers'). To this extent - and also in the way they dealt with the left - the allies did 'prevent a new order' in Germany. It was this together with the rapid absorption of the German problem into the wider issues of the emerging Cold War, the division of the country and the legacies of Nazi crimes which, still today, constitutes much of what is now commonly called the German 'identity crisis'.

The Military Occupation of Germany: the Deployment of Allied Troops in April/May 1945

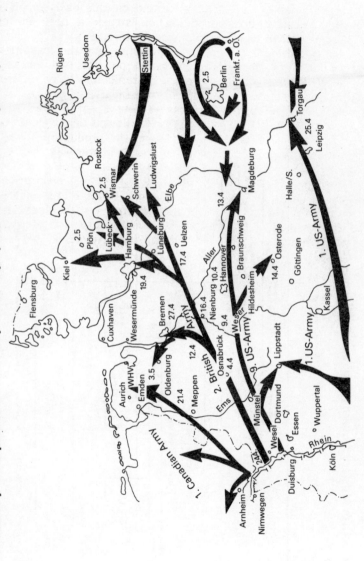

The British Military Government Structure (September 1946)

C-in-C and Military Governor
Marshall of the Royal Air Force Sir Sholto Douglas
(British Member of the Control Council)

POLITICAL ADVISER
(Sir William Strong)

DEPUTY MILITARY GOVERNOR
(Lieut. Gen. Sir Brian H. Robertson,Bart)
(British Member of the Co-ordinating Committee)

VACBNG
(Vice-Admiral
Sir Harold
T.C. Walker)

GOC-in-C BAOR
(Lieut. Gen.
Sir Richard
McCreery)

AOC-in-C BAFO
(Air Marshal
Sir Philip
Wigglesworth)

DCOS (OPG)

DCOS (E/EC)
(Maj. Gen. W.H.A. Bishop)

DCOS (POL)
(Maj. Gen. W.E.J Erskine)

SECRETARIAT

STAFF GROUP

PRESIDENT
ECONOMIC SUB-COMMISSION
(Sir Cecil Weir)

DEPUTY PRESIDENTS

PRESIDENT
GOVERNMENTAL SUB-COMMISSION
DCOS (POL) (ACTING)
DEPUTY PRESIDENT
(Mr. A.H. Albe)

INTELLIGENCE
(Maj. Gen.
J.S. Lethbridge)

PR/ISC GROUP
(Brig. W.L. Gibson)
(Acting)

POLITICAL
(Mr. C.E.
Steel)

MANPOWER
(Mr. R.W. Luce)

PW and DP
(Brig. A.G.
Kenchington)

IA and C
(Mr. J.H.
Simpson)

LEGAL
(Mr. N. Macaskie)

(Brig. J.G. Cowley)

(Brig. D.I. Anderson)

RD and R
(Mr. G.S.
Whitham)

NAVY
(VACBNG)

AIR
(AOC-in-C
BAFO)

FINANCE
(Mr. S.P.
Chambers)

TRANSPORT
(Mr. R.J.M. Inglis)

ARMY
(Brig. C.J.G. Dalton)

TRADE and
INDUSTRIES
(Mr. E.A. Seal)

FOOD
and AGRICULTURE
(Mr. G.E. Hughes)

BERLIN
(Maj. Gen.
E.P. Mares)

NORD RHEIN WESTFALEN
REGION
(Mr. W. Asoury)

SCHLESWIG-HOLSTEIN
REGION
(Air V. Marshal H.V.
Champion de Crespigny)

HANNOVER
REGION
(Lt. Gen. Sir Gordon Macready, Bart)

HANSESTADT
HAMBURG
(Mr. H.V. Berry)

L/R DET
COLOGNE

L/R DET
OLDENBURG

L/R DET
DUSSELDORF

L/R DET
BRUNSWICK

L/R DET
AACHEN

L/R DET
AURICH

L/R DET
MUNSTER

L/R DET
HANNOVER

L/R DET
ARNSEBERG

L/R DET
LUNEBURG

L/R DET
MUNDEN

L/R DET
STADS

L/R DET
HILDESHEIM

L/R DET
OSNABRUCK

Correct at 30th Sept. 1946

APPENDIX III

Statistical Annexe

1. <u>Area of town</u> 13,429 hectares (approx. 5,371 acres)

<u>Population statistics</u> (per 1,000 inhabitants)

	November 1945	1939
Marriages	8.2	13.5
Births	11.6	17.3
Deaths	15.0	12.4

<u>Population according to sex and age in comparison with 1939</u>

For 100 men there were the following numbers of women:

	0-14 years	14-65 years	over 65	Total
1945	96.0	132.0	113	124
1939	96.3	112.1	123	110

2. <u>Number of Inhabitants</u>

Columns:

2	3	4
	Established population	Refugees & evacuees
<u>Population on 17.5.1939</u>		
471,186	301,313	3,747

5	6	7
German soldiers, held as POWs	Foreigners	Others (pupils, hospital patients)
7,227	19,530	3,000

8
Total population
present in
the town
334,817

Columns 3-4
represent population
on 1.11.1945

3. <u>Population density</u>

<u>Comparative figures</u>

17.5.1939	1.11.1945	Col 4 as % of Col 3	Col 6 as % of Col 3	Col 3 as % of Col 8
3,516	2,497	1.2	6.5	90

Percentage change in population 1.11.1945 as against:
17.5.1939	1.6.1945
-29.0	+9.5

4. <u>Health statistics</u>

Infant mortality	18 (per 100 live births) 1939:5.1
Suicides (highest number)	22 in May 1945
Number of doctors	264
Doctor-patient ratio	1 doctor to 1,140 inhabitants
Number of hospital beds	about 3,000

5. <u>Cost of living index</u>

1913/14 = 100   July 1939 = 127.3
                       July 1945 = 149.3

6. <u>Percentage of population in employment</u>

1939 - 49.4%   1950 - 46.5%

7. Social strata of those employed

	1939	%	1950	%
Self-employed or in family business	30,230	13.3	27,573	13.3
Official/civil servant	18,497	8.2	13,772	6.7
White collar worker	54,403	24.0	60,570	29.3
Blue collar worker	123,423	55.0	104,901	50.7

8. Total number of businesses

	1939	1945	1955
Total	19,048	7,776	22,701
of which:			
Industrial	1,264	587	1,932
Wholesale	1,436	704	2,207
Retail	6,049	2,576	9,664
Transport	968	436	1,304
Hotels & restaurants	1,589	436	1,136
Banks & insurance	252	81	458
Crafts	7,472	3,009	6,000

9. The extent of war damage to buildings

Type of building	Destroyed %	Badly Damaged %	Some Damage %	Little or no damage %
Houses	50	11.0	33.0	6.0
Flats		51.2	43.6	5.2
Public buildings	44	35.0	15.0	6.0
Shops and storehouses	36	14.0	42.0	8.0
Industrial premises	33	28.0	33.0	6.0

10. The development of crime rates 1945 - 1949

Survey:	1945	1946	1947	1948	1949
Total entries	72,028	57,176	61,846	53,020	44,405
Crimes reported	47,562	31,610	32,224	32,795	21,882
Arrests	10,387	7,541	14,439	17,934	14,599
Germans	9,163	7,224	14,146	17,868	14,536
Foreigners	1,224	317	293	66	63
Murders	70	19	13	24	7
Robberies	18,407	255	242	211	149
Looting	1,488	126	22	-	-
Sex offences	294	157	439	601	889
Grand larceny	4,879	6,521	4,717	4,632	3,003
Petty larceny	4,331	11,574	15,763	14,043	8,832
Motor vehicle theft	893	578	453	426	223
Bicycle theft	4,048	4,571	3,914	2,497	1,891
Embezzlement	1,782	2,029	1,451	1,668	1,279
Fraud	276	639	1,158	2,071	1,992
Forgery of documents	238	422	265	374	225
Drug offences	18	95	9	49	21
Economic offences	413	3,141	2,598	1,814	581

From: NStAH, ZGS 1/5 Entwicklung der Polizei Hannover seit 1920 (Pol Oberinspektor Kürschner)

Appendix source: SAH-II-L-40b

APPENDIX IV

Election Results. City of Hanover 1920-1933

	Entitled to vote	Poll	NSDAP	DNVP	DVP	Z	DDP	Guelphs	SPD	KPD	others
1920	2772	2375	–	162	456	111	102	356	1159	11	9
v.H.		85,7	–	6,8	19,2	4,7	4,3	15,0	48,8	0,5	0,4
1924 I	2913	2421	207	239	303	105	88	289	724	285	49
v.H.		83,1	8,6	9,9	12,5	4,3	3,6	16,1	29,9	11,8	2,0
1924 II	2981	2444	66	330	340	123	102	349	889	200	17
v.H.		82,0	2,7	13,5	13,9	5,0	4,2	14,3	36,4	8,2	0,7
1928	3129	2555	58	208	338	110	93	170	1295	141	111
v.H.		81,7	2,3	8,1	13,2	4,3	3,6	6,7	50,7	5,5	4,3
1930	3236	2880	594	119	234	117	79	143	1295	181	66
v.H.		89,0	20,6	4,1	8,1	4,1	2,7	5,0	45,0	6,3	2,3
1932 I	3230	2904	1160	130	43	132	26	40	1061	271	23
v.H.		89,9	39,9	4,5	1,5	4,5	0,9	1,4	36,5	9,3	0,8
1932 II	3346	2936	1018	233	72	125	25	45	987	377	33
v.H.		87,8	34,7	7,9	2,5	4,3	0,9	1,5	33,6	12,8	1,1
1933	3367	3123	1311	240	47	131	29	39	986	389	23
v.H.		92,8	42,0	8,7	1,5	4,2	0,9	1,2	31,6	9,3	0,7

Election Results. City of Hanover 1946 – 1949

	Entitled to vote	Poll	DRP	DP	FDP	CDU	DZP	SPD	KPD	RSF	others
1946		826	–	112	104	133	–	422	54	–	–
v.H.		80,1	–	13,6	12,6	16,1	–	51,1	6,5	–	–
1947	2658	1686	34	228	167	253	26	852	126	–	–
v.H.		65,5	2,0	13,6	9,9	15,0	1,5	50,5	7,5	–	–
1948	2934	4495	–	591	490	866	–	2322	227	–	–
v.H.		56,6	–	13,1	10,9	19,3	–	51,6	5,1	–	–
1949	3041	2247	172	259	231	347	10	1104	108	14	–
v.H.		75,0	7,7	11,5	10,3	15,5	0,5	49,1	4,8	0,6	–

From: G. Franz, Wahlen in Niedersachsen, p.126.

REFERENCES

UNPUBLISHED SOURCES

British Archives

Foreign Office: FO 371; FO 936; FO 1010
War Office: WO 171; WO 220
Labour Party: 'Reports to International Sub-Committee'
Trade Union Congress
BBC Written Archives
Imperial War Museum

German Archives

Stadtarchiv Hannover
Sitzungs- und Beschlussprotokolle des Rats 1946-49
Niederschriften über die Besprechungen mit den
    Dezernenten und dem Stadtbeirat, März - Oktober 1945
Niederschriften über die Sitzungen des Bauausschusses 1946-
    49
Protokolle der Besprechungen zwischen Oberbürgermeister
    Bratke mit den Standtkommandanten 1945-46
Nachlass Bratke. Vier ungeordnete Pakete mit insgesamt 32
    Unterakten
Nachlass Stadtdirektor Lindemann
Akte C Nagel (Gesundheitsdezernent)
Hauptregistratur, Stadtverwaltung II: Zusammenarbeit mit
    der Besatzungsmacht (seven 'Unterakten')
Hauptregistratur, Stadtverwaltung XXI Allgemeine
    Polizeisachen

References

Neuer Hannoverscher Kurier 1945/46 (Nachrichtenblatt der
    alliierten Militärregierung)
Hannoversches Nachrichtenblatt der alliierten Militärre-
    gierung 1945/46

Staatsarchiv Hannover
Staatskanzlei (NdS Z50)
Ministerium des Innern (NdS 100)
Regierungspräsidium Hannover (NdS 120A und Hann II)
Nachlass Kwiecinski (VVP 5)

Material relating to denazification in Lower Saxony is not
open to the public (Law concerning the conclusion of
Denazification in Lower Saxony, 18.12.1951).

The following material is at present in the Universität
Hannover, Politisches Seminar (it is used for the 'Projekt
Arbeiterbewegung Hannover' which the Seminar has been
running over several years and is quoted in the text as
'Projekt Arbeiterbewegung').

Protokolle der Delegiertenversammlungen des Ortsvereins
    Hannover Stadt 1946-49
Rechenschaftsberichte des Ortsvereinvorstands 1947-49
Akte 'Untersuchungsausschuss - Ehrenrat'
Protokollbuch der 40. Abteilung des SPD-Ortsvereins 1946
Diverse kleinere Schriften
Material des SPD-Bezirks, Hannover
    Schriftwechsel 1945-48
    Personalien 1946
    Ordner 'Falken' 1947
    Rechenschaftsbericht für den Bezirksparteitag 1948

Archiv der sozialen Demokratie Friedrich-Ebert-Stiftung,
    Bonn-Bad Godesburg
Nachlass Schumacher

Archiv beim Bundesvorstand des DGB, Düsseldorf
Material betr. 'Allgemeine Gewerkschaft Niedersachsen'

References

Nachlass Albin Karl

Archiv der Industrie- und Handelskammer, Hannover
Only official publications were made available. The files remained closed to the author 'because our material has not yet been sorted out' (letter from the Chamber to author, 12.1.1981).

Works Archives
Bahlsen
Bennecke
Günther Wagner
Works Council Minutes in 'Material Hartmann'. Copies made available by Franz Hartmann, Stuhr/Bremen.

The following Works Archives were not open to the author because the firms refused access:
Sprengel (Works Archive in the Staatsarchiv)
Continental

Interviews
Lord Annan 25.4.1985
Sir A. Bramall 16.10.1984
H. Hasselbring 4.3.1981
A. Holweg 11.5.1981

Newspapers

Hannoversche Presse
Hannoversche Neueste Nachrichten
Niedersächsische Volksstimme
Deutsche Volkszeitung
Abendpost

PUBLISHED SOURCES

A. Adamthwaite, 'Britain and the World: A View from the Foreign Office 1945-49'. Paper given at a conference organised by University Association for Contemporary European Studies. Kings College, London. 27.9.1984.

References

'Anpacken und Vollenden'. Hannover 1949. Städtisches
     Presse-und Kulturamt Hannover (ed)
C.R Attlee, As It Happened. London, 1954.
M. Balfour, Four Power Control in Germany and Austria
     1945-46. Survey of International Affairs, London, 1956
W. Benz & H. Graml (eds), Aspekte deutscher Aussenpolitik,
     1976
Bericht des deutschen Gewerkschaftsbundes Bezirk
     Niedersachsen über die Gewerkschaftsbewegung in
     Niedersachsen seit der Kapitulation 1945 für die
     Bezirkskonferenz Niedersachsen am 30.3.1949, 1971
R. Billerbeck, Die Abgeordneten der ersten Landtage (1946-
     51) und der Nationalsozialismus, Düsseldorf, 1971
A. Bullock, Ernest Bevin. Foreign Secretary. Oxford, 1985
R.W. Carden, 'Before Bizonia: Britain's Economic Dilemma
     in Germany 1945/46', in JCH 14/3/1979
L.D. Clay, Decision in Germany, London, 1950
L.D. Clay, Papers, vol. 1 J.E. Smith (ed), Bloomington and
     London, 1974
CCG (BE) Monthly Report of the Control Commission for
     Germany
W.C. Cromwell, 'The Marshallplan, Britain and the Cold
     War', in International Studies, VIII/1982
H. Dalton, High Tide and After: Memoirs 1945-1960,
     London, 1962
J. Diefendorf, 'Organisationsfragen beim Wiederaufbau
     deutscher Städte nach 1945' in Die Verwaltung, 18/4
     1985
Drei Schwere Jahre. Ein Bericht der Bauverwaltung der
     Haupstadt Hannover für die Zeit vom Beginn der
     Besetzung (April 1945) bis zur Währungsreform (Juni
     1948), Hanover
R. Ebsworth, Restoring Democracy in Germany. The British
     Contribution, London and New York, 1960
R.A. Eden, The Reckoning, The Eden Memoirs, vol. 2,
     London, 1965
L.J. Edinger, Kurt Schumacher, a Study in Personality and
     Political Behaviour, Stamford and London, 1965
W. Fesefeldt, Der Wiederbeginn des Kommunalen Lebens in
     Göttingen. Die Sadt in den Jahren 1945 bis 1948,
     Göttingen, 1962
U. Fischer, Der Bode-Panzer Streik. Staatsexamensarbeit,
     Göttingen 1973
O. Flechtheim, Die deutschen Parteien seit 1945. Quellen
     und Auszuge, Berlin, 1957

214

References

J. Foschepoth, 'British Interest in the Division of Germany
    after the Second World War', in JCH 21/1986
J. Foschepoth (ed), Kalter Kreig und Deutsche Frage.
    Deutschland im Widerstreit der Mächte 1945-52,
    Stuttgart, 1985
J. Foschepoth & R. Steininger (eds), Britische Deutschland-
    und Besatzungspolitik 1945-49, Paderborn, 1985
K. Franke, Die Niedersächsische SPD Führung im Wandel
    der Partei nach 1945, Hildesheim, 1980
G. Franz, Wahlen in Niedersachsen, Bremen, 1950
A. Fratzscher, CDU in Niedersachsen. Demokratie der
    ersten Stunde, Rosdorf/Göttingen, 1972
H.J. Fricke, Die Neuerrichtung der Industrie-und
    Handelskammer Hannover vor 10 Jahren, Hanover, 1955
Die Gewerkschaftsbewegung in der Britischen Zone.
    Geschäftsbericht des Deutschen Gewerkschaftsbundes
    (Britische Besatzungszone) 1947-49, Cologne
J. Gimbel, A German City under American Occupation,
    Stamford, 1951
J. Gimbel, The American Occupation of Germany, Stamford,
    1968
J. Gimbel, The Origins of the Marshallplan, Stamford, 1976
A. Glees, Exile Politics during the Second World War,
    Oxford, 1982
T. Grabe, R. Hollmann, K. Mlynek, Wege aus dem Chaos.
    Hannover 1945-49, Hanover, 1985
H. Grebing, Entscheidung für die SPD. Briefe und
    Aufzeichungen linker Sozialisten, Munich, 1984
H. Grebing ao, Die Nachriegsentwicklung in
    Westdeutschland 1945-49, Stuttgart, 1980
H. Grebing, B. Klemm, Lehrstücke in Solidaritat. Briefe und
    Biographien deutscher Sozialisten, 1945-49, Stuttgart,
    1983
Hannover im 20 Jahrhundert. Aspekte der neueren
    Stadtgeschichte, Hanover, 1978
Hansard, Parliamentary Debates
F. Hartmann, Entstehung und Entwicklung der
    Gewerkschaftsbewegung in Niedersachsen nach dem
    Zweiten Weltkrieg, PhD Thesis, 1977
F. Hartmann, Geschichte der Gewerkschaftsbewegung in
    Niedersachsen, 1972
J. Hengst, Der Wiederaufbau einter lokalen SPD-
    Organisation 1945/46 im Kontext der Neugründung auf
    Westzonenebene am Beispiel Hannovers. Staatsexa-
    mensarbeit, 1975

215

E.U. Huster, Determinanten westdeutscher Restauration
    1945-49, Frankfurt, 1972
E.U. Huster, Die Politik der SPD 1945-1940, Frankfurt, 1978
H. Ingrams, 'Building Democracy in Germany', in The
    Quarterly Review, 572/1947
Institut für Zeitgeschichte (ed), Westdentschlands Weg zur
    Bundesrepublik, 1945-49, Munich, 1976
A. Kaden, Einheit oder Freiheit. Die Wiedergründung der
    SPD 1945/46, Berlin/Bonn, 1964
L. Kettenacker, 'The Anglo-Soviet Alliance and the Problem
    of Germany 1941-1945', in JCH, 17/1982
I. Kirkpatrick, The Inner Circle, London, 1959
J. Klein, Vereint sind sie alles? Untersuchungen zur
    Entstehung der Einheitsgewerkschaften in Deutschland,
    Phd, Hamburg, 1972
A. Lefevre, 100 Jahre Industrie-und Handelskammer zu
    Hannover, Hanover, 1966
B. Marshall, 'German Attitudes to British Military
    Government 1945-47', in JCH, 15/1, 1980
B. Marshall, 'German Reactions to Military Defeat, 1945-47:
    the British View', in V. Berghahn & M. Kitchen (eds),
    Germany in the Age of Total War, 1981
H.G. Marten, Die FDP in Niedersachsen. Demokratie der
    ersten Stunde, Hanover, 1972
A.J. & R.L. Merritt, Public Opinion in Occupied Germany.
    The OMGUS Surveys 1945-49, 1970
H. Meyn, Die Deutsche Partei. Entwicklung und Problematik
    einer national-konservativen Rechtspartei nach 1945,
    Opladen, 1965
B. Montgomery Viscount, The Memoirs of Fieldmarshall
    Montgomery, London, 1958
L. Mosley, Report from Germany, London, 1946
L. Niethammer ao Arbeiterinitiative 1945, Wuppertal, 1976
B. Ruhn von Oppen, Documents of Germany under
    Occupation 1945-54, Oxford, 1955
R. Ovendale (ed), The Foreign Policy of the British Labour
    Governments, 1945-51, Leicester, 1984
H. Pietsch, Militärregierung, Bürokratie und Sozialisierung.
    Entwicklung des politischen Systems in den Städten des
    Ruhrgebiets, 1945-48, Duisburg, 1978
F. Pingel, 'Die Russen am Rhein? Die Wende der britischen
    Besatzungspolitik   im   Fruhjahr   1946',   in:
    Vierteljahreshefte für Zeitgeschichte 30/1982
T. Pirker, Die blinde Macht. Die Gewerkschaftsbewegung in
    Westdeutschland, Munich, 1960

T. Pirker, Die verordnete Demokratie, Grundlagen und Erscheinungen der Restauration, Berlin, 1977

T. Pirker, Die SPD nach Hitler, Munich, 1965

H. Plath, H. Mundhenke & E. Brix, Heimatchronik der Hauptstadt Hannover, Hanover, 1956

S. Pollard, The Development of the British Economy 1914-1967, London, 1976

B. Pollmann, Reformansatze in Niedersachsen, Hanover, 1977

Protokoll der ersten Gewerkschaftskonferenz der britischen Zone vom 12. - 14 März 1946 im Katholischen Vereinshaus in Hannover-Linden

Protokoll der Gewerkschaftskonferenz der britischen Zone vom 21-23 August 1946 in Bielefeld

Protokoll des Parteitags der SPD 1946 in Hannover, 1947

U. Reusch, 'Die Londoner Institutionen der britischen Deutschlandpolitik 1943-48. Eine behördengeschichtliche Untersuchung, in Historisches Jahrbuch 100/1980

F. Roberts, 'Bevin and Eden: Some Personal Impressions'. Paper given at UACES Conference, King's College, London, 27.9.1984

W.R. Robson, 'Local Government in Occupied Germany', in Political Quarterly, XVI/1945

V. Rothwell, Britain and the Cold War, 1941-47, London, 1982

W. Rudzio, Die Neuordnung des Kommunalwesens in der britischen Zone. Zur Demokratisierung und Dezentralisierung der politischen Struktur: eine britische Reform und ihr Ausgang, Stuttgart, 1968

K. Sainsbury, 'British Policy and German Unity at the end of the Second World War', in English Historical Review, 44/1979

C. Scharf, H.J. Schroder (eds), Die Deutschlandpolitik Grossbritanniens und die britische Zone, 1945-49, Wiesbaden, 1979

C. Scharf, H.J. Schroder (eds) Politische und ökonomische Stabilisierung Westdeutschlands, 1945-49, Wiesbaden, 1977

E. Schmidt, Die verhinderte Neuordnung, Frankfurt, 1970

U. Schneider, Britische Besatzungspolitik 1945, PhD Thesis, Hannover, 1908

U. Schroder, 'Der Ausschuss für Wiederaufbau und die antifaschistische Bewegung in Hannover, in Niethammer ao (eds), op.cit.

K. Schutz, Parteien in der Bundesrepublik. Studien zur

Entwicklung der deutschen Pareien bis zur Bundestagswahl 1953, Bonn, 1953

R. Schulze, 'Bürgerliche Sammlung oder Welfenpartei? Ergänzungen zur Entstehungsgeschichte der Niedersächsischen Landespartei 1945/46', in Jahrbuch für Niedersächsische Landesgeschichte, 57/1985

H.P. Schwarz, Vom Reich zur Bundesrepublik. Deutschland im Widerstreit der aussenpolitischen Konzeptionen in den Jahren der Besatzungsherrschaft 1945-49, Stuttgart, 1980

L. Schwering, Frühgeschichte der CDU, Recklinghausen, 1963

A. Sharp, The War-time Alliance and the Zonal Division of Germany, Oxford, 1975

M. Steinert, Hitler's War and the Germans, Ohio, 1977

Lord W. Strang, Home and Abroad, London, 1956

D. Tasch, Hannover-1945. Series of articles in Hannoversche Allgemeine Zeitung 3.4.-14.4.1965

T. Vogelsang, Hinrich Wilhelm Kopf und Niedersachsen, Hanover, 1963

Vom Plan zur Wirklichkeit. 4 Jahre Ratsarbeit Hannover

R. Wagnleiter, 'Die Kontinuität der britischen Aussenpolitik nach dem Wahlsieg der Labour Party im Juli 1945', in Zeitgeschichte, 5/1978

D.C. Watt, Britain looks to Germany. British Opinion and Policy towards Germany since 1945, London, 1965

Westdeutschlands Weg zur Bundesrepublik, 1945-49, 1976

H.G. Wieck, Die Entstehung der CDU und die Wiedergründung des Zentrums, Düsseldorf, 1953

H.A. Winkler, Politische Weichenstellungen im Nachkriegsdeutschland, 1945-53, Göttingen, 1979

C.W. Zöllner, Aspekte kommunalpolitischer Entscheidungsprozesse dargestellt an der Entwicklung der Stadt Braunschweig nach 1945. PhD Thesis, Braunschweig 1971

G. Zorn, Widerstand in Hannover, Hanover, 1977

INDEX

Adenauer, Konrad 194

Barth, Emil, Director of
Police 35, 48, 57, 77, 81
basic German services,
restoration of 34, 38-42
Bevin, Ernest, Foreign
Secretary, 1945-51 135,
139, 200
Bratke, Gustav, Oberburger-
meister of Hannover 35,
36, 41, 43, 44, 45, 48, 49,
57, 77, 81, 97, 99, 100,
111, 142, 143, 167, 170
Brenner, Otto, Trade Union
leader and member of
SPD 64, 66, 89, 120, 134,
160, 164, 166, 200, 201
British Foreign Policy
general 8-9
post-war treatment of
Germany 9-14; 198-200
war-time plans for
Germany 1-3

CDU 66, 76, 82, 83, 84, 98,
100, 101, 102, 115, 121,
174, 175-81, 183, 185,
187, 194, 195, 201, 202
Chamber of Industry and

Commerce 78, 124-7, 184
COGA 14-17, 21, 22
Committee for Reconst-
ruction (RC) see Reconst-
ruction Committee
Committee of Ex-Concent-
ration Camp Inmates 52-3
Control Commission for
Germany (CCG)
organisation 20-3, 104,
126
war-time plans for 3-5

Denazification 47-57
German attitudes to 48,
52, 56-7
of the economy 53-6
of the German administ-
ration 49, 51
of the police 50
Displaced Persons (DPs) 36-
7, 41

EAC 3

FDP 83, 84, 98, 100, 101,
102, 174, 181-5, 189
finance 45-7
food 10, 41-2, 127-34

219